Praise for

THE RESURRECTED JESUS

"My friends Christen Bloom and David Limbaugh have done every Christian a singular service with this wonderful exegesis of the Apostle Paul's final letters to the early Christian churches. *The Resurrected Jesus* is a book that is useful, moving, and profound all at the same time. I highly recommend it."

—**AINSLEY EARHARDT, co-host of *Fox and Friends* and author**

"David Limbaugh and Christen Bloom deliver. This book will not only renew your mind, it has a devotional feel that will nourish your soul. Like skilled storytellers, this father-daughter team will make you think the apostle himself has come back to narrate and expound his own letters! An enlightening read for both the new believer and longtime Christian. Highly recommended."

—**FRANK TUREK, author of *I Don't Have Enough Faith to Be an Atheist* and president of CrossExamined.org**

"What an outstanding book! David Limbaugh and his very capable coauthor Christen Limbaugh Bloom bring to life Paul's letters to the early church, teachings that remain the bedrock of our faith. Brilliant commentary and essential reading."

—**SEAN HANNITY, host of *Hannity* on Fox News and *The Sean Hannity Show***

THE RESURRECTED JESUS

THE RESURRECTED JESUS

The CHURCH in the NEW TESTAMENT

DAVID LIMBAUGH
CHRISTEN LIMBAUGH BLOOM

Regnery Publishing
WASHINGTON, D.C.

First trade paperback edition published 2023

ISBN: 978-1-68451-424-3
Library of Congress Control Number: 2022941096

Published in the United States by
Regnery Publishing
A division of Salem Media Group
Washington, D.C.
www.Regnery.com

Manufactured in the United States of America

10 9 8 7 6 5 4 3 2 1

Books are available in quantity for promotional or premium use. For information on discounts and terms, please visit our website: www.Regnery.com.

To my brother and Christen's uncle, Rush, whose entire life was inspiring to me, and particularly his last year after receiving his diagnosis. During that year he grew closer and closer to Jesus Christ, thanking God for every precious day of his life. His courage in the face of this life-ending challenge and his open demonstration of faith, thankfulness, and love touched me and countless others. He was a brother like no other, who opened so many doors to me. I can't begin to express my gratitude. We also want to dedicate this book to Rush's fans who have reached out to us in droves to express their sympathy and their own sense of deep loss with his passing. God bless all of you, and thank you, sincerely.

CONTENTS

INTRODUCTION

Prior to this book, I had written four Christian-themed books: *Jesus on Trial*, *The Emmaus Code*, *The True Jesus*, and *Jesus Is Risen*. I asked my daughter Christen to write this book with me. She is a spirit-filled Christian, a prayer warrior, and a wonderful writer, who sometimes writes Christian opinion pieces for the Fox News website. Several years ago she launched Haplous, an online Christian blog and Bible study community that seeks to help people strengthen their relationship with God. She has a heart for Christ and has great insight into the application of biblical principles to our daily lives. I thought it would be a great blessing for us to work together on this project and that with her perspective she could add a great deal to this pbook.

As explained in *Jesus Is Risen*, the New Testament contains twenty-seven books. The four gospels and the Book of Acts are historical books: the gospels are accounts of Jesus' life, death, and resurrection, and Acts is the history of the early church. The final book of the New Testament is Revelation, which is categorized as apocalypse, prophecy, or revelation. The other twenty-one books are epistles, which are letters written mostly by apostles to churches or individuals. They deal with matters of doctrine, problems in local churches, Christian living, and other matters. Paul wrote thirteen epistles, known as the Pauline epistles, and the other eight are known as the general epistles. Seven of those were written by John, Peter, and Jesus' brothers James and Jude. John wrote three, Peter two, and James and Jude each wrote one. The author of the other one—the Book of Hebrews—is unknown.

In *Jesus Is Risen*, I covered the Book of Acts and the Apostle Paul's six missionary epistles—Galatians, 1 and 2 Thessalonians, 1 and 2 Corinthians, and Romans, which most scholars believe were written during Paul's three missionary journeys and before his other seven epistles. This was in keeping with my approach in *The True Jesus* of presenting the gospel events in chronological order rather than their canonical order—the order in which the books appear in the Bible.

In this book, Christen and I continue this practice and explore Paul's remaining seven epistles in the order most scholars believe he wrote them. These letters fall into two categories—the prison epistles and the pastoral epistles. It's widely believed that Paul writes the four prison epistles—Colossians, Philemon, Ephesians, and Philippians—while under house arrest in Rome. We know Paul is imprisoned when writing these letters because he says so (Eph. 3:1, 4:1; 6:20; Col. 4:18; Philem. 10, 13; Philip. 1:7, 13). Though he doesn't specify whether he is under arrest in Caesarea or Rome, scholars believe he pens these epistles during the Roman imprisonment.

Paul likely writes Colossians first to warn the church at Colossae against a dangerous heresy circulating there. Around the same time, he pens a personal letter to one of the church's congregants, Philemon, and also prepares his letter for the Ephesians and other churches in that area. (He probably writes Philippians after the other three,[1] though many scholars believe he wrote it before.)[2]

Though under house arrest for two years, Paul has the freedom to greet guests and preach the gospel to them "with all boldness and without hindrance" (Acts 28:30, 31). There, he learns of the heresies circulating in Ephesus, Colossae, and the surrounding areas. He addresses these issues in the epistles to the Colossians and Ephesians, and he writes a separate letter to his friend Philemon partially concerning Onesimus, a slave whom Paul led to Christ. After Epaphroditus brings him a gift from the church in Philippi, Paul reciprocates with a letter of encouragement and gratitude to the church, which he delivers through Epaphroditus.[3]

Many scholars believe Paul is released from prison by Roman authorities and embarks on more missionary journeys before they imprison him again. Most scholars contend that during the interval between his imprisonments, he writes the three pastoral epistles, 1 and 2 Timothy and Titus.[4] Others believe he probably writes 2 Timothy during his second Roman imprisonment.[5] Though known as the pastoral epistles, the addressees are not pastors of certain churches but those who helped to organize the churches in Ephesus and Crete at the direction of other leaders.[6] In these letters Paul confirms instructions to Timothy and Titus that he had earlier imparted verbally.[7] Though the letters are written to individuals and even have a personal flavor, they are apparently intended to be read to the churches.[8]

Paul is a tireless evangelist; he plants many churches throughout his missionary journeys, and the new faith takes off like wildfire, with thousands becoming believers committed to Christ and to growing the church. But Paul realizes the church won't continue to flourish on its own, especially given Rome's hostility to the burgeoning movement as well as the aging of the apostles. He knows it's imperative to equip younger leaders and workers with the practical knowledge to carry on their work.

Despite his strong personality and determination to accurately present the gospel, Paul's letters reveal he is unafraid to delegate critical leadership tasks to younger trusted believers he mentored such as Timothy and Titus. They, in turn, are meant to raise up other leaders who will effectively multiply Paul's and their work. As Paul writes to Timothy, "And the things you have heard me say in the presence of many witnesses entrust to reliable people who will also be qualified to teach others" (2 Tim. 2:2).[9] But Paul is not about to send his lieutenants out without further instruction, as he knows formidable opposition awaits them and that Satan specializes in misinformation. Diluting the gospel and conflating it with heretical ideas could destroy Christianity in its infancy. While God in His sovereignty superintends the spread of the message, He accomplishes that through His evangelistic foot soldiers and leaders like Paul who direct them.

Paul doesn't choose his proteges lightly. He adores Timothy as a "dear son" (2 Tim. 2) and is convinced of the sincerity of his faith, which his believing grandmother Lois and mother, Eunice, modeled to him while teaching him the Bible (2 Tim. 1:5, 3:15). With a Greek father and Jewish mother (Acts 16:1), Timothy's fine reputation in his community (Acts 16:2) and his unique character traits particularly impress Paul, as he testifies to the Philippians, "I have no one else like him, who will show genuine concern for your welfare. For everyone looks out for their own interests, not those of Jesus Christ" (Philip. 2:20–21). Indeed, such was Timothy's devotion that he traveled on evangelistic missions with Paul despite his "frequent illnesses" (1 Tim. 5:23).

Timothy is not an apostle because he was not chosen by Christ as His direct representative. But his work is extraordinarily important as he is, notes J. P. Lilley, "a general missionary superintendent, highly qualified to preach and teach, and empowered by the Apostolic Church to arrest the progress of error and guide organization in districts that had special needs."[10] Since few things are more important to Paul than the purity of the gospel, his high regard for Timothy is shown by his delegation to him of the task of proclaiming and defending the truth, thereby preserving that purity.

Paul also led to Christ the young Greek Titus, who accompanied him and Barnabas to Jerusalem, where he presented the gospel to Jews and introduced Titus to them as a Gentile convert. Though not an apostle, Titus is a committed believer willing to undertake challenges and hardship to spread the gospel. Paul sees Titus as more of a leader—enthusiastic and willing to act on his own initiative (2 Cor. 8:17)—than Timothy, who sometimes might need gentle nudging (2 Tim. 1:6).[11] Paul has great confidence in Titus, whom he entrusts with the job of helping to resolve conflicts among congregants of the Corinthian church (2 Cor. 8:6; 1 Cor. 1:11). Paul tells the Corinthians, "I urged Titus to go to you and I sent our brother with him. Titus did not exploit you, did he? Did we not walk in the same footsteps by the same Spirit" (2 Cor. 12:18)?

As we delve into the richness packed within Paul's divinely inspired letters to the early churches and his proteges, we ask that throughout these pages you join us in prayer. We begin with the one on the following page:

Prayer

Holy Spirit, we thank You for every single person who will read this book. We lift them up to You and ask that Your favor be upon their lives. Increase in each of them a desire to know You more deeply, and we humbly ask that the pages within this book help them in their unique journey to grow in their knowledge and love for You. Open our hearts and minds to hear Your voice clearly through the messages penned in Your holy word. Guide each reader through this book with faith in believing that You have specific love notes for each of them within its pages. We honor and thank You for Your love which knows no bounds. In Your Heavenly Name,

Amen.

CHAPTER ONE

COLOSSIANS

A DEFENSE AGAINST EARLY HERESIES

As you read Paul's letter to the Colossian believers, use your God-given mind to evaluate your own belief system. Is it based on God's Word and centered on Christ? Or do you rely on human philosophy and your ability to think?

—Bruce Barton[1]

Paul, likely during his first imprisonment in Rome, writes this letter to the infant church at Colossae, which was founded by his friend Epaphras (Col 1:7). Paul had led Epaphras to Christ during Paul's three-year ministry in Ephesus (A.D. 52–55),[2] where Paul's preaching at the hall of Tyrannus was so powerful that Luke claimed, "All the Jews and Greeks who lived in the province of Asia heard the word of the Lord" (Acts 19:10). Located about one hundred miles east of Ephesus on the southern bank of the Lycus River (in modern Turkey), Colossae had once been populous and prosperous. By the time the church was founded, however, it had diminished into a small town surpassed in importance by Laodicea and Hierapolis, two other cities in the Lycus valley.[3]

One of Paul's shortest epistles, Colossians clarifies the gospel message and encourages believers to grow in the faith and to live as authentic followers of Christ (Col. 2:6–8). Crucially, it starkly warns against false teachings. The enemy can quickly attack a church from within, and such is the case in Colossae, which commentator Richard Melick describes as having "a complex and confusing intellectual climate" where misguided notions present "a major threat to Christianity's very existence."[4] Paul has to correct these false ideas to preserve the purity and impact of the gospel, which is a pervasive theme in his letters. The errors, which we discuss in greater detail below, go to the heart of the gospel because they devalue Christ's supremacy and the biblical teaching that salvation can be found only through Him.[5]

Heresies have plagued orthodox Christianity since its inception. Many involve some distortion of the teaching that Christ is both fully God and fully human. Let's briefly survey some of the major heresies.

- ★ The second-century heresy of Adoptionism rejected the pre-existence of Christ and thus His deity. It held that Jesus was a man of extraordinary virtue whom God adopted into divine sonship.[6]
- ★ Around the same period, Docetism, viewing physical matter as intrinsically evil, taught that Jesus appeared to have a physical body but actually did not, and that He neither suffered on the cross nor was resurrected. The early church fathers denounced these views as heretical denials of Christ's incarnation.[7]
- ★ In the fourth century, Apollinarianism denied Christ's humanity, claiming His mind was divine and not human.[8]
- ★ Also in the fourth century, Arianism declared that Jesus was not divine but a created being begotten of the Father. He was nevertheless deemed worthy of

worship because He was God's first created being and He created the universe.[9]

★ Fifth-century Nestorianism held that Jesus was two persons, one human and one divine, and that Mary gave birth to his human nature. Christianity, however, teaches that Christ has two natures that are unified in one person. Nestorianism was officially condemned at the church councils of Ephesus in A.D. 431 and Chalcedon in A.D. 451.[10]

★ In that same century Monophysitism, also formally rejected at Chalcedon, taught that Jesus was of one nature only.[11] In the seventh century, Monothelitism arose to counter Monophysitism but still ran afoul of scriptural truth in teaching that Jesus had dual natures but only one will.[12]

The false teachers at Colossae insist that Christ could not have been both human and God and that man's salvation depends on special human knowledge accessible only to the intellectual elite[13]—doctrines that partially resemble the second-century heresy of Gnosticism. Moreover, such heretics cannot accept that Christ could be human because they believe matter is inherently evil and only the spiritual is good, as the later heresy of Docetism taught. By this logic, God couldn't possibly take on an evil body.

Another seductive error is the argument that Christianity can't be exclusively true—it is just one of many religions.[14] This belief is widespread today among those who reject absolute truth and insist all philosophical beliefs are equally valid. Just as it was in Paul's time, however, this demand for "tolerance" is actually a sinister refusal to distinguish between truth and error. If all ideas are correct, then no ideas can be wrong, including mutually contradictory ones.

Ironically, those preaching the new tolerance are blind to their own intolerance and judgmentalism for they condemn, in a self-defeating way, those who believe in absolute truth and who clearly distinguish between right and wrong.[15]

Adherents of the new tolerance present themselves as morally superior because they supposedly accept all views. Even if they did accept all views, which they don't, is it moral to falsely claim two mutually contradictory positions are both true? Is it right to deny truth? Is it morally right to contradict the Son of God who so clearly stated that He is the only way to the Father and eternal life? Indeed, would it be moral for those of us who accept Christ's teaching to pretend there are other avenues when we believe this mistaken notion could lead to the damnation of souls? Should we really engage in this charade just so we can avoid judgment by people who claim to be nonjudgmental? In sum, don't we have a duty to preach what we believe to be the truth even though it runs afoul of today's cancel culture?

Of course Christians are tolerant—we advocate treating all people with dignity and respect and defending their right to express beliefs, especially religious and political beliefs, with which we disagree. But that does not mean we must validate every personal belief, and in some cases we have a moral duty not to, such as the notion that all religious beliefs are equally true. Let's not fool ourselves to please man. God Himself is intolerant toward sin because it is against His holy nature and because it leads to death and destruction. Falsely proclaiming spiritually deadly ideas is not virtuous—it is morally wrong, no matter how vehemently the finger-wagging virtue signalers claim otherwise.

This is a central component of Paul's teaching. In this epistle, he sets the record straight, refusing to allow the fruit of the new believers' conversion to be poisoned by false doctrine or their assurance of salvation to be diminished. The epistle's message of the centrality of Christ, salvation by faith alone, the indispensability of correct theology, and right Christian living remains as relevant today as when Paul wrote the letter. "One theme predominates" in Colossians, writes Melick. "The centrality of Christ. No other epistle is as Christocentric as this one.... Every encounter with the text brings one face to face with the Lord."[16] Indeed, no biblical book is more Christ-centered than this one. Christ is creator and Lord of the universe, ruling over the world and the unseen spiritual realm. In Him we have everything we need. Our salvation is by faith in Christ alone. He is our all in all.

PRAYER

Jesus, we come to You seeking to know You fully and to make You the center of our lives. May we neither settle for watered-down nor overly religious versions of You. Instead, may Your Holy Spirit draw us toward Your true nature through prayer, Bible study, and other spiritual disciplines. We ask for Your Holy Spirit to give us divine encounters that will strengthen our relationship with You on a personal level. In Your Holy Name,

AMEN.

CHAPTER 1

Paul begins the letter by identifying himself as its author and as an apostle of Christ Jesus by "the will of God." He doesn't use the word "apostle" lightly, as apostles were directly chosen by Christ and served not as mere messengers but as His official representatives.[17] He isn't asserting this pridefully but to establish his authority to deliver this message, which would become part of scripture. Paul also mentions Timothy, not as a coauthor but as a trusted companion and supporter and possibly his *amanuensis* (transcriber).

Paul addresses the letter to "the saints and faithful brothers in Christ at Colossae" (1:2). He greets them with grace—recipients of God's unmerited favor—and peace, which they find in God, based on their faith in Christ and His death on the cross.[18] Significantly, Paul calls the Colossian believers "holy." "That is an astonishing thing for a Jew to say of non-Jews," writes commentator John Woodhouse. "Israel was God's holy people (Exodus 19:6).... Yet Paul calls this gathering of mainly non-Jewish Colossians 'holy.' It is not a description of their character or conduct. They are holy in the sense that Israel was holy: set apart by God and for God."[19] Woodhouse notes, however, this is not a status that believers earn but a matter of God's grace.[20] As Christ's ambassadors, they must reflect Him in their lives. As Paul says later in the letter, "Put on then, as God's chosen ones, holy and beloved, compassion, kindness, humility, meekness and patience" (3:12).

Paul constantly thanks God for the congregants' faith and their love for their fellow believers—a faith and love that come from the hope they gained by accepting the true message of the gospel (1:3–5). Paul is delighted because the gospel is bearing fruit and spreading throughout the world, just as it has been among the Colossians since Epaphras taught it to them (1:6–7). Epaphras told Paul about their "love in the Spirit" (1:8), which F. F. Bruce describes as "the mutual love implanted and fostered in their hearts by the Holy Spirit who dwelt within them and united them in a living bond."[21]

Paul prays that they be filled with the knowledge of God's will through the wisdom and understanding the Spirit gives (1:9). Why? "So as to walk in a manner worthy of the Lord, fully pleasing to him: bearing fruit in every good work and increasing in the knowledge of God" (1:10). That is, to please God, we must understand what pleases Him—we must come to understand His will. The Old Testament includes the same teaching: God is the source of all wisdom (Prov. 2:6; Psalm 147:5), and a wise person is a godly person (Hosea 14:9).[22] But is Paul repeating himself in saying that believers must learn God's will so they can grow in their knowledge of God? No. Woodhouse argues this is intentionally circular: "It is how the Christian life works. As we are filled with the knowledge of God's will, we will live more and more in the way that pleases God, bearing good fruit, and so we grow in the knowledge of God!"[23]

Though we increase in our knowledge of God through the power of the Holy Spirit, this won't happen automatically. We must place ourselves before the Holy Spirit and allow Him to enlighten us and to work in our lives. We must regularly and carefully study the Bible, pray, and exercise the other spiritual disciplines. "Fruit does not come automatically," writes S. R. Leach, "but rather is cultivated as believers, like branches, remain dependent on Christ, our Vine."[24] We must be cautious, however, not to engage in the spiritual disciplines as a matter of duty alone. Psalm 100:3 tells us God wants us to serve Him with gladness!

In sum, new believers are declared righteous and given eternal life upon their conversion through faith in Jesus Christ, but they don't instantly become holy or Bible scholars. They might just have a rudimentary understanding of God's will. They must proactively pursue biblical knowledge and holiness through the exercise of the spiritual disciplines. As we allow the Spirit to work in our lives, we grow in biblical knowledge and spiritual maturity and bear the fruit of godly behavior. It's an interconnected process because as we learn God's will, we conform our behavior to please Him, thereby growing closer to God and godly wisdom. Our understanding of the Holy

Spirit's role is essential. We won't grow in godly knowledge and become more Christlike except through His power.

Trying to understand God's will on our own accord, untethered to the Spirit, could lead us into misunderstanding and even heresies, which is another reason Paul repeatedly stresses the importance of acquiring godly knowledge and correct doctrine. Heresies are deadly to the life of the believer and to the growth of the church, and refuting heresies that afflict the church at Colossae is one of Paul's primary motivations in writing this letter. "The Colossians demonstrated a desire to obey by their continuous love for other Christians," notes Leach, "so what they needed now was the direction and guidance given by the Word of God and not by the [heretical] teachers."[25]

Paul's timeless advice must sink into our very souls. Do we really grasp the importance of understanding God's will? If so, do we act on our awareness? Do we regularly read the scriptures and pray that the Spirit will illuminate our comprehension?

PRAYER

Jesus, give us a hunger to learn Your word and spend time in Your presence. You are the author and perfecter of our faith. May our love for You drive us to study Your word and truly know it, keeping it hidden in our hearts, that we may have confidence in our knowledge of You and refuse to be tempted by half-truths and flat-out lies woven into so much of today's culture by the enemy. Shield us from the seductive messages and promises of cultists and false teachers. As You describe in Ephesians 6, may we treat Your word as a coat of armor around our hearts and minds and stand firm in Your truth when our faith is tested.

▶

Holy Spirit, I thank you for your presence in my heart. I come to You now and ask that in this moment, my thoughts and desires may become less and Your thoughts and desires may become more in my heart and mind. Lord, I confess that as a flawed human being, I often fail to actively pursue Your divine will. I ask that You'll expand and elevate my carnal perspective. Teach me to search for Your will not only in my own life but across the earth and the Heavenly realm as well. Increase a desire in my heart to seek out Your purposes by spending time with You daily, studying Your word and maintaining an ongoing conversation with You through my prayers. Help me to become more sensitive to Your still voice and instruction so that my heart and mind may be aligned with You on a moment-by-moment basis. I cast off any spirit of pride or guilt that might tempt me to try to accomplish Your will through my own power and efforts. Instruct me as I learn to walk hand-in-hand with You on this ongoing journey of seeking out Your loving, all-powerful, and perfect plans. With faith and love,

AMEN.

Continuing, Paul says that growing in the knowledge of God will also build endurance and patience (1:11). As he is entrusting Timothy and his congregation with the important task of taking on the false teachers, they must be armed with God's word against these enemies of scripture, and they will need the strength, patience, and endurance to oppose them.[26] Scripture is part of "the whole armor of God" that we must use to "stand against the schemes of the devil" (Eph. 6:11).

Finally, Paul prays that the Colossians be filled with joy and always give thanks to the Father, who has enabled them to share in the inheritance of his holy people and "delivered [them] from the domain of darkness and transferred [them] to the kingdom of his beloved Son, in whom [they] have redemption, the forgiveness of sins" (1:10–14).

Believers must always be grateful to God because He makes them His holy people. God chose the Jews as His special people—His inheritance—but now He is bringing in Gentile believers in Christ to share in this inheritance. Some interpreters believe Paul means that Gentiles are now included in God's promise to Israel of their land as an everlasting possession. But F. F. Bruce argues that "the inheritance in view here belongs to a higher plane and a more enduring order than any terrestrial Canaan." Although Gentiles by birth, "they have been reborn into the family of God, thanks to their all-enabling Father."[27]

Since one of the primary purposes of this letter is to address errors circulating in the church about Christ's nature, Paul now turns to describing Christ. He has just referred to Him as the Father's "beloved Son," and now he elaborates: He is "the image of the invisible God, the firstborn over all creation. For in him all things were created; things in heaven and on earth, visible and invisible, whether thrones or powers or rulers or authorities; all things have been created through him and for him. He is before all things, and in him all things hold together (1:15–17)."

With this description Paul is hardly paving new doctrinal ground. He is affirming what he'd written to the Corinthians: "The god of this age has blinded the minds of unbelievers, so that they cannot see the light of the gospel that displays the glory of Christ, who is the image of God" (2 Cor. 4:4). Thus we see that Paul ties Christ's deity to the gospel message. Our salvation depends on our trusting in Christ, but we can't do that if we don't recognize that He is God.

Some cults wrongly teach that Christ was a special human messenger and salvation-agent but not Himself God. Dr. M. R. De Haan corrects the record: "Jesus Christ is the inescapable Christ. All men will meet Him either as God's Lamb who died for their sins or as the Judge when He comes to punish the sinner because he has rejected Him. Christ is to you either the Lamb or the Lion. If you come to Him as a lost and guilty sinner and receive by faith the sacrifice He accomplished on Calvary and allow Him to apply the blood of the Lamb to your soul, then you will become a child of God." He continues, "If you reject this offer, some day, as surely as He came the first time, He will come again as a roaring Lion, to judge you and cast all the wicked in the lake of fire and brimstone."[28] This is reminiscent of the cogent words of British apologist C. S. Lewis:

> I am trying here to prevent anyone saying the really foolish thing that people often say about Him: "I'm ready to accept Jesus as a great moral teacher, but I don't accept His claim to be God." That is the one thing we must not say. A man who was merely a man and said the sort of things Jesus said would not be a great moral teacher. He would either be a lunatic—on a level with the man who says he is a poached egg—or else he would be the Devil of Hell. You must make your choice. Either this man was, and is, the Son of God: or else a madman or something worse. You can shut Him up for a fool, you can spit at Him and kill Him as a demon; or you can fall at His feet and call Him Lord and God. But let us not come with any patronizing nonsense about His being a great human teacher. He has not left that open to us. He did not intend to.[29]

A word of caution to those—alluded to earlier—who elevate their distorted concept of "tolerance" as the greatest human virtue: such proud people, certain that their own standards are superior to the Bible's "antiquated" principles, militantly reject Christianity's exclusive truth claims. Faith in Christ might be one way to salvation, they say, but there are plenty of others, and for us to claim there is only one is egotistical and intolerant. Their overall view is, "That may be true for you, but not for others."

But Christians don't hold themselves out as the judge. There is only one judge: Jesus Christ. He tells us He is the way, the truth, and the life, and no one comes to the Father except through Him (John 14:6). He unambiguously denies there are other avenues, and He did not vacillate about His deity. "I and the Father are one," He declared (John 10:30). So condemn Christ for intolerance if you dare, but don't pretend He was tentative whatsoever in His pronouncements about who He is and that He is the sole way to salvation. You are free to deny Jesus' unequivocal assertions of deity and insist that your concept of tolerance trumps biblical morality, but you do so at your own peril.

The Apostle John was just as explicit as to Christ's divinity, His equality with the Father, and the Father's invisibility: "No one has ever seen God, but the one and only Son, who is himself God and is in closest relationship with the Father, has made him known" (John 1:18). We read in the Old Testament that some did "see" God but not fully, as Christ did.[30] Yet Christ, though visible to man in His human form, is the precise image of the Father—something impossible for a mere human, especially since the Father is invisible. But can a human being be the image of someone who is invisible? Certainly not in the physical sense. As early church father John Chrysostom explains, "Whose image then will you have him be? God's? Then he is exactly like the one to whom you assign him. If you compare him to a human image, say so, and I'll be done with you as a madman.... 'The image of the invisible' is itself also invisible, and invisible in the same way, for otherwise it would not be an image. For an image, so far as it is an image, even on a human level, ought to be exactly similar."[31]

But what does Paul mean in verse 15 when he calls Christ "the firstborn?" The Greek word used is *protokos*, which emphasizes Christ's preeminence.[32] It doesn't mean the Son had a physical origin or was created—an error long ago debunked as the classic Arian heresy, as noted. Transcending time, He has existed eternally with the Father and the Holy Spirit. In fact, Paul affirms that Christ preceded creation in three successive verses, illustrating the importance of the revelation: he is "the firstborn over all creation" (1:15), "in him all things were created" (1:16), and "He is before all things, and in him all things hold together" (1:17).

In speaking of the firstborn son, Paul is analogizing Christ, for example, to the son of a monarch who would inherit his rulership together with the rights and privileges of the firstborn son.[33] The firstborn has supremacy and priority of rank over others.[34] Paul's revelation that Christ preceded and was involved in creation further establishes His deity. "We see here that the whole Trinity is involved from the beginning in the generation and ordering of the universe," declares Augustine.[35] A human being could not have created the physical universe, nor would it have been created "for him," that is, for his benefit. The very idea of it is absurd, which is one of many reasons you can't credibly claim to be a biblical Christian if you deny Christ's deity. The ESV Study Bible affirms that "since Jesus is in this sense the goal of creation, he must be fully God."[36]

The writer of Hebrews also validates Christ's deity. "The Son is the radiance of God's glory and the exact representation of his being" (Heb. 1:3). Christ does not just reflect God's glory as the moon reflects the light of the sun, but He generates that very radiance Himself as intrinsic to His deity.[37] "Jesus is the effulgence of God's glory because he shares the same divine nature as the Father, yet he is distinct from the Father in his person," explains David

Allen. He notes that the Council of Nicaea, which confirmed Christ's deity, addressed this issue directly: "The Council of Nicaea said, regarding the relationship of the Son to the Father in reference to the Son's essential deity, that Jesus is 'light from light.'"[38]

Let's not overlook Paul's declaration that in Christ "all things hold together." The writer of Hebrews corroborates this point, affirming that the Son "[sustains] all things by his powerful word" (Heb. 1:3). "Sustaining all things" is synonymous with holding together all things. Christ exists apart from the universe and is sovereign over all of it, which is a divine function. He created the universe and is in charge of it from beginning to end. Unlike the mythical god of the deists, God is not an indifferent watchmaker who created the world and then left it to its own devices. "As the pre-creational Wisdom of God, the Son not only embodies God's glory but also reveals this to the universe as he sustains all things and bears them to their appointed end by his omnipotent word," writes William Lane.[39]

Importantly, Christ sustains the universe dynamically, not passively, says David Allen, and He carries it along or guides "it towards its intended goal."[40] "Christ does not physically hold up the world, as was said of the mythical Atlas," argues Bruce Barton, "but he guides the world toward its appointed future—the time when he will receive it as his inheritance.... All things are held together in a coherent or logical way, sustained and upheld, prevented from dissolving into chaos. In him alone and by his word, we find the unifying principle of all life."[41]

PRAYER

Jesus, thank you for creating us and for creating the universe. Since the beginning of time, You have held all things together on earth and in the Heavenly realm. It is awe-inspiring to realize that nothing happens throughout all the earth, in our relationships, even ▶

down to our innermost thoughts, that You do not see. Before the creation of the world, You knew we would fall away from Your divine plans, Yet You chose to create us anyway. Thank you, Lord! Thank You for counting the cost and loving us enough to say that despite how much we would hurt and disappoint You (even to the point of Your own sacrificial death), You decided we were worth it all. We offer a moment of silence to sit gratefully in Your presence.

AMEN.

Paul now turns to Christ's leadership of the body—His church—toward redemption. Christ created the universe for a purpose—man's redemption—and He sustains it and guides us toward it for that purpose despite our fallen nature. Paul writes, "For God was pleased to have all his fullness dwell in him, and through him to reconcile to himself all things, whether things on earth or things in heaven, by making peace through his blood, shed on the cross" (1:19–20). What a rich, glorious assurance. Here again, Paul stresses through repetition an important truth: Christ is God. He is God's exact image and all of God's fullness; every bit of God inheres in Christ.

Christ, through His sacrificial work on the cross, reconciles men to God—men who were separated from God through sin. Paul homes in on the importance of Christ's incarnation and passion: "But now he has reconciled you by Christ's physical body through death to present you holy in his sight, without blemish and free from accusation" (1:22). This is "the hope held out in the gospel. This is the gospel that you heard and that has been proclaimed to every creature under heaven, and of which I, Paul, have become your servant." (1:23–24). Our redemption and our reconciliation to God are neither universal nor automatic. They require faith in Christ's finished work on the cross. "Reconciliation basically means 'the removal of God's enmity toward fallen man' and, because enmity has been removed, all men are rendered savable," writes Arnold Fruchtenbaum. "Reconciliation itself does not save anyone; it merely renders people savable. They are saved now only when they believe in Jesus the Messiah."[42]

Do we really believe this? If so, do we act on our belief? Do we evangelize with the committed purpose of bringing the good news to unbelievers and explaining to them the opportunity of redemption and reconciling themselves to God through faith in His son? If we believed this as fervently as we profess, wouldn't we work harder to this end?

PRAYER

Lord, You have called us to be the salt of the earth, sharing the good news about the salvation available to all of us through Your Son, Jesus. Give us the passion to share our personal stories of salvation with the people You have placed right in front of us. Help us not to disqualify ourselves, assuming we are not the right people to share this hope with others. We ask Your Holy Spirit to empower us, encourage us, and to guide us to the people You want to reach through our lives. May we daily offer ourselves as living sacrifices to You.

AMEN.

False teachers and similar heretics couldn't be more off-base in dismissing the reality of Christ's humanity and His actual suffering on our behalf. John assured us that "the Word became flesh and made his dwelling among us" (John 1:14). Christ's material existence was essential for God's salvation plan to work. Reconciliation required a physical sacrifice—"by making peace through his blood, shed on the cross" (1:20) and "by Christ's physical body" (1:22).

This is Paul's shot across the bow to the false teachers, leaving no doubt he is addressing and refuting them directly. Paul is consistent. He had written to the Romans, "God presented Christ as a sacrifice of atonement through the shedding of his blood—to be received by faith" (Romans 3:25). The shedding of blood—as physical as it gets—was imperative, as is our appropriation of His sacrifice through our faith in Him. Likewise, the writer of Hebrews assures us, "But we do sec Jesus, who was made lower than the angels for a little while, now crowned with glory and honor because he suffered death, so that by the grace of God he might taste death for everyone" (Hebrews 2:9).

No, Christ didn't just *appear* to be physical, and His death on the cross was not some theoretical fiction. It was abundantly real and full of anguish and suffering. In almost every Christian-themed book I (David) have written, I have felt compelled to reiterate evangelist John Stott's gripping description of the impact of Christ's physical and spiritual suffering on His own faith. Please indulge us as we repeat it here because if just one person profits from this as much as we have, it will be worth others' having to bear its repetition. Stott wrote,

> I could never myself believe in God, if it were not for the cross. The only God I believe in is the One Nietzsche ridiculed as "God on the cross."... For the real sting of suffering is not misfortune itself, nor even the pain of it or the injustice of it, but the apparent God-forsakenness of it. Pain is endurable, but the seeming indifference of God is not. Sometimes we picture him lounging, perhaps dozing, in some celestial deck-chair, while the hungry millions starve

> to death. We think of him as an armchair spectator, almost gloating over the world's suffering and enjoying His own insulation from it. Philip Yancey has gone further and uttered the unutterable which we may have thought but to which we have never dared to give voice: "If God is truly in charge, somehow connected to all the world's suffering, why is He so capricious, unfair? Is He the cosmic sadist Who delights in watching us squirm?" Job said something similar: God "mocks the despair of the innocent" (Job 9:23). It is this terrible caricature of God which the cross smashes to smithereens. We are not to envisage Him on a deck-chair, but on a cross. The God Who allows us to suffer, once suffered Himself in Christ, and continues to suffer with us and for us today.[43]

Having described Christ's essence and His role in creation and redemption, Paul transitions to describing his own evangelical role in general and on behalf of the Colossians in particular. "Now I rejoice in what I am suffering for you, and I fill up in my flesh what is still lacking in regard to Christ's afflictions, for the sake of his body, which is the church. I have become its servant by the commission God gave me to present to you the word of God in its fullness—the mystery that has been kept hidden for ages and generations but is now disclosed to the Lord's people" (1:2426).

What is this mystery? Paul discloses it in his epistle to the Ephesians: "This mystery is that through the gospel the Gentiles are heirs together with Israel, members together of one body, and sharers together in the promise in Christ Jesus" (3:6). The Old Testament revealed that God would bless all people through Abraham by making salvation available to them (Gen. 12:3; 22:18), which Paul later identifies as God's announcement of the gospel to Abraham in advance (Gal. 3:7–9). With Christ's coming, all believers in Him would be equal and united in the body of Christ (Eph. 2:11–22).[44]

Paul closes the chapter proclaiming his commitment to help believers become fully mature in Christ—knowledgeable in doctrine, steadfast in faith, and Christlike in their behavior. Paul understands this is only possible through the work of the Holy Spirit indwelling believers. Though there is nothing we can do to earn our salvation, human effort is not entirely irrelevant in the Christian life. As noted, we acquire all our spiritual power from the Spirit, but we must place ourselves before Him and exercise the spiritual disciplines. To facilitate the growth of believers, Paul would "contend with all the energy Christ so powerfully works in me" (1:29). While all the power and credit belong to the Spirit, Paul, empowered by the Spirit, would do his part as Christ's obedient servant to evangelize, plant churches, combat heresies, and encourage other leaders and believers.

CHAPTER 2

Paul explains that he is working mightily on behalf of those at Laodicea and for all who have not met him personally (2:1). He intends to encourage their hearts—a recurring theme in his epistles—and unite them in love so they can enjoy "the full riches of complete understanding." They will then come to know the mystery of God in Christ, "in whom are hidden all the treasures of wisdom and knowledge" so "that no one may delude [them] with plausible arguments" (2:3–5). Paul is urging congregants to embrace the gospel intellectually and emotionally, preach it, and build one another up through their shared mission. They must be united in love for one another, and their love must be grounded in their mutual love for Christ and their commitment to grow together as a unified body.

Paul directs their focus squarely on Christ, the fountain of wisdom and knowledge. This contrasts with the false teachers, who tout their own special knowledge and seek to delude them with "plausible arguments"—seductive ideas that sound reasonable on their face. Believers must be thoroughly convinced of the truth of the gospel and committed to it. This will lead not only to their salvation and the spread of the gospel but to a bond of love among believers in the church. "Paul has in mind a Spirit-shaped conviction about the truth of the gospel (the knowledge, the mystery)," explains Scot McNight. "Knowledge promotes unity in love, just as love promotes unity in knowledge. The focus for Paul... is a fellowship that exhibits a supernaturally based union through the Spirit. Love and knowledge for Paul are thoroughly ecclesial (church) virtues."[45]

Some commentators particularly highlight Paul's opening words in this chapter, "I want you to know." Of course, he wants them to know—he could precede his every utterance with that phrase. So why say it here, since he normally doesn't waste words? It's because Paul wants to emphasize how hard he has been working for them, but not to boast or gain their sympathy. Rather, he wants them to understand how much God values them as He is working through Paul to grow their faith and knowledge and to multiply the effects of their spiritual maturity as they work together in love as Christ's body.[46]

In what way, though, is Paul working? John Woodhouse believes one strenuous activity Paul has in mind is praying. That is certainly counterintuitive, as we don't normally consider praying to be work at all, much less hard work—we usually ask God to do the work for us or thank Him for already having done so. But Woodhouse argues that Paul saw prayer as "very hard work," noting that at the end of this letter he describes Epaphras' prayer on behalf of the Colossians as "struggling" on their behalf in his prayers.[47] Indeed, the NIV says Epaphras "is always wrestling in prayer for you, that you may stand firm in all the will of God, mature and fully assured" (4:12). Several times in the letter Paul assures them of his work on their behalf, in prayer. "This is what the gospel servant does," says Woodhouse. "Praying is a struggle. It takes effort and discipline. 'I want you to know that,' says Paul. And I want you to know that that struggle is happening."[48]

Paul's profession of struggling in prayer should comfort and encourage us. We often struggle to bring ourselves to pray and also struggle during prayer. We don't always want to do it, and when we do, we sometimes aren't sure we are doing it correctly or effectively. We wonder: Are we truly connecting with God or just going through the motions? Paul's description assures us we are not abnormal in struggling with prayer and that it doesn't always come naturally. We know it sometimes takes effort and discipline, which is why it is considered one of the spiritual disciplines. That it could be difficult for Paul and Epaphras tells us we aren't necessarily doing it incorrectly just because it's challenging.

We must discipline ourselves to pray frequently. We shouldn't consider it a chore; at its core, after all, it is a conversation with the God of the universe, even if it doesn't seem so at times. If we bear this in mind it might make it easier and even more awe-inspiring. We all sometimes get lazy, however. There's no question that we deeply love our families and close friends, yet at times we don't feel like picking up the phone to call them. Even if we don't, we must discipline ourselves to remain in touch to preserve, strengthen, and refresh those relationships.

Moreover, consider that when we do pick up the phone and make that call, we are usually glad we did. Prayer can be similar. Our carnal nature beckons us away from God, but we must practice opening our hearts to him by daily prayer and Bible study. Let's quit thinking so much about it and just do it. There is no shame in having to condition ourselves to practice the spiritual disciplines, but there is a spiritual cost if we do not do so, in that our relationship with God will suffer. Paul validates this as he tells the Colossians he is delighted by their discipline and the firmness of their faith in Christ (2:5).

Paul also touched on this theme in chapter one, when he conveyed that he is exerting strenuous effort "in warning everyone and teaching everyone with wisdom, that we may present everyone mature in Christ" (1:28). He described his efforts as toiling and "struggling with all his energy," noting, however, that this energy derives from God, who is "powerfully" working within him (1:29).

Again, Paul seeks no personal credit for his labors but wants congregants to know that God-inspired labor is being exerted on their behalf to bring them to maturity in their faith. By emphasizing the work involved and God's commitment to them, he is giving them a priceless gift: quickening their awareness of God's love for them. They must mature in their faith to reap the full benefits of the Christian life, the most important of which is love.

In our efforts to mature in the faith, as Paul instructs, we must remember that the church is Christ's body of believers—his bride—and that we must love and pray for one another as Paul prays for the Colossians. We shouldn't see Paul's role as an intercessor as exclusive to him or his time. Paul writes that it was God who ignited a deep burden in his heart to pray for the church body. As believers today, we cannot overlook the importance of the church and of the superior power of the whole body, which we can't match through our individual work. The same Holy Spirit who ignited Paul's prayers is just as alive and active on the earth—and in the hearts of modern-day believers—today as He was in Paul's era.

So let's not miss out on God's calling for us to pray frequently for the church as a whole and for our individual congregations, encouraging all members to participate and contribute their gifts to the body, striving to set aside our petty quarrels in favor of the overall mission. Let us be gracious and loving toward one another, mindful that we are working toward a common goal of maturing in our faith and growing in our Christian love for God and for one another.

PRAYER

Father, we pray that you will help us not to fall into complacency about Your purposes throughout the earth. Give us hearts that seek to empower Your church body rather than focus on our individual comforts and desires. We want to be sold out for You and Your greater plans. Please empower and encourage us in regularly praying for the church and its members, that they mature in their faith and grow in Your perfect love, knowledge, and understanding and in doing Your will.

AMEN.

Continuing, Paul again repeats themes he articulated earlier in the letter—telling believers that just as they received Christ as Lord they must continue to grow in their faith and gratitude. As believers we can't rest on our laurels after having received Christ.

We must keep living our lives "rooted and built up in him," "strengthened in the faith," and "overflowing with thankfulness" (2:6–7), Paul declares. Douglas Moo pinpoints this passage, together with the next section in which Paul condemns false teachings, as the heart of the letter. "We are to continue," writes Moo, "to live in him, to work out just what it means in both our thinking and our acting to live under the Lordship of Christ." We "must continue looking to Christ, and Christ alone, for all [our] spiritual needs."

Furthermore, to have "received Christ" doesn't just mean accepting the teaching or the word of God "but of Christ himself." You must believe in His person and commit "to the apostolic teaching about Christ and his significance."[49]

Having instructed believers to live and grow in Christ, Paul segues into a warning about the heresy threatening their church and diverting them from Christ. "See to it that no one takes you captive by philosophy and empty deceit, according to human tradition, according to the elemental spirits of the world, and not according to Christ" (2:8).

This is a lesson to us all. Usually when people come to Christ they are enthusiastic, attentive to the gospel, excited to have found and embraced Christ, and anxious to learn all they can about Him and the Bible. Here Paul is exhorting us to carry that enthusiasm forward. But he knows this will be difficult if we are led astray by false teachings, which undermine our understanding of Christ's divine nature and His sacrificial work. Paul makes clear that we must be centered on Christ, which will keep us grounded and allow us to continue to grow. As Paul told the Ephesians, "Then we will no longer be infants, tossed back and forth by the waves, and blown here and there by every wind of teaching and by the cunning and craftiness of people in their deceitful scheming" (Eph. 4:14). In Colossians, Paul denounces this false teaching as "hollow and deceptive philosophy" that depends on human tradition and spiritual forces of the world rather than Christ. In Ephesians he condemns those who spread these lies as cunning, crafty, and deceitful. Whether or not everyone who preaches a false gospel does so maliciously, conscious of their deceit, Paul stresses they are disseminating man-made, spiritually depraved lies and contradicting divine revelation.

Paul continues to make Christ the focus—the be-all, end-all—reiterating and expanding upon what he wrote earlier: "For in him the whole fullness of deity dwells bodily, and you have been filled in him, who is the head of all rule and authority. In him also you were circumcised with a circumcision made without hands, by putting off the body of the flesh, by the circumcision of Christ" (2:9–11). We used to be ruled by the flesh, says Paul, but that all changed when Christ "circumcised" us. We were buried with Him in baptism and raised with Him through our faith in Him and in God, who raised Him from the dead. Before, we were dead in our sins, but through our faith God resurrected us and made us alive with Christ. He forgave us all our sins, taking away our legal indebtedness and nailing it to the cross (2:12–14).

Paul is using the term "circumcision" metaphorically. "A circumcision made without hands" is a spiritual phenomenon whereby believers have "put off the body of the flesh," meaning they have cast aside their sinful nature and now live under Christ's lordship and not the authority of the world. As Paul told the Galatians, "Those who belong to Christ Jesus have crucified the flesh with its passions and desires. Since we live by the Spirit, let us keep in step with the Spirit" (Gal. 5:24–25).

In the Old Testament, physical circumcision was a sign of Jewish identity within the covenant and was therefore the first order of business under the law, introducing a Jew to the law's duties. Jews firmly believed that no one could live under the law's requirements unless first circumcised.[50] But even the Old Testament teaches the significance of the circumcision of the heart (Deut. 10:16; Jer. 4:4). Paul is confirming the importance of spiritual circumcision and telling the Colossians they have already been spiritually circumcised with Christ, which was symbolized by their baptism. The sacrament of baptism identifies Christians with Christ's crucifixion and His triumph over sin. Baptism leads not only to the believer's identification with Christ in His death but also in His resurrection (2:12).

Though this identification with resurrection is metaphorical in this context, believers will later actually be physically resurrected with Christ (1 Cor. 15:12–58).

Our salvation wouldn't be possible but for Christ's cancelation of our debts with His death on the cross. Our slate is wiped clean in God's eyes, and we are purified for salvation purposes. British pastor Charles Spurgeon put it best, explaining that when God looks at believers, He no longer sees our grotesque sin but sees Jesus Himself covering us with His veil: "When the Lord looks this way we hide behind the veil, and the eyes of the Lord behold the exceeding glories of the veil, to wit the person of His own dear Son, and He is so pleased with the cover that he forbears to remember the defilement and deformity of those whom it covers. God will never strike a soul through the veil of His Son's sacrifice. He accepts us because He cannot but accept His Son, who has become our covering."[51]

Paul asserts that Christ "disarmed the rulers and authorities and put them to open shame, by triumphing over them" (2:15). Christ forgave our sins and in the process "disarmed" the authorities and made them a public spectacle. We marvel at the irony of considering Jesus victorious when the earthly powers killed *Him*. What they didn't know is that He came to earth precisely to die and to achieve victory over Satan, sin, and death. As Paul told the Corinthians, "None of the rulers of this age understood it, for if they had, they would not have crucified the Lord of Glory" (1 Cor. 8). It is fitting that Paul couches this in martial language—He "disarmed" them. Understand that Paul isn't only referring to earthly authorities when he declares that Christ achieved a humiliating victory over the rulers and authorities. He is mainly talking about evil spiritual forces—the demonic powers who orchestrate such evil. Though Christ defeated the devil in His death and resurrection, depriving him of his ability to destroy the eternal life of believers, the devil and his forces remain alive and active in the world.

Thus, we remain in the throes of a spiritual battle with earthly forces ruled by Satan (Col. 1:13; 2 Tim. 2:26; John 12:31; 1 John 5:19; Eph. 2:2). In His sacrificial death, Christ not only gave eternal life to those with faith in Him, but He empowered them, through the Holy Spirit, to conquer Satan and sin every day of their earthly existence. Satan no longer rules the spirit-empowered believer. Christ's victory over these forces is complete ("God left nothing that is not subject to them"), "yet at present we do not see everything subject to them" (Heb. 2:8). "In the Garden of Eden, God assigned Adam and Eve to rule over all the earth (Genesis 1:28–30)," writes Bruce Barton. "But they sinned, and God took away their authority over all the creation. Today everything is obviously *not* under our control."[52] But we will regain that control in the future. As F. F. Bruce reminds us, "All creation will ultimately 'be set free from its bondage to decay and obtain the glorious liberty of the children of God'" (Romans 8:21). "A day is coming when, in the wonderful plan of God, the dominion that man lost will be given to him again," writes John MacArthur.[53]

Note Paul's paradoxical statement that Christ not only triumphed over the rulers and authorities but made a public spectacle of them by dying on the cross. He not only defeated the evil spiritual and earthly powers by allowing them to kill Him and thus fulfill His divine purpose in saving us, but He thereby publicly humiliated *them*. We should be consoled by this perspective and apply it to our own lives. Today, we see ungodly forces imposing their values on the world, smugly virtue-signaling the apparent victory of secular morality. They are misguided and contradicting biblical values, but, as scripture assures us, the truth will triumph in the end.

PRAYER

Jesus, we thank you for finishing Your work on the cross, assuring us that if You are for us, no one can be against us (Romans 8:31) and that nothing shall separate us from Your love (Romans 8:38–39). May we keep our eyes fixed on this promise as truth because You are perfectly faithful and cannot lie (Heb. 6:13–20). Give us the strength to believe with all our hearts that because You, the Creator and ruler of the universe, are on our side, we have nothing to fear. Let us take John's words to heart: "There is no fear in love, but perfect love casts out fear" (1 John 4:18). You have already fought and won the greatest battle for us. Your victory over death assures our victory as well, through faith in You. Though You told us we will have trouble in this world, You also assured us You will never leave us or forsake us (Heb. 13:5). Remind us of your presence in our daily struggles. Help us not to keep any doubt or concern from You. There is no problem too great or too small for You. Give us a heavenly perspective of the strength we can access through communing with You, and help us to keep our intentions pure. In Your Holy Name,

AMEN.

Paul reminds the Colossians that through Christ's sacrificial death, Christians are free from the law of sin and death (Romans 8:2), so he warns them not to return to bondage by following the rules of the authorities on such matters as food and drink, festivals, new moons, or the Sabbath (Col. 2:16). After all, Christ Himself declared all foods clean (Mark 7:19). As Paul told the Galatians, "For freedom Christ has set us free; stand firm therefore, and do not submit again to a yoke of slavery" (Gal. 5:1).

Note that freedom in Christ doesn't mean freedom from obedience to God and His moral standards. In fact, through our love of Christ we follow *higher* standards, for the standards Christ articulated in the Sermon on the Mount were far more demanding than those in the Mosaic Law. Following them, however, is not a matter of legalism. John MacArthur explains that "Christ set us free from the 'guilt-establishing and deadening power of the law' through His death and resurrection. Going back into a yoke of slavery is absurd."[54] Luther describes this freedom as "freedom from God's everlasting wrath."[55] In short, it is a matter of grace rather than law. Warren Wiersbe expressed this point beautifully: "'Your doctrine of grace and liberty is dangerous!' Paul's enemies argued. 'Why, if Christians are free from the Law, they will live wicked lives! We need the Law to control them!' So people have argued down through the centuries, little realizing that grace, not law, is the greatest teacher and 'controller' in the world."[56]

Paul elaborated on grace in his letter to Titus, writing, "For the grace of God has appeared that offers salvation to all people. It teaches us to say 'No' to ungodliness and worldly passions, and to live self-controlled, upright and godly lives in this present age, while we wait for the blessed hope—the appearing of the glory of our great God and Savior, Jesus Christ, who gave himself for us to redeem us from all wickedness and to purify for himself a people that are his very own, eager to do what is good" (Titus 2:11–14). You see, freedom in Christ does not mean a license to sin but living godly and self-controlled lives. It means actually being eager to do the right thing, not simply going through the motions of obeying the law without the proper spiritual mindset. Along these lines, Paul admonished the Romans that Christians are not free to sin because they are under grace and not law: "But thanks be to God that, though you used to be slaves to sin, you have come to obey from your heart the pattern of teaching that has now claimed your allegiance. You have been set free from sin and have become slaves to righteousness" (Romans 6:17–18).

There you have it—freedom from the bondage of sin means we are bound to righteousness. We must think of it in a positive way, deemphasizing the negative. That is, we mustn't think of it as a matter of avoiding sin but of seeking righteousness.

PRAYER

Lord, true devotion to You develops when we understand Your loyal love and sacrifice, which seems too good to be true. The Psalmist writes, "How precious are your thoughts about me, O God. They cannot be numbered" (139:17). It is humbling, almost embarrassing, to think that You, the perfect, Holier than Holy God, think countless, precious thoughts about us. And yet, we accept Your word as truth. Thank you, Lord! May this word be buried deep in our beings, for that is what will ultimately spur our desire to serve You. Infuse us with Your love and a desire to serve You because of that love, rather than trying to live up to religious rules for their own sake and through our own feeble efforts. We recognize true righteousness comes from You and You alone. We ask You to show us areas we must surrender to You, and we thank You for the freedom You provide.

AMEN.

Paul next commands the congregants not to allow anyone to judge them based on what they eat or drink or on matters concerning religious festivals or Sabbath days. "These are shadows of the things to come, but the substance belongs to Christ" (2:16–17). (The writer of Hebrews echoed this truth: "For since the law has but a shadow of the good things to come instead of the true form of these realities, it can never, by the same sacrifices that are continually offered every year, make perfect those who draw near" [Heb. 10:1]). Nor must they let anyone who delights in false humility and the worship of angels disqualify them. Such people are proud of their unspiritual minds and provide "great detail" about what they've seen. "They have lost connection with the head, from whom the whole body, supported and held together by its ligaments and sinews, grows and God causes it to grow" (2:18–19). Why would they submit to the "elemental spiritual forces of this world" when they died with Christ to them? These are fleeting things based not on godly commands but human ones. These teachings are seductive because they have "an appearance of wisdom" and the trappings of "false humility" and are supported by "self-imposed worship." While following these rules results in the "harsh treatment of the body," they "lack any value in restraining sensual indulgence" (2:18–23). Obeying rules for the sake of appearances or bringing credit upon yourself is not the proper motivation.

Scripture prohibits the worship of anything or anyone other than God—which includes angels (Exodus 20:3–4) because angels are servants like we are (Rev. 22:8–9). The heretics among the Colossians self-servingly depict their worship of angels as virtuous humility, but it is actually their pride. They elevate themselves with idle notions inspired by their unspiritual minds. Conceit is the devil's playground. To ascribe deity to anyone or anything other than the Father, the Son, and the Holy Spirit is rank idolatry and diminishes the deity of Christ. Christians should not be influenced by those who would "disqualify" them—that is, who would deny their Christian authenticity—based on some cultish rules they impose on the church. False teachers rely on themselves rather than scripture and Christ, who is the head of the church. They insert themselves between the body (members) of the church and Christ. The body grows through essential contact with the head (Christ), so false teachers impede vital contact between the head and the body and stifle the spiritual growth of the church.[57]

Paul again warns Christians against legalism—the following of man-made rules—as an avenue to spirituality. Legalism is both wrong and spiritually damaging. These ceremonial rules empower the authorities who issue them and confer on them a veneer of wisdom and false humility. Instead of promoting spirituality, these rules blunt it and deter true dependence on Christ, which is liberation from the bondage of rules made by "elemental spiritual forces of this world." Christ's sacrificial death nullified those rules (2:20). Church father Origen offers an interesting insight into false humility, reminding us of Peter's objection to Christ's washing his feet. Peter obviously intended well—he thought it presumptuous and inappropriate to have his feet washed by the Savior—but he was unwittingly keeping himself from bonding with Jesus.[58]

Moreover, as Christians we are in the world but not of the world (John 15:18–19). If we dishonor this truth, we are enemies of the cross of Christ (Philip. 3:18), whose "destiny is destruction, their god is their stomach, and their glory is in their shame. Their mind is set on earthly things. But our citizenship is in heaven" (Philip. 3:19–20). We know people who make an idol out of dietary rules—who cultishly ascribe a false spirituality to adherence to certain guidelines. It's wise to promote healthy living and healthy eating, for example, but let's not derive our sense of spiritual self-worth from such practices.

The false teachers pursued righteousness through self-denial.[59] It's one thing to deny oneself certain privileges as a spiritual discipline, such as fasting, but the focus there is always on God, not on the person submitting to the discipline. There is a marked distinction between obedience and self-promotion. John MacArthur reminds us of the monks who "mistakenly thought the path to spirituality lay in exposing" their bodies to the elements and withdrawing from the world. Self-denial in itself is not the problem and may even be admirable so long as it is not the final goal or perceived as a substitute for the worship of Christ. "God may call some to a life of self-denial," writes MacArthur. "Many missionaries, for example, have by necessity led ascetic lives. They did not do so, however, as an attempt to gain spirituality."[60]

Nor should Christians practice self-denial as a means of advertising their own piety. "Beware of practicing your righteousness before other people in order to be seen by them, for then you have no reward from your Father who is in heaven," warns Christ. "Thus, when you give to the needy, sound no trumpet before you, as the hypocrites do in the synagogues and in the streets, that they may be praised by others." He adds, "And when you fast, do not look gloomy like the hypocrites, for they disfigure their faces that their fasting may be seen by others. Truly, I say to you, they have received their reward. But when you fast, anoint your head and wash your face, that your fasting may not be seen by others but by your Father who is in secret. And your Father who sees in secret will reward you" (Matthew 6:1–2, 16–18).

PRAYER

Lord, we recognize there are evil spirits who actively use "religion" to deceive us into thinking we deserve credit and recognition for our devotion to You. Protect us from the temptation to pat ourselves on the back for our perceived piousness. Help us also to recognize it is Your Holy Spirit who compels us to devote our time and energy to You; we can take no credit. You alone are our saving grace. Replace our hardened hearts with hearts of compassion, humility, and gratitude for Your sacrifice. We thank You for the astounding lengths You go to bring us into Your presence. May we never take that for granted. In Your Holy Name,

AMEN.

CHAPTER 3

Next, Paul transitions from railing against the false teachers to instructing the Colossians to live in a Christlike manner. Since they "have been raised with Christ," they must set their "hearts on things above, where Christ is, seated at the right hand of God." They must not focus on "earthly things." As they have died and been raised with Christ, their lives are now hidden with Christ in God. Christ is their life, and when He appears they will appear with Him in glory (3:1–4). Christ is everything to the believer. He is not an enhancement to life. "He *is* life," and we must orient our lives around Him.[61]

Upon their conversion Christians are united with Christ and spiritually enter his death and resurrection, which enables them to understand spiritual truths and the will of God. We have acquired our new spiritual life, though our physical resurrection with Christ will occur in the future. This "already–not yet" concept appears elsewhere in the Bible concerning the coming of the kingdom of God, as discussed in *The True Jesus*: "The idea is that the kingdom of God is here now but is also coming in the future in a different way that is tied to the original and will complete it."[62]

In Jesus' first coming He ushered in the kingdom of God, which was not, as the Jews expected, a military triumph over the earthly authorities. Jesus indeed inaugurated the kingdom of God, but He will not consummate His kingdom rule until He returns. Closely related to the already–not yet aspects of the kingdom of God, believers are presently (already) indwelled by the Holy Spirit and empowered to live godly lives and overcome sin. Not yet, but in the future, we will be totally free of sin upon our physical resurrection and glorification with Christ. In the meantime, we are to set our minds on the things above. "We are not simply awaiting Christ's return, when we will receive our inheritance and enter our heavenly home," writes Grant Osborne. "We *already* have entered heaven spiritually and are already part of that new reality. Our physical environment is still earthly, but our hearts and minds are focused 'above,' giving us an entirely new set of priorities."[63]

These "things above," explains MacArthur, are the privileges and riches of the heavenly kingdom, which are accessible to believers.[64] Here, Paul further contradicts the false teachers who masquerade as spiritual elites with secret wisdom, claiming a direct line to God and spiritual knowledge. To the contrary, they have nothing but an illusion, while believers have access to the true things above through the Holy Spirit.[65] "The false teachers centered in visions (2:18), believing that they provided transport to the heavenly realm," explains Osborne. "Paul is showing the error of such merely human techniques for gaining access to heaven—which is real, not something we need to 'see' in a vision. The believer already dwells there."[66] As Paul explains, however, the believer's life in Christ is hidden from unbelievers who do not know Him and therefore can't comprehend the believer's relationship with Christ.[67]

Paul is saying that Christians in Colossae are, in a sense, resident aliens, as their actual identity is heavenly and not worldly. Upon their conversion they had died to Christ (2:20) and been spiritually reborn as new creations (2 Cor. 5:17), so their citizenship is in heaven. This timeless scriptural lesson has profound implications for us and how we should live, and thus deserves our attention. We must presently seek these heavenly things. "The world needs heavenly people as never before, and this is what Christians are when they live up to their true identity," writes J. Philip Arthur. "The message of this passage to Christians, whether in the first or twenty-first century, then, is: 'Be what you are!'"[68]

Christians have all they will ever need in Christ while the false teachers are selling something useless and even harmful to them. One can't improve on godly truths and on the supremacy and sufficiency of Christ. Christians must embrace their new identity because it is their true identity and because it will make this world a more heavenly place. "In calling upon Christians to be what they are, Paul set before the Colossians the challenge to live as heavenly people and, in doing so, to bring some of the quality of heaven to earth to irradiate and suffuse all their relationships and life situations," says Arthur.[69]

Believers must actively "put to death" those things that are part of their earthly nature, including "sexual immorality, impurity, lust, evil desires and greed" (3:5). As they have taken off their old selves, they must purge themselves of "anger, wrath, malice, slander," obscene language, and lying (3:8). In his other writings, Paul similarly warns us against sinning (see Romans 1:29–31; 1 Cor. 5:11; 6:9; Gal 5:19–21; Eph. 5:3–5).[70]

Pastor and professor Sam Storms raises an interesting question about Paul's teachings: Why does Paul so roundly condemn rules about eating, drinking, and religious festivals in chapter two and elsewhere, then impose his own list of forbidden behaviors? Why isn't this legalism as well? Storms's answer is that legalists, such as the false teachers, typically impose their rules concerning acceptable and unacceptable conduct as a means to gain favor with God or induce Him to grant life. Paul and other New Testament writers, by contrast, lay down these standards as evidence of the fruit of the believer's already acquired favor with God. "We already are the favored and beloved of God, made such by sovereign grace alone, and it is on the basis of this glorious truth that we are inwardly impelled (rather than outwardly compelled) to express life, not earn it," writes Storms. We aren't encouraged to do certain things and avoid others to gain Christ. Rather, we pursue holiness because we have already received Christ and been raised with Him spiritually.

"We pursue purity and eschew evil not in order to be hidden with him but because we already are."[71]

Paul continues, declaring that the believer's new self is being renewed in knowledge after the image of its creator (3:10). Norman Geisler explains that Paul's term "being renewed" means this "new self" requires constant refreshing to keep us victorious over sin. This idea is vital to Paul, as shown in his second letter to the Corinthians: "Though our outer self is wasting away, our inner self is being renewed day by day" (2 Cor. 4:16); in his epistle to the Romans: "Do not be conformed to this world, but be transformed by the renewal of your mind" (Romans 12:2); and in his letter to the Ephesians: "to be renewed in the spirit of your minds, and to put on the new self, created after the likeness of God in true righteousness and holiness" (Eph. 4:23).

There is no distinction between Gentile or Jew, circumcised or uncircumcised, barbarian or Scythian, slave or free. That is, every person, regardless of race, culture, nationality, or economic status, becomes a new creation. It is solely about our faith in Christ. "Christ is all, and in all" (3:11). As Geisler observes, "All barriers are destroyed in Christ, and all believers are truly 'created equal.'"[72] Consequently, all believers should discard their sinful practices and live consistent with their "new self."

Not only must we avoid the sins of the flesh but fervently pursue the heavenly things in Christ. "Put on then, as God's chosen ones, holy and beloved, compassionate hearts, kindness, humility, meekness, and patience, bearing with one another and, if one has a complaint against another, forgiving each other; as the Lord has forgiven you, so you also must forgive. And above all these put on love, which binds everything together in perfect harmony. And let the peace of Christ rule in your hearts, to which indeed you were called in one body. And be thankful." (3:12–15).

PRAYER

Lord, often when we read Your commands, our minds immediately rush to all our shortcomings. In these moments, remind us that when we accepted Jesus, His holiness enveloped us and gave us a new life! Help us to see ourselves as Your beloved adopted children, heirs to Your heavenly kingdom who should no longer approach You as orphans begging for bread. Instead, may we take direction from the first line of the Lord's prayer, imploring You to bring Your will and Your heavenly kingdom to the world we live in. May we seek Your presence constantly, asking You to show us how You are working all things for good behind the scenes, and how we can play a part in that process. We ask for Your Holy Spirit to give us supernatural perspective so that we may see from the heavenly perspective rather than through our marred, human viewpoint. In Jesus' name,

AMEN.

Having received eternal life by God's grace and through no merit of our own, believers should respond in grateful obedience and dedicate themselves to pleasing God and emulating Christ. We must adopt the behaviors Paul describes, and our will to do so should flow naturally from our faith and position in Christ. We should freely forgive others as God has forgiven us—because grudges may lead to sinful behavior, but above all, because it is the right thing to do.[73] Illustrating this point, D. L. Moody imagined Christ telling Peter, "Go, hunt up the man who put the crown of thorns on My head and tell him that I love him. Tell him that he can have a crown in my kingdom, one without a thorn. Find the man who spat in my face and preach the gospel to him. Tell him that I forgive him and that I died to save him. Find the man who thrust the spear into my side and tell him that there is a quicker way to my heart."[74]

It makes sense that Paul follows his command to forgive with his exhortation that we cloak ourselves with love. Just as unforgiveness leads to dark-heartedness and sin, love is the apex of Christlikeness, and Christlike behavior necessarily proceeds from it. Love is the foundation of all other virtues.[75] D. L. Moody's depiction of Christ's forgiveness illuminates that forgiveness springs from love. In his first letter to the Corinthians, Paul succinctly captures the paramount importance of love, insisting that we can have all the spiritual gifts in the world and even strong faith, but they won't matter if we don't have love: "If I speak in the tongues of men and of angels, but have not love, I am a noisy gong or a clanging cymbal. And if I have prophetic powers, and understand all mysteries and all knowledge, and if I have all faith, so as to remove mountains, but have not love, I am nothing. If I give away all I have, and if I deliver up my body to be burned, but have no love, I gain nothing" (1 Cor. 13:1–3). He adds, "So now faith, hope, and love abide, these three; but the greatest of these is love" (1 Cor. 13:13). Jesus underscored this in identifying love as the greatest commandment. "You shall love the Lord your God with all your heart and with all your soul and with all your mind. This is the great and first commandment. And a second is like it: You shall love your neighbor as yourself. On these two commandments depend all the Law and the Prophets" (Matt. 22:37–40).

Christ's love—described with the Greek term *agape*—is exemplified by the selfless, sacrificial love that led Jesus to the cross. So when Paul tells us to "put on love," as it binds everything together in perfect harmony, he's telling us that love is quintessentially Christlike. "Love...holds Christians together in fellowship under the strain of all common life," writes J. Moffatt. "It is the link of the perfect life.... Love checks the selfish, hard tempers which keep people apart and thus militate against the maturing of good fellowship. Here...is the full expression of the divine life in the Community, devoid of bitter words and angry feelings, and freed from the ugly defects of immorality and dishonesty. The argument is a parallel to that of Matthew 5:43–48."[76]

As the Gospel according to John confirms, "Anyone who does not love does not know God, because God is love" (1 John 4:8). Furthermore, "God is love and whoever abides in love abides in God, and God abides in him" (1 John 4:16). It's not simply that God acts lovingly toward us; it's that He *is* love. It is His nature. To "put on love" is to put on godliness.

PRAYER

Lord, our human nature constantly tempts us to spiral into self-pity, resentment, and anxiety. Help us combat these feelings by following Your command to "rejoice always, pray continually, and give thanks in all circumstances" (1 Thess. 5:16–18). Worshipping You is our greatest weapon because it increases Your presence. Help us to step outside our feelings and to practice thanking You regularly for the many blessings You've showered upon us. Point us to worship music and Bible verses we can sing and memorize in our hearts, and may those words flow from us on a daily basis, acting as a barrier between us and the schemes of the enemy to separate us from You. Thank You, Lord!

AMEN.

Paul teaches that believers must also let the peace of Christ rule in their hearts (3:15). Christ has won this peace for us through His sacrificial death, and we must avail ourselves of it. It is an inner contentment in Christ that transcends the ups and downs of life on earth. This peace that we have been given individually also unites us corporately as a church. And for these unmerited gifts, we must be grateful to God. The word of Christ must dwell in us richly, says Paul, teaching and admonishing one another in all wisdom (3:16).

Here again Paul reminds us of the importance of God's word. The word of Christ—scripture—is the means by which God's peace is assured to us.[77] Christ's teaching should dwell in us through our study and knowledge of the Bible—the living, breathing word of God. It is never changing, and it will keep us attuned to the mind of God and encourage us toward Christlike behavior. We must certainly pray for God's wisdom (1:9), but a direct line to that wisdom is His word, which we must read daily while praying that He opens its rich meaning to us. We must share the word with believers and instruct one another with its wisdom.

Paul tells the Colossians they should do everything—words and deeds—in the name of Jesus and give thanks to the Father through Him (3:17). Commentator Richard Melick notes that Paul is teaching that God comes to the world and the world comes to God through Jesus. Jesus' sacrificial death on the cross gives us access to the Father through Him. In turn, we must express our gratitude to the Father through Jesus.[78] This, of course, doesn't mean we can't thank the Father directly, but it underscores our real, tangible access to the triune God of the universe because His Son became man, lived among us, died for us, and was resurrected so that we too could be resurrected.

Paul closes this chapter with instructions for Christian households: "Wives, submit to your husbands, as is fitting in the Lord. Husbands, love your wives, and do not be harsh with them. Children, obey your parents in everything, for this pleases the Lord. Fathers, do not provoke your children, lest they become discouraged" (3:18–21).

The notion of wives' submitting to their husbands doesn't sit well with today's culture, and Paul is frequently attacked for these and other so-called harsh teachings. Many modern commentators discount these instructions either by rejecting the Bible's divine authority or by claiming that Paul's teaching only applied to the particular culture he was addressing. Wrestling with this passage can indeed be difficult. There is, however, a strong argument that Paul meant exactly what he said. First, the Bible's divine authority, including Paul's writings, is recognized by the vast bulk of Christendom, and we cannot transform God's word into a mere fictional allegory simply to annul some teaching that may offend modern sensibilities. And second, Paul laid down similar admonitions elsewhere, including in Ephesians (5:22–6:9) and First Corinthians (11:2–16). But if Paul meant for these rules to apply universally to all cultures in all times, there are some accompanying truths that should ease believers' angst.

God, through Paul, is establishing rules for households patterned on the interrelationships of the three persons of the Trinity. The functional distinctions between husbands and wives, in fact, do not detract from the equality of women. Jesus, who is Himself God, is functionally subordinate to the Father, which in no way diminishes His deity or His equal essence with the Father and the Holy Spirit. Jesus set the pattern for servanthood; though He is God, He came not to be served but to serve. He voluntarily surrendered His divine attributes in His incarnation. As Paul wrote to the Philippians, "Christ Jesus, who, though he was in the form of God, did not count equality with God a thing to be grasped, but emptied himself, by taking the form of a servant, being born in the likeness of men. And being found in human form, he humbled himself by becoming obedient to the point of death, even death on a cross" (Philip. 2:5).

The husband is commanded to love his wife as Christ loved the church (Eph. 5:25). Remember that Christ loved the church—His believers—so much that He died for it. There is no higher love. In

Jesus' own words, "Greater love has no one than this, that someone lay down his life for his friends" (John 15:13). Paul's directives for husbands and wives pertain to domestic relationships, and they apply on earth, not in heaven.[79] Another mitigating factor, according to Melick, is that while children and slaves are told to obey in the passage above, wives are not. Their submission is voluntary, and obedience is not directly commanded. "Paul made it clear that such submission is an outworking of the lordship of Christ," notes Melick. "It is part of the Christian order.... Voluntarily taking a position of submission is a matter of a wife's relationship to the Lord, not to her husband. It is 'fitting in the Lord.'"[80]

In other words, the wife is not instructed to submit to the husband because he's superior and she's inferior. Rather, it is a matter of obedience to God, who has ordained a functional subordination within the household. If a husband loves his wife as Christ loves the church—sacrificially—the household should be harmonious. A sacrificially loving husband is not insensitive or domineering. Indeed, if a husband truly loves his wife as Christ loves the church and treats her accordingly, he will be more, not less, deferential in his interactions with her, which should ease any tension resulting from her functional subordination to him in household matters.

We may struggle to fully understand certain passages of scripture, but we don't presume to put our discomfort ahead of the Lord's commands. We can't wish away portions of God's word simply because they don't sit perfectly well with us. We would all be better served if we didn't take the bait of modern culture—which often pits man against woman and race against race—but instead love and treat one another as Christ loved and treated the church.

Paul continues unfolding God's design for family relationships in setting out the relationships between parents and children. Children should obey their parents in everything, as this pleases the

Lord. Children learn the importance of obedience, respect, and authority in their relationship with their parents, who groom them for adulthood and lend stability to society. This pleases God, who defines authority. In turn, Paul admonishes fathers not to discourage their children by aggravating them. The themes are consistent. Just as the husband authority figure has no license to be harsh with his wife and must love her like Christ loved the church, parents are not to abuse their authority over their children but to treat them lovingly. Discipline is important, but ridicule and derision are forbidden.

In another controversial passage, Paul instructs slaves ("bondservants") to obey their earthly masters "not by way of eye-service, as people pleasers, but with sincerity of heart, fearing the Lord. Whatever you do, work heartily, as for the Lord and not for men, knowing that from the Lord you will receive the inheritance as your word. You are serving the Lord Christ" (3:22–24). The *New Living Translation* is a bit clearer here—instead of using "eye-service" and "people pleasers," it says, "Try to please them all the time, not just when they are watching you." Many people are troubled by these passages, arguing that Paul is apparently condoning slavery. But we must distinguish between Paul's comments on slavery and his remarks on family relationships. "The relationships between husbands and wives and parents and children are ordained by God from creation," explains the ESV Study Bible. "Hence, Paul's instructions on marriage represent the perfect will of God. Slavery, on the other hand, is something created by human beings and does not represent God's will from creation; the Scriptures regulate the institution without commending it."[81]

Furthermore, it's important to understand that Roman bondservants were quite different from North American chattel slaves. Bond servants were sometimes allowed compensation and to eventually purchase their freedom. The Bible reveals that some masters entrusted their servants with significant responsibilities, including the management of their financial resources. The ESV Study Bible notes that slaves constituted an estimated one-third of the population of cities like Colossae and Ephesus. They were sometimes considered family members and often remained as workers for the family after acquiring their freedom. This does not mean their masters didn't abuse them, which is one reason Paul issues instructions on the proper treatment of servants.

Paul, then, isn't recommending slavery but is laying out rules and attitudes regarding an already existing institution, which ultimately died out partially due to the influence of his writings.[82] These "household codes" Paul prescribes "did not set out to abolish or reshape existing social structures, but to christianize them," writes F. F. Bruce.[83] To the extent that Paul addresses servants here, he treats them with dignity and sympathy, instructing them to fear and work hard for the Lord and promising they will be rewarded for doing so. He says their true master is the Lord Jesus, signifying that in God's eyes they are as important as any other human being, including their masters.

Clearly, if Paul had considered them chattel, he never would have addressed them as children of God who are invited to partake of their divine inheritance through faith in Christ.[84] He certainly would not have directed masters to treat their servants "justly and fairly, knowing that [they] also have a Master in heaven" (Col. 4:1). After all, in a little-quoted passage of the Bible—First Timothy 1:9— Paul condemns "enslavers."[85]

We further consider Paul's writings on the master-servant relationship in our chapters on Philemon and Ephesians.

CHAPTER 4

Paul next directs the believers to continue steadfastly in prayer (4:2), as he did elsewhere (1 Thes. 5:17). They must be "watchful" in prayer and do it with thanksgiving (4:2). Commentators infer that being watchful means they should remain alert and focused on their devotion to God during prayer as well as attentive to answers to their prayers. They have plenty to be thankful to God for, including their reconciliation to Him through their faith in Christ and that He is sustaining and restoring the fallen world.

That Paul highly respects the new believers and regards them as his brothers in Christ is shown by his earnest request that they pray for him and his fellow evangelists—that their work for the Lord may open more doors to advance the gospel (4:3–4). They are to behave like Christ—to "walk in wisdom," make "the best use of the time," and let their "speech always be gracious" (4:5-6). People often say that Christians win more hearts for Christ through their behavior than their words, and Paul here affirms the importance of a winsome Christian witness.

Paul closes his letter with an extensive list of greetings. Importantly, he urges the believers to share his letter with the church in Laodicea. Remember that at this time, the New Testament had not yet been officially compiled, and Paul wanted his instructions to the Colossian believers to aid other believers in the surrounding churches—and all believers everywhere and throughout the ages.

CHAPTER TWO

PHILEMON

"NO MORE AS A SLAVE"

Christianity arose in a complex social setting. Many conflicting religions and philosophies contributed to a pluralistic environment where anyone could justify anything in the name of a personal god. Secularism rose to new popularity as Greeks and Romans often made only a token acknowledgment of the place of religion in society. Christianity met these challenges. Christians claimed that faith in Christ brought a totally new way of thinking and acting. Everywhere Christianity spread, a sense of morality and social justice naturally went with it. The Epistle to Philemon illustrates this truth. It is an informal letter addressed to a man converted to Christ by the apostle Paul.

—Richard Melick[1]

Most commentators believe this letter was written during Paul's first Roman imprisonment, about the same time as the epistle to the Colossians. Philemon was an affluent resident of Colossae whom Paul brought to Christ (Philem. 19).[2] The letter concerns relationships between Christians and how they should treat one another, including forgiveness and reconciliation in the spirit of Christ's love.

Philemon's slave Onesimus had stolen from him and escaped captivity. While Onesimus was on the run, he met Paul and through him became a believer. Thus, the three principals involved in this letter are interconnected through Paul's evangelism. In this letter Paul appeals to Philemon, a leader of the church in Colossae who hosted church services in his home, to show grace to Onesimus by allowing him to return as a Christian brother. Paul's plea to Philemon gives concrete meaning to this oft-quoted verse from Galatians: "There is neither Jew nor Greek, there is neither slave nor free, there is no male and female, for you are all one in Christ Jesus. And if you are Christ's, then you are Abraham's offspring, heirs according to promise" (3:28–29).

Christianity is the great equalizer—all Christians, regardless of race, gender, creed or other background, are equals in Christ (Acts 10:34–35). Paul isn't trying to shame Philemon but to appeal to him as a brother, and interestingly, Paul writes as if he expects Philemon to agree and honor his suggestion. He doesn't seem the slightest bit concerned that Philemon might exercise his rights under Roman law to punish Onesimus. It is not only a wonderful letter that encapsulates the Christian concept of love, but it's also a refreshing refection of Paul's true attitude toward slavery.

PRAYER

Basil the Great once warned of the temptation to let our emotions drive us when correcting others, writing, "The superior should not administer a rebuke to wrongdoers when his own passions are aroused. By admonishing a brother with anger and indignation, he does not free him from his faults but involves himself in the error."[3] Lord, when we are clearly called to correct or rebuke another, help us to take a pause, inviting the Holy Spirit to give us the direction we need to handle such situations with proper care. If we show no restraint in regard to our heightened emotions, we will most assuredly give the enemy a foothold. Guard our hearts and help us to submit our plans to You. With reverence for Your knowledge and authority over all things we lift these things to You.

AMEN.

CHAPTER 1

Paul opens by calling himself "a prisoner for Christ Jesus"—meaning he is literally in prison for preaching the gospel. Paul identifies Timothy as a co-author of the letter, but most scholars don't believe he actually helped draft the epistle. As F. F. Bruce notes, "Throughout the body of this letter one man (Paul) addresses one man (Philemon)."[4] Rather, Timothy is Paul's trusted companion who spent much time visiting Paul during his house arrest in Rome. By mentioning him up front, Paul is acknowledging their close relationship and spiritual solidarity.

In addressing the letter primarily to Philemon, Paul describes him as a beloved fellow worker (1:1), indicating that Paul loves him dearly precisely because he is a co-worker for Christ and the advancement of the gospel. At the opening of the letter, then, Paul highlights his spiritual bond with Philemon, which will be important for the request that follows.[5] Paul includes "the church in your house" as one of the addressees, which tells us that Philemon conducts services in his home.

Paul assures Philemon that he thanks God every time he remembers Philemon in his prayers—because he has heard of Philemon's love and faith toward Jesus and the church (4–5). Paul says he prays that the sharing of Philemon's faith "may become effective for the full knowledge of every good thing that is in us for the sake of Christ" (6). Paul expresses his gratitude for Philemon's Christian love and faith, noting that these qualities will enhance believers' deeper understanding of the many blessings they have in Christ and of His goodness.

Paul recognizes the synergies that occur through the shared love and faith among individual believers and the church. "Real faith and love will inevitably result in a concern for fellowship," writes John MacArthur. "There is no place in the Body of Christ for an individualism that does not care about others."[6] The Christian faith is relational and communal based on the relationship of the three persons of the Holy Trinity. What each member does affects the whole body. All believers are united to Christ and with one another. As we will discuss in Chapter 3, Paul describes the interdependency of these relationships in Ephesians, declaring, "Speaking the truth in love, we are to grow up in every way into him who is the head, into Christ, from whom the whole body, joined and held together by every joint with which it is equipped, when each part is working properly, makes the body grow so that it builds itself up in love" (Eph. 4:15–16). Likewise, Paul tells the Corinthians, "For just as the body is one and has many members, and all the members of the body, though many, are one body, so it is with Christ. For in one Spirit we were all baptized into one body—Jews or Greeks, slaves or free—and all were made to drink of one Spirit. For the body does not consist of one member but of many.... God arranged the members in the body, each one of them, as he chose. If all were a single member, where would be the body be? As it is, there are many parts, yet one body" (1 Cor. 12:12–15, 18–20).

Paul is continuing to lay a foundation for his appeal to Philemon that he do a good thing—the Christian thing—and reconcile himself with Onesimus.[7] By effectively and energetically sharing his faith and his blessings, Philemon's godly wisdom and his gratitude for Christ would grow, which would move him to do the right thing by Onesimus.[8] We marvel at Paul's revelation that our Christian works help not only those to whom we witness but ourselves as well. Good works beget more good works. Acts of love multiply and rebound.

Philemon's act of Christian grace wouldn't simply bless Onesimus but would also be a powerful witness that would strengthen the local church and the entire body of Christ. "If Christianity could work in such tension-filled relationships, it could work anywhere," argues Richard Melick. "Paul, Philemon, Onesimus, the church, and all of Christianity had much at stake in Philemon's response. Paul prayed that Philemon would make the correct choice."[9]

Paul is reiterating the connection between Christian behavior and knowledge of God's word and His will. The more believers act on their faith, the more they grow in their understanding of God and God's will because they will see the fruit of their actions, including a strengthening of the bond between believers, which will further reinforce their faith. In turn, their active pursuit of God's wisdom by staying in His word will lead them to more effectively practice their faith to the benefit of the full church and those to whom they evangelize. Here, Paul is commending both knowledge of the word and the importance of the experiential wisdom you gain when you put the word into practice.[10]

In a culture highly focused on individualism, it's unusual for us to think of ourselves as being part of a great entity. Even much of today's Christian messaging focuses on discovering our individual purposes in God's kingdom. This is not necessarily a bad thing, but we must direct our attention beyond ourselves if we really want to experience the fullness of God's design for our lives. Do we have believers in our lives to whom we regularly go for prayer? Do we open ourselves enough to them, allowing them to see our messy lives and struggles? Do we ask God how we in turn can use our individual gifts to build others up and walk alongside them in their journeys?

Prayer

Lord, You lovingly assure us in Hebrews 13:5, "I will never leave you nor forsake you." Open our eyes to see how You use people in our lives to fulfill this promise. How can we be a blessing to Your church body? Give us hearts that increasingly think of ourselves

▶

less and hunger more for communion with fellow believers. Please place people in our lives whom we can trust, and who in turn can trust us as we seek to serve You in different, yet complementary ways. You could have asked us to do this life alone, but we praise You for designing us to live in community and family with others—what a beautiful gift! We entrust these requests to You and will wait patiently and faithfully for You to highlight these people in our lives. Thank You, Jesus!

AMEN.

Paul tells Philemon he has derived much joy and comfort from Philemon's love because Philemon has refreshed the hearts of believers (7). What could warm Paul's heart more than Philemon's demonstrating his love for his brothers in Christ and thereby encouraging and leading them to imitate that love and spread it throughout the body of Christ? Paul continues to praise Philemon—though not flatter him—in advance of his request. Paul is reminding him of the benefits to Philemon and to the body of Christ in living out Christ's love. Philemon will experience those same blessings if he does the right thing in this case.

Paul next appeals to Philemon on behalf of Onesimus. He explicitly says he has sufficient confidence and authority in Christ to command Philemon to grant his request, but he's instead asking him to be lenient and forgiving not under coercion but in the spirit of Christ's love. Perhaps by mentioning but not invoking his apostolic authority, Paul is underscoring the authority and reliability of the message he is delivering. He is also implying he is by no means asking Philemon to do something that he himself wouldn't do and hasn't done countless times already. The mere mentioning of Paul's credentials should capture Philemon's sober attention.

Paul's approach to Philemon strikes us as analogous to his teaching, especially in Romans, that the Christian is not under law but under grace (Romans 6:15). Having died to the law through Christ's death and resurrection, Christians now belong to Him and so will bear fruit for God (Romans 7:4). "But now we are released from the law," says Paul, "having died to that which held us captive, so that we serve in the new way of the Spirit and not in the old way of the written code" (Romans 7:6). He further explains that yes, we have been set free from sin, but we have become slaves of righteousness (Romans 6:18).

Don't misunderstand. We are not trying to stretch Paul's appeal to Philemon to suggest he's directly applying his teaching in Romans. But when we read his words to Philemon, we can't help but remember these passages in Romans and conclude that Paul really is asking Philemon to serve in the new way of the Spirit—to bear fruit for God because he belongs to Christ and is full of His love. Philemon must show he is a slave of righteousness. Paul is asking him to take stock of his position in Christ, to be mindful of the grace that Christ has shown him, and to extend that same Christian grace to Onesimus. Paul does not indicate he expects Philemon to do otherwise, but rather he seems confident that Philemon will comply because he has shown that spirit of grace before.

Paul intensifies his appeal by sharing that Onesimus is Paul's spiritual child, having developed that relationship while Paul was imprisoned. In an interesting twist, Paul notes that Onesimus was essentially useless to Philemon while under Paul's servitude, or at least after he ran away, because he was not yet a fellow believer. Thanks to his conversion, however, he is now useful to both Paul and Philemon (10–11). He is a changed man, transformed by the Spirit of Christ.

As much as Paul has grown attached to Onesimus (he describes him as his "very heart" [12]), he is sending him back to Philemon.

He would have been pleased to keep Onesimus with him to serve him on behalf of Philemon, says Paul, but he prefers not to do that without Philemon's consent (13–14). Again, Paul doesn't want Philemon to act under compulsion but of his own accord, out of his own goodness. Church father Jerome offers a fascinating insight into this verse that addresses a deep theological question: Why didn't God just create man irreversibly good from the beginning—the type of beings who could not have fallen? "This verse answers the question of why God, in creating human beings, did not constitute them invariably good and upright," writes Jerome. "If indeed, God is good not out of some impersonal necessity but because in his essence he freely wills his own goodness, he should in making man have made him to the divine image and likeness, that is, that he be good willingly and not by necessity."[11]

Most commentators suggest Paul's statement that Onesimus could serve him on Philemon's behalf implies that if Philemon could, he would be with Paul helping to advance the gospel. Since he cannot, Onesimus could serve nicely in his absence, which further confirms that Onesimus had served him well. He is not simply a nominal brother in Christ—he is actually proving his worth as a laboring servant of the Lord.

Paul says that maybe the reason Onesimus fled in the first place (presumably through God's providence) was that he would return forever—no longer as a bondservant but as a beloved brother to Paul and even more to Philemon (15–16). He would be returning both as a free man and as a brother in Christ. Paul could be stressing that for Philemon to fully profit from Onesimus' changed nature, he must accept him as a brother in Christ—his new status alone wouldn't be sufficient.[12]

Scholars debate whether Paul is requesting full emancipation for Onesimus or just a new relationship between the two as brothers in Christ. Though Paul had elsewhere urged slaves to seek their liberty if possible (1 Cor. 7:21), his intention here is ambiguous because he doesn't explicitly ask for Onesimus to be freed. That is, while he does say "no longer as a bondservant," he also says "more than a bondservant." So he could mean that it's Philemon's prerogative as to whether he frees him, but even if he doesn't, he'll henceforth be honor-bound to accept Onesimus as an equal in Christ, which would create an entirely different relationship between the two. "In other words, whether Onesimus remained a slave or not, he could no longer be regarded *as* a slave," writes Peter O'Brien. "A change had been effected in him independent of his possible manumission."[13]

So Paul is talking about the objective status of Onesimus now that he is a Christian, not how Philemon might regard him. "The 'no more as a slave' is an absolute fact, whether Philemon chooses to recognize it or not," observes Joseph Lightfoot.[14] Regardless of whether Paul is issuing a firm directive, Philemon would surely find it hard to continue to enslave a man whom Paul is now imploring him to recognize as an equal brother in Christ.

Paul tells Philemon that if he considers Paul his partner, he should receive Onesimus as he would receive Paul (17). So Paul is interceding for Onesimus, and he is also identifying himself with Onesimus.[15] He is demanding not only that Onesimus be treated respectfully and lovingly but in the highest sense of those terms—as an intimate friend—just as Philemon would doubtless treat Paul.[16] The unstated implication here too is that, as much weight as Paul's vouching for Onesimus should carry, God's is infinitely more important. And God had adopted Onesimus, via Onesimus' faith in Christ, as His son. The inescapable conclusion is that "Philemon should open his arms to welcome Onesimus back to his household and, as a new believer, to the church," writes Barton. "God had welcomed Onesimus; so should Philemon."[17] Robert Wall frames it even more emphatically:

> [Paul] realizes that religious conversions, such as those experienced by both Philemon and Onesimus, have very public results; they are not events that just happen to one and are then privatized and compartmentalized so they do not intrude on one's other activities. Conversion joins the believer with Christ in the cosmic salvation of God, whose grace transforms every aspect of human life.... The previous arrangement between Onesimus and Philemon as slave and owner has been changed by their experience of grace. They are now partners in a [communion of faith], where they share a new capacity to love one another as never before.... Philemon is no longer his lord but a brother; they are partnered together with the Lord Jesus for their mutual salvation.[18]

Barton and Wall give us the eternal perspective, bidding us to recognize Paul's endorsement of the spiritual realities over man's temporal and artificially established hierarchies. Christ is the great equalizer.

The *Life Application Study Bible* points out, "As Paul interceded for a slave, so Christ intercedes for us, slaves to sin." What a beautiful parallel! Romans 8:34 gives us a picture of Jesus at the right hand of God the Father, interceding for us day in and day out. May we fix our eyes on this image that reminds us of how blessed we are to have a Savior who, even in His elevated state of glory, never ceases to fight for the lives of His sheep.

PRAYER

Jesus, we thank You for being our Savior and Intercessor. You told us that in Your kingdom the last shall be first (Matthew 20:16). May we be reminded that we are all equally created and equally loved by You, and that You call us to serve others because that is what You have

▶

done for us. Help us to follow Your example in washing Your disciples' feet and to remember the promise that followed: "Now that you know these things, you will be blessed if you do them" (John 13:17). In Your precious name,

AMEN.

Anticipating Philemon's possible objections or misgivings about his request, Paul instructs Philemon to charge it to Paul's account if Onesimus has wronged him or is indebted to him (18). "I, Paul, write this with my own hand: I will repay it—to say nothing of your owing me even your own self" (19). Commentators interpret this literally—if there is an outstanding debt, Paul will be happy to pay it. This intent is reinforced by Paul's declaration that he writes these words with his own hand, as if to say, "Here is my promissory note, with my own signature attached to it."[19]

Paul puts a fine point to the matter when he reminds Philemon that he owes Paul his very self. Many scholars believe this debt is Philemon's debt to Paul for Paul's role in his conversion—his path to eternal life.[20] After all, Paul elsewhere wrote that bringing one to Christ left the beneficiary with a debt to the evangelist. "Paul considered the gospel that he preached to be a gift that implied obligatory actions from those who received it," writes Seth Ehorn.[21] As Paul wrote to the Romans, "For Macedonia and Achaia have been pleased to make some contribution for the poor among the saints at Jerusalem. For they were pleased to do it, and indeed owe it to them" (Romans 15:26–27).

Ehorn also notes that Paul only invokes this argument when it helps to advance the gospel—he is not seeking monetary remuneration. But he is implying he could repay a monetary debt (that of Onesimus to Philemon) with a spiritual debt. Paul had established precedent for this, says Ehorn, when he told the Romans that if the

Gentiles come to share in the Jews' spiritual blessings, they should be of service to them in material blessings (Romans 15:27).[22]

Next, Paul tells Philemon, "Yes, brother, I want some benefit from you in the Lord. Refresh my heart in Christ" (20). N. T. Wright argues this translation doesn't fully capture Paul's meaning. A better rendering might be, "Yes, my dear man—now I come to think of it, I want some return from *you*!" Moreover, "Refresh my heart in Christ" might be understood as, "It is now *my* turn to be refreshed."[23]

Scholars interpret these passages differently. Some maintain that Paul is not making an additional request but merely strengthening the request he makes in verse 17: that Philemon welcome back Onesimus because it would greatly please Paul.[24] Others contend that Paul is supplementing his request—he's asking that Philemon also return Onesimus to Paul to serve with him in the spread of the gospel.[25] Still others confess that it's unclear what benefit Paul is seeking to derive.[26] The *ESV Study Bible* speculates that Paul intentionally omits specific directions in order to give Philemon the freedom to decide the best course of action. This, it seems, would be consistent with the spirit of Christian love Paul is promoting. If he acts voluntarily to extend Onesimus or Paul greater benefit, then he is certainly acting out of his Christian love and not out of coercion.

Regardless, we shouldn't overly concern ourselves with the specific benefit Paul is requesting. We must simply recognize that any such benefit is selfless, even though it will bring him joy—it is to glorify Christ through demonstrations of mutual Christian love and forgiveness and to advance the gospel. R. C. H. Lenski directs attention to Paul's words "in the Lord" and "in Christ." The profit Paul seeks is "in the Lord," Lenski says, and specifically, the profit is to be refreshed in Christ. In other words, as we can see, Paul is seeking nothing for himself other than the satisfaction he'll derive from two

Christian brothers' reconciling and joining in fellowship despite their different stations in life.[27]

PRAYER

Jesus, thank You for living the perfect human life and for giving us so many examples of how we are to walk out our faith. Just before You went to die on the cross, You spoke to God the Father in the Garden of Gethsemane. Even in Your weakest moment when You asked Him to take this cup from You, You immediately followed with, "Yet not My will, but Yours be done." Jesus, please convict us to present ourselves to You in this way; may we submit to Your Will despite our greatest fears. Help us to surrender the things we hold on to the tightest, both the good and the bad. May no desire be too precious or past grudge be so strong that we cannot offer it fully to You.

AMEN.

Mixed in with final greetings, Paul concludes this letter by saying, "Confident of your obedience, I write to you, knowing that you will do even more than I say. At the same time, prepare a guest room for me, for I am hoping that through your prayers I will be graciously given to you" (21–22). Early church father Chrysostom was impressed by the tenderness of this passage. "What stone would not these words have softened?" asked Chrysostom. "What wild beast would not these requests have rendered mild and prepared to receive him heartily?" More than this, Paul is expressing confidence that Philemon will do as he asks and even more. He will obey not just in fellowship to Paul but to honor and please Christ. Paul, it should be noted, is acting confidently but not presumptuously. He trusts God to inspire Philemon to rise to the occasion.[28]

Is there a contradiction, however, between Paul's giving Philemon total freedom to act and then insisting that following Paul's request is a matter of obedience? This gets back to the point above—that doing the right thing voluntarily, rather than blindly obeying the rules, is a greater expression of Christian love. "In the Bible... true obedience and true freedom are not viewed as mutually exclusive," writes Daniel Migliore. "Obedience in Christian life is not the same as grudging compliance to a burdensome order or unwilling submission to a superior power. God's grace sets us free, and our freedom takes the shape of free and glad obedience to God's will that Jesus summarizes as love of God and love of neighbor. Just for this reason, Paul can speak of 'the obedience of faith' (Romans 1:5; 16:26) and never considers such obedience to conflict with genuine human freedom."[29]

Paul also exudes confidence in unhesitatingly assuming that Philemon will happily provide lodging for him. The *NIV Cultural Backgrounds Study Bible* notes that hospitality was viewed as a great virtue in antiquity, and people considered it an honor to host respectable guests, which shows that Paul knows Philemon respects him.[30] By requesting hospitality for himself, just as he does throughout the letter on behalf of Onesimus, Paul identifies himself with Onesimus as a fellow Christian facing some of the same difficulties and having the same needs.[31]

This verse signals that, because of his strong faith, his certainty that his fellow believers will pray for him, and his corresponding belief in the power of prayer, Paul is confident God will enable his release from prison and let him continue his ministry. Paul's constant mentioning of his own prayers and his requests for the prayers of others demonstrates his fervent belief in the indispensability and effectiveness of prayer. "Here again you see that although Paul is a saint and a 'chosen instrument,' nevertheless he everywhere requests prayers and support for himself and asks that others stand by him in battle," writes Martin Luther. "Thus every one of us needs the prayer of others even more, we who are conscious of being in the same Christ, but are far inferior to him."[32]

PRAYER

Lord, You told us in Matthew 18:19, "If two of you agree on earth about anything they ask, it will be done for them by my Father in Heaven." May we never take for granted the access to the power You have granted each of us by the Holy Spirit living in our hearts—and the even greater power of praying together. The *Life Application Study Bible* elaborates on this: "In the body of believers (the church), the sincere agreement of two people is more powerful than the superficial agreement of thousands, because Christ's Holy Spirit is with them. Two or more believers filled with the Holy Spirit, will pray according to God's will, not their own; thus their requests will be granted." When we feel hesitant to share our prayer requests with others due to shame or simply a lack of conviction, point us back to this verse where You instruct us to seek support from fellow Christians as we offer our prayers and petitions to You, believing in faith that You will grant us these things.

AMEN.

Paul closes his letter with personal greetings (23–24) and a benediction: "The grace of the Lord Jesus Christ be with your spirit" (25). Gordon Fee and Douglas Stuart argue this "semiprivate letter" from Paul to Philemon is included in the Bible "because the truth of the gospel lies not only in its history and the theological interpretation of that history; it is also anecdotal. God's story has been told a million times over in stories like this one."[33] Indeed, these kinds of stories add authenticity and intimacy to the theological lessons they impart. The characters in the Bible were real people with real lives and real struggles. Stories of such struggles help us relate to biblical figures and their problems, and make the Bible's lessons concrete and specific, not abstract and theoretical.

CHAPTER THREE

EPHESIANS

A BLUEPRINT FOR SPIRITUAL EMPOWERMENT

More than any other book in the Bible, Ephesians displays the great purpose and plan of God for the church. It provides a perspective that is unique: God's—and the believer's—view from the "heavenly realms."

—Walter L. Liefeld[1]

Paul's epistle to the Ephesians has been called "one of the most sublime compositions of the kind, that ever came from the pen of man;" "the jewel case of the Bible;" and the "Canyon of Scriptures."[2] But we believe John MacArthur's description of this powerful letter more trenchantly captures its unique value. MacArthur recalls the story of Hetty Green, reputed to be America's greatest miser. She died in 1916 with a net worth of $100 million but was so cheap that she ate her oatmeal cold to avoid the expense of heating water. Ephesians, notes MacArthur, informs believers of the vast spiritual resources accessible to them and warns them not to neglect those resources like Hetty Green neglected her material resources. "Such believers are in danger of suffering from spiritual malnutrition," argues MacArthur, "because they do not take advantage of the great storehouse of spiritual nourishment and resources at their disposal."[3] What a marvelous way of focusing our attention on the incomparable riches of this book!

We mustn't read this book—or any biblical book—simply to gain knowledge. We must take its lessons to heart and avail ourselves of its treasures. Let's not stop at the intellectual level and merely nod our heads approvingly when we read Paul's revelation of the "unsearchable riches of Christ." Let's be inspired to dive in, partake of His divine glory, invite His Holy Spirit to lead us into closer communion with Him and fellow believers, and pray that the Spirit empowers us to advance Christ's kingdom for His glory.

It's believed Paul wrote Ephesians during his first imprisonment in Rome. As certain ancient manuscripts omit "Ephesus" as the specific addressee, some scholars believe the letter was intended for circulation to churches throughout that area. They note that Paul doesn't address specific problems in Ephesus as he does for certain churches in other epistles.[4] Although they're interesting, such questions ultimately matter little because God intended that all of Paul's letters—indeed, all letters in the New Testament—would ultimately circulate to the ends of the earth.

That Paul's epistles were eventually distributed worldwide, even though Paul wrote some of them from prison, is a testament to God's sovereignty. "Although the Roman government was able to imprison Paul the apostle, it was not able to imprison the Gospel of Jesus Christ," writes Gary Everett.[5] The profundity of the prison epistles illustrates that God blesses believers through their hardships and those of others, as Matthew Henry observes: "When his tribulations did abound, his consolations and experiences did much more abound, whence we may observe that the afflictive exercises of God's people, and particularly of his ministers, often tend to the advantage of others as well as to their own."[6]

Many scholars draw parallels between Ephesians and the Old Testament Book of Joshua. The Old Testament books preceding Joshua record Israel's wanderings, while Joshua describes the nation's coming into possession of the promised land. Ephesians, they say, tells of the spiritual possessions of believers—"those who have entered the Canaan of the soul by faith in Jesus Christ."[7] That observation aside, most commentators agree this letter is rich in theology, perhaps second only to the Book of Romans as a comprehensive doctrinal exposition of the Christian faith.[8]

The letter probably includes more teaching about spiritual warfare than any other epistle. Christians have long relied on Ephesians as a guidebook for combatting evil forces. This book reminds us that our struggle is against unseen forces that are every bit as real as tangible opponents. We ignore these threats at our own peril. Understanding that invisible, yet powerful forces underlie monumental evil helps us to make sense of the otherwise incomprehensible. This letter informs us that we cannot fight these battles on our own—clothed with "the whole armor of God" (6:11), we must rely on divine strength.

Ephesians emphasizes that all Christians, irrespective of ethnicity and nationality, are united in Christ. God's mystery, hidden throughout the ages until he revealed it through Paul, was that His salvation plan would be available to all mankind, Jews and Gentiles alike, and that they would all be one in Christ. Accordingly, we must treat others with dignity and respect, and diligently promote harmony in the church. Assaults on individual believers are assaults on the entire body of Christ. Disharmony in the church grieves God, who wants us unified in love, in doing His will, and in advancing the gospel. Let's keep these things in mind as we go through this wonderful book.

Prayer

Father God, *The Message* paraphrases Ephesians 1:6 as follows: "Long, long ago He decided to adopt us into his family through Jesus Christ. (What pleasure he took in planning this!) He wanted us to enter into the celebration of his lavish gift-giving by the hand of his beloved Son." What a breathtaking depiction of Your heart! As we study this book, may we remember that the reality we live in as Your adopted children was planned long ago. You always intended to bring us home to You. The Old Testament prophet Isaiah wrote, "Behold, I am doing a new thing; now it springs forth, do you not perceive it? I will make a way in the wilderness and rivers in the desert" (43:19). That word had significance to Isaiah's contemporary audience but also foretold the time we live in today. We have a new life in Jesus Christ! May we turn our backs on our former ways of thinking and focus our eyes on the solution to every struggle we face—You.

Amen.

CHAPTER 1

Paul identifies himself as an apostle of Jesus Christ by the will of God and addresses the letter to the believers in Ephesus. As noted, however, some scholars conclude it was also intended for believers in the surrounding areas and their churches. Paul offers his readers grace and peace from God the Father and Jesus Christ. He explains that Christianity is different from other religions in that the others are works-based, whereas Christianity is based on grace and centers on the person of Jesus Christ.

Grace is a unique, counterintuitive feature of Christianity. R. P. C. Hanson defines God's grace as "the free, unmerited, unexpected love of God, and all the benefits, delights, and comforts which flow from it. It means that while we were sinners and enemies we have been treated as sons and heirs."[9] Many people believe we can earn our way to salvation through our own good works—if the good works outweigh the bad, i.e., if we are "good people," we will get to heaven. But people who are honest with themselves—assuming they are not in abject spiritual darkness—realize their thorough sinfulness. They instinctively understand the wisdom in Christ's teaching that our evil *thoughts*, not just our evil actions, make us sinful. We must realize that no human being is holy in God's sight except through his faith in Jesus Christ. Apart from Christ, we have no righteousness to offer God that will lead to our eternal life with Him. Our salvation is purely a gift from God, and to receive it we must appropriate Christ's finished work on the cross through faith in Him. This letter elucidates this concept as well as any other.

Paul tells us of the peace available to all Christians—the peace that comes from God the Father and His Son. This is not a throw-away platitude. God is a God of peace (Romans 15:33; Phil 4:9; 1 Thess. 5:23; Heb. 13:20). The Bible describes the good news itself as the gospel of peace (Acts 10:36; Eph. 6:15). God's sacrificial death establishes peace between God and those who believe in His Son. (Romans 5:1; Col. 1:20).[10] Human beings truly cannot enjoy inner peace apart from faith in Christ. But with salvation that comes through faith, believers receive an internal tranquility and assurance of the presence of the Holy Spirit.

Moreover, believers are united in this gift of peace from God, which He ordained from the very beginning. With Jesus lying in the manger wrapped in swaddling clothes, a multitude of the heavenly host praised God, saying, "Glory to God in the highest, and on earth peace among those with whom he is pleased" (Luke 2:13–14). Jesus confirmed this before He left the world, saying, "Peace I leave with you; my peace I give to you. Not as the world gives do I give to you. Let not your hearts be troubled, neither let them be afraid"

(John 14:27). We are to intentionally share this gift of peace with one another to ensure that God will be with us: "Finally brothers, rejoice. Aim for restoration, comfort one another, agree with one another, live in peace; and the God of love and peace will be with you" (2 Cor. 13:11).

Let us be forever grateful for God's gifts to us of grace and peace, and remember that they are not simply soothing words. They bring life and contentment to us individually and unite us as Christ's body of believers. "Both grace and peace remove contention. They convey the will of God," writes early church father Marius Victorinus. "Since therefore they were in the grip of error, grace was first sought on their behalf, in order that they should know God and fully obey God and Christ, putting all trust in Christ and nothing else."[11]

PRAYER

Lord, thank You for giving us this revelation: "He does not deal with us according to our sins, nor repay us according to our iniquities. For as high as the heavens are above the earth, so great is his steadfast love toward those who fear him; as far as the east is from the west, so far does he remove our transgressions from us" (10–12 ESV). If we do not fully acknowledge this as truth, we will never experience Your peace. Help us to understand that part of our faith depends on our truly accepting Your gift of grace and forgiveness. This is crucial for our walk with You because until we understand how deeply we have been forgiven, we will not be able to forgive and live at peace with others. May Your Holy Spirit fill us with Your abounding love and may it spill out into the lives of every person we encounter. Thank you, Holy Spirit.

AMEN.

Continuing this long, forceful introduction, Paul writes, "Blessed be the God and Father of our Lord Jesus Christ, who has blessed us in Christ with every spiritual blessing in the heavenly places, even as he chose us in him before the foundation of the world, that we should be holy and blameless before him" (1:3–4). We praise God because of the extraordinary spiritual blessings He has showered upon us. These blessings, says Paul, are "in the heavenly realm." The heavenly realm or heavenly places, according to scholars, is the place to which Christ has been raised and where believers, through faith in Him, have also been raised.

Notice that Paul describes these blessings as having already occurred. As earlier discussed, we have been spiritually raised but not yet physically raised. "Even if [believers] live on earth in mortal bodies, they can enter into the good of their heavenly inheritance here and now through the ministry of the Spirit," writes F. F. Bruce.[12]

Even before God created the world, He chose us for salvation by faith in His Son. Despite His foreknowledge that man would fall into sin and be unholy in His sight, He arranged for our individual redemption and eternal life in Jesus Christ. Through faith in Christ our unholiness becomes holiness for salvation purposes because God, when judging us, looks not at our sinfulness but at the sinlessness of Christ, which we have appropriated for ourselves through faith in Him. While believers will never be sin-free until they are glorified in heaven, they will, through the power of the Holy Spirit, become holier. This process of growing in holiness through the power of the Spirit, who indwells believers upon their conversion, is known as sanctification.

Believers are immediately "justified" upon their conversion, which means they are declared just before God for purposes of eternal salvation because Christ's righteousness is imputed to them. Upon conversion they begin the process of sanctification, which they will continue until they part from the earth. Later, upon their physical resurrection, they will become sin-free—that is called glorification.

Paul explains that in addition to indwelling believers and empowering them to become more Christlike, the Holy Spirit performs another important function—He is our spiritual guarantor. When people place their faith in Christ and become believers, they are "sealed with the promised Holy Spirit, who is the guarantee of our inheritance until we acquire possession of it, to the praise of his glory" (1:13–14).

Paul assures us that God predestined us to be adopted as sons through Jesus Christ, that our sins are forgiven, and that we are redeemed wholly through His grace, "which he lavished upon us" (1:8). Paul is making it quite clear that God has bathed us in grace and that nothing we have done entitled us to any of these blessings. As he wrote to the Romans, "By works of the law no human being will be justified in his sight.... For there is no distinction: for all have sinned and fall short of the glory of God, and are justified by his grace as a gift, through the redemption that is in Christ Jesus, whom God put forward as a propitiation by his blood, to be received by faith" (Romans 3:20, 22–25).

Paul says that God's plan, which will be realized in "the fullness of time," is "to unite all things in [Christ], things in heaven and things on earth" (1:10). Paul offered a similar revelation to the Colossians, saying that God reconciled "to himself all things, whether things on earth or things in heaven, by making peace through [Christ's blood], shed on the cross" (Col. 1:19–20). What does Paul mean by this, exactly? Bruce Barton explains, "At that time, God is planning to bring all things in heaven and on earth together under one head, even Christ. God is planning a universal reconciliation—all of creation will be reinstated to its rightful owner and creator—Christ. Just as Christ administered God's plan of redemption by carrying it out as a human on this earth, so he will ultimately be in charge of 'all things in heaven and on earth.' All of creation (spiritual and material) will be brought back under one head."[13]

Paul now grows personal, relating that because he has heard of his correspondents' faith in Christ and love for fellow believers, he prays ceaselessly for them, giving thanks for them and asking God to give them "the Spirit of wisdom and of revelation in the knowledge of him" (1:17). He prays that God will enlighten the "eyes of their hearts" so they may understand the "hope to which he has called you, what are the riches of his glorious inheritance in the saints, and what is the immeasurable greatness of his power toward us who believe, according to the working of his great might that he worked in Christ when he raised him from the dead and seated him at his right hand in the heavenly places, far above all rule and authority and power and dominion, and above every name that is named, not only in this age but also in the one to come" (1:18–21).

New believers have an incomplete knowledge of God, so Paul is asking God to increase their understanding through the power of the Holy Spirit as they mature in the faith. Specifically, he prays that they come to understand their future hope, God's inheritance in the saints, and their power in Christ.[14] He doesn't simply want them to understand these things intellectually but with "the eyes of their hearts." As the heart is life's central organ, it is the fountain of our feelings and will, as well as our intellect.[15] Church father Marius Victorinus notes that we discern the knowledge of divine things through two avenues—our own rational insight and God's direct revelation to us, through His Spirit, of His divinity.[16] We believe Paul is saying he wants us to understand and embrace these truths on a deep, spiritual level. We must own them completely.

What is their future hope that he wants them to understand? It is the future riches God has in store for them. "Hope" in this context isn't how we define it today. There is no doubt as to whether their promised riches will be realized—it is a certainty. God has redeemed believers and adopted them as His sons, so they will enjoy eternal life with Him. As noted, believers receive some of these blessings presently through the indwelling and empowering of the Holy Spirit, but there are far greater things to come when we join Christ in glory with our physical resurrection. In the meantime, the Holy Spirit protects us until that day.[17] Of these things we can be sure because God has promised them, and God cannot lie (Heb. 6:18).

Paul assures us that "saints," that is, believers, are God's inheritance, meaning that as His adopted children, we are His treasured possession and will be united with Him forever in eternity. It is awesome to contemplate that God loves us so much that He savors the notion of our living in His presence.

We must be certain of the "immeasurable greatness" of God's power toward believers by virtue of Christ's sacrificial death, His resurrection, and His sovereignty over all earthly and heavenly authorities, now and forever. God is omnipotent and will use His power to bring about His promises on our behalf. This is just further reinforcement of these essential truths Paul wants us to embrace, both because it is important that we believe them and so we can rest assured and secure in them. "The point of this great petition is that we might comprehend how secure we are in Christ and how unwavering and immutable is our hope of eternal inheritance," writes John MacArthur. "The power of glorification is invincible and presently operative to bring us to glory."[18]

I (David) once told my friend and noted apologist Frank Turek about a person who doubts his self-worth and is struggling to find his identity. Frank said we must understand that as believers our identity is something we do not *achieve* through our own efforts but *receive* from God. This resonated with me, so I researched it further and found this compelling explanation by David Appleby and George Ohlschlager: "Changed identity flows from the fact of our changed ownership. The Christian is no longer his or her own; each of us who has yielded to the call now belongs to God." They add, "Our new identity in Christ also reflects our new citizenship." This view echoes Paul's teachings here in Ephesians and elsewhere (we are waiting for Christ to "transform our lowly bodies into our new glorious bodies" [Phil. 3:20–21]). Appleby and Ohlschlager note other New Testament inferences as well: "This heavenly citizenship is what allows us to come boldly to the throne of grace (Heb. 4:16) to petition our King for the holy transformation of everything—for that which is impossible for us to do on our own."[19]

Appleby and Ohlschlager provide a final insight that is especially relevant for us today. Our new identity in Christ trumps any other identity we have—racial, ethnic, or otherwise. And here, we believe, they capture Frank's point to me: "Critically important is the recognition that our identity in Christ will most often bring peace and harmony and forge the healing path to maturity and integrity. By contrast, the assertion of any other identity tends to create dissension and division."[20] Like Frank, they are asserting that once we are in Christ, we receive our identity from Him, not through our own power. And if we resist that and try to forge our own identity, we'll harm ourselves and others. It's hard for us to suppress our pride and accept that our salvation and all the other blessings that flow from our faith in Christ come from God, but until we grasp it, we'll be flailing aimlessly and working against ourselves. In short, we must surrender to Christ's Lordship and accept His gift of grace.

Prayer

Lord, we are grateful to You as members of the body of Christ that we can claim for ourselves these promises You first gave

▶

to Your chosen people, the Israelites: "Fear not, for I have redeemed you; I have called you by name, you are mine. When you pass through the waters, I will be with you; and through the rivers, they shall not overwhelm you; when you walk through fire you shall not be burned, and the flame shall not consume you" (Isaiah 43:1–2). May these words open the eyes of our hearts to the identity You have given us—You say it Yourself, we are Yours! Later You reinforce this: "Behold, I have engraved you on the palms of my hands" (49:16). Thank You, Lord! When we are tempted to find our identity in anything but You, imprint on our minds the image of our individual names written in the palm of Your hand. Holy Spirit, fill our minds with images of Jesus' face smiling upon us, that we may develop a tangible sense of His presence and the reality of the glory that awaits us when we are physically reunited in Heaven.

AMEN.

In concluding this chapter, Paul expands on the revelation that the Father put Christ in charge over all creation in describing Christ's relationship to His church: "And he put all things under his feet and gave him as head over all things to the church, which is his body, the fullness of him who fills all in all" (1:22–23). We noted earlier that in this letter and others Paul depicts the church as a human body with Christ as its head. The head and the body are incomplete without each other. Paul isn't saying that Christ—the Son of God—is incomplete without us but that the church is incomplete without both. John Calvin took it as a high compliment to human beings. "The highest honor we in the church can be given is for Christ to say that without it he is somehow incomplete," argued Calvin. "What an encouragement for us." So as not to leave the wrong impression, Calvin added that Christ "fills everything in every way."[21]

Indeed, Christ fills us. He is everything to us, and we need Him for our very lives. He doesn't need us in the sense that he is lacking anything, but He deeply loves and values us and, by definition, there is no church without us. It is His will that there be a church and that it be His "body." As usual, John MacArthur sheds light on this paradox: "As a head must have a body to manifest the glory of that head, so the Lord must have the church to manifest His glory. . . . He has chosen us to display His incomparable majesty."[22] But let's be clear: It is He who fills the church in every way. "The fullness of deity resides in [Christ]," writes F. F. Bruce, "and out of that fullness his church is being constantly supplied."[23]

We must mention a separate but equally profound point that Paul makes throughout this section. Though he is not addressing false teachers in this letter, his emphasis on Christ's completeness and indispensability to us implies that we need nothing besides Christ. Any suggestion otherwise is a fatal scriptural error. "All these statements about the magnificence and power of Christ have this purpose: To prove that nothing further is to be received, no other thought required to complete the revelation," writes church father Marius Victorinus. "The Ephesians are therefore in error if they add anything further and introduce anything from the teaching of the Jews or of the world."[24]

Prayer

Heavenly Father, thank You for the endless riches of wisdom You provide us in Your living word. It's a marvel that even when we don't fully comprehend certain messages, You use our questions or doubts to pique our interest, drawing us further into Your presence and revelation. You assure us, "It is the glory of God to conceal things; but the glory of kings is to search things out" (Prov. 25:2). Thank

►

you for showing us this aspect of your character! Verses like this remind us that life with You is meant to be an adventure and one of continual growth—one where we expectantly wait for You to lead us to places we'd never dream of going and explore thoughts and concepts we never could have imagined comprehending. Holy Spirit, please stoke a fire within our hearts that burns to discover more of who You are, and may this flame never burn out.

AMEN.

CHAPTER 2

After explaining God's gift to humanity and His provision of redemption through faith in Jesus Christ, Paul begins this chapter with the jolting, unpleasant reality of a person's spiritual condition apart from saving faith in Christ: "And you were dead in the trespasses and sins in which you once walked, following the course of this world, following the prince of the power of the air, the spirit that is now at work in the sons of disobedience—among whom we all once lived in the passions of our flesh, carrying out the desires of the body and the mind, and were by nature children of wrath, like the rest of mankind" (2:1–3). Paul doesn't mince words. There is no gray here. We are hopeless without Christ. While we come into this world physically alive, we are *spiritually* dead, part of the fallen race of Adam. People uncomfortable with the notion of original sin should be honest enough to recognize that even if we were not fallen as a result of Adam's sin, we would be immediately fallen due to our own.

Paul is clear that all men are afflicted. In fact, you cannot embrace scripture as God's word and deny the devil exists. Paul isn't talking metaphorically in identifying him as "the prince of the power of the air" who rules his rebellious followers. Christ described the devil similarly: "Now is the judgment of this world; now will the ruler of this world be cast out" (John 12:31). Though these concepts may seem troubling, we must understand the totality of man's helplessness apart from God if we are to fully appreciate the magnitude of His gift of life to us. Douglas Moo suggests this is why Paul uses the plural synonyms "trespasses and sins": "to highlight the severity and variety of our deliberate and willful rebellion against God's holiness and righteousness."[25] None of us is exempt from this condition, and there is no way out of it but faith in Christ. Don't fool yourself into believing "good people" will be judged favorably by their works. "Good works and purity are of no use to anyone who is an unbeliever," writes church father Ambrosiaster.[26]

Just as soon as he underscores our spiritual lifelessness apart from Christ, Paul reiterates the path to regeneration. And he does so with special emphasis on the glory of God's gift of Christ, which is rooted in His immense love for us even while we were in our wretched, fallen state: "But God, being rich in mercy, because of the great love with which he loved us, even when we were dead in our trespasses, made us alive together with Christ—by grace you have been saved—and raised us up with him and seated us with him in the heavenly places in Christ Jesus" (2:4–6).

Note that in Chapter 1, Paul stressed that God raised Christ and seated him at his right hand in the heavenly places, and now he is saying that He raised us up and seated us right along with Christ. Think about that. Even Jesus' disciples longed to be seated alongside Christ, both on earth and in the spiritual life to come, but Paul is clear that we all are given that privilege as believers. It's no accident that he uses a parallel construction to compare our position in eternity to Christ's in the sense that we, too, will be seated alongside Him. We won't have to make an appointment to visit Him. We will live with Him and alongside Him. Paul provides one reason God extends us this grace: "So that in the coming ages he might show the immeasurable riches of his grace in kindness toward us in Christ Jesus" (2:7). He cares that we understand His grace. He is showing it to us and to all future generations, and Paul deems it essential that we know that. God knows every hair on our head; how much more does he care about the path to redemption He has provided us?

Next Paul lays out one of the most central gospel truths and one of the most wonderful passages of scripture: we are saved *only* by our faith in Christ, as a matter of God's grace. "For by grace you have been saved through faith. And this is not your doing; it is the gift of God, not a result of works, so that no one may boast" (2:8–9). To make it clear, Paul repeats the concept four times—in different words—in the successive clauses:

1. It is not our doing;
2. It is God's gift to us;
3. It is not a result of our works;
4. So that we may not boast.

In the next verse, he continues the theme: "For we are his workmanship, created in Christ Jesus for good works, which God prepared beforehand, that we should walk in them" (2:10). Robert Bratcher and Eugene Nida say that Paul is not referring to God's initial act of creating us. Rather, this refers to His redeeming us through Christ, making us new creations. God has provided everything we need through our faith in Christ, and as a result we are prepared for good works. These good works don't save us—that occurs upon our conversion. But once converted, we are empowered for good works through the indwelling Holy Spirit.

PRAYER

Jesus, we ask that Paul's message that our salvation comes exclusively through Your sacrifice and grace would penetrate our hearts and minds. You created us with a desire and capacity to mature in our faith, but may we never let those desires confuse us about our immovable status in Heaven. The day we each accepted Your gift of salvation we became Your co-heirs, and we freely received this standing as a gift from You! (Romans 8:17). What you did on the cross was more than enough to save us completely. Hallelujah! We stand amazed, contemplating the reality of salvation. As C. S. Lewis described it, Christianity "is a religion you could not have guessed. If it offered us just the kind of universe we had always expected, I should feel we were making it up. But, in fact, it is not the sort of thing anyone would have made up. It has just that queer twist about it that real things have."[27] While the salvation story seems too good to be true, it is in fact the truest thing in all of existence. May we keep Your words etched on our hearts: "My grace is sufficient for you, for my power is made perfect in weakness" (2 Cor. 12:9). Let us never lose sight of the fact that Your grace, Your power, Your provision is all we have and will ever need. Thank you, Jesus! We praise Your wonderful name!

AMEN.

The next section involves the unity of all believers in Christ, Jews and Gentiles alike. Paul, appointed apostle to the Gentiles, informs his Gentile readers that they used to be called "the uncircumcision" by those called "the circumcision." The Jews correctly regarded the Gentiles as wholly separated from God and alienated from Israel. We were "strangers to the covenants of promise" (2:12), and we had no hope because we were without God. The Jews were God's chosen people, set apart by Him and under His protection to be guardians of the law. Through them would come the Messiah and thus the possibility of salvation for Jews and Gentiles as well. Until God's appointed time, it was a great hidden mystery, as noted, that Gentiles are also heirs of God's covenantal promises" (Eph. 3:6). He promised to bless *all* people through Abraham (Gen 12:3), and Paul elsewhere identifies that blessing as God's provision of salvation for all people who believe in His Son, that is, the gospel (Gal 3:7–9).

Though Paul is announcing this great unity, he notes that before this mystery was unveiled, the Gentiles had it doubly bad—they neither had Christ nor any relationship with God at all. The irony is that the Gentiles thought they had many gods, but there has never been but one God. "When [Paul] says 'having no hope, without God in the world,' he does not deny that the Ephesians had many gods before they believed in Christ," writes church father Jerome. "His point is that the one who is without the true God has no god worthy of the name."[28] Unlike the Jews, we were not then set apart. But though we "once were far off," we have now "been brought near by the blood of Christ" (2:13). Christ has ended our alienation and unified all of us, Jews and Gentiles, through faith in Him. There is no longer a distinction between Jew and Greek, slave or free, male or female, for we are all one in Christ (Gal. 3:28).

It is especially fitting that Christ is the unifying agent because while on earth He prayed to the Father for His people to experience a unity that would mirror the unity of the Trinity. "The glory that you have given me I have given to them, that they may be one even as we are one, I in them and you in me, that they may become perfectly one, so that the world may know that you sent me and loved them even as you loved me" (John 17:22–23).

Christ is our peace (2:14). Through His death He ended the "dividing wall of hostility" between us (2:14). Instead of two men, we are now one new man, unified "in one body through the cross, thereby killing the hostility" (2:15–16).

Christ not only unified in Himself all peoples and thereby provided peace; as the divine antidote to sin He also brings peace in our individual lives. In other words, He is not just a peacemaker, that is, someone who has brought two alienated or warring factions together, but He has also brought peace to us by reconciling us to God. Formerly alienated from one another and from God, we are now privileged, through the blood of Christ, with actual access to God because of the indwelling Spirit (2:18).[29] We are no longer at odds with God, living in spiritual darkness and separation, but are united with Him as His adopted children. As Paul told the Romans, "For you did not receive the spirit of slavery to fall back into fear, but you have received the Spirit of adoption of sons, by whom we cry, "Abba! Father!" (Romans 8:15). Indeed, we are so much at peace with God that, in calling to Him, we are invited to use the intimate term Hebrew children use to address their earthly fathers: "Abba." We mustn't miss this profundity, as "Abba" is the equivalent of "Daddy" or "Papa."[30]

Having spiritual peace in Christ does not exempt us from earthly troubles, but it does give us strength and solace through these times. Believers should have less anxiety about the afterlife and an inner calm realizing no matter what happens, in the end God is in control. Christ's peace is enduring, not a false sense of security. The prophet Jeremiah spoke of the counterfeit version when he noted that people say, "'Peace, peace,' but there is no peace" (Jer. 6:14). Jesus offers us something entirely different. As He said, "Peace I leave with you; my peace I give to you. Not as the world gives do I give it to you. Let not your hearts be troubled, neither let them be afraid" (John 14:27).

Paul assures his readers they "are no longer strangers and aliens" but "are fellow citizens with the saints and members of the household of God, built on the foundation of the apostles and prophets, Christ Jesus himself being the cornerstone, in whom the whole structure, being joined together, grows into a holy temple in the Lord. In him you also are being built together into a dwelling place for God by the Spirit" (19–22).

Believers are united as Christ's church, which is built on the foundation of the apostles and prophets who originally proclaimed the gospel, but Christ Himself is the cornerstone upon which this foundation rests.[31] The imagery is of a vibrant, growing church, with each believer fitting perfectly into the structure and resting on the cornerstone. The church is a holy temple because it is grounded in Christ Jesus and filled with the Holy Spirit, who indwells individual believers and unites them corporately.

Imagine the impact this revelation had on Paul's contemporary readers, whom Paul is firmly informing that by faith they are connected to God in the heavenly realm through the Holy Spirit as a result of Christ's death and resurrection.[32] Warren Wiersbe traces the history of God's dwelling, observing that in Genesis God "walked" among His people, and in Exodus, he dwelt with them in the tabernacle, but His glory left them due to Israel's sins. He next dwelt in the temple and, in the New Testament, in the body of Christ (John 1:14). Today, God dwells in the church through His Holy Spirit. He does not dwell in a man-made temple, including the physical churches of today. Rather, He dwells in the hearts of believers and the church as a whole.[33]

PRAYER

Holy Spirit, we thank You for dwelling inside us. Thanks to You, we can obey Christ's direction to be His lights of the world, shining Your light before others (Matt 5:14–16). Help us to understand that "church" is not a place or an event—it is us, your

▶

people! We ask that You open our eyes to new opportunities to share Your light with others, in ways big and small. Whether it's following a nudge to talk about You with a friend, asking a co-worker how we can be praying for him or her, or simply showing patience and kindness to people who try our own patience, help us BELIEVE that You can and will use us when we are willing. We are Your church, and each of us makes up a piece of Your holy temple that You carefully designed. May we confidently walk that out.

AMEN.

CHAPTER 3

Though Paul is a prisoner of the Romans and awaiting trial, he repeatedly refers to himself as Christ's prisoner because his devotion to Christ and the gospel, along with his refusal to stop preaching salvation to the Gentiles, led to his legal jeopardy. He begins this chapter with the words "For this reason," which refer to his preceding discussion of the unveiling of God's mystery, which was that salvation is available to the Gentiles, just as to the Jews, through faith in Jesus Christ, and that Jews and Gentiles would now be united in Christ and not separated by race or ethnicity. It is initially difficult to follow this section because Paul breaks off mid-sentence in verse 1 ("For this reason I, Paul a prisoner of Christ Jesus on behalf of you Gentiles—") and doesn't return to the thought until verse 14, where he repeats his opening words, "For this reason." In the intervening thirteen verses he describes his role as God's minister—his duty to shine light on God's special revelation to him concerning the mystery of Christ. With that explanation he implores his readers not to be discouraged by his imprisonment and suffering, especially considering that it is ultimately for their benefit.[34]

He reminds them that God, by His grace, entrusted him and his fellow apostles and prophets with the mystery of Christ, though it had been hidden from previous generations. As we've discussed, he specifically defines the mystery: "that the Gentiles are fellow heirs, members of the same body, and partakers of the promise in Christ Jesus through the gospel" (3:6). Paul relates that God, through His grace, assigned him—"the very least of all the saints"—the task of preaching the gospel ("the unsearchable riches of Christ") to the Gentiles.

It is ironic, yet fitting, that God sent Paul to the Gentiles because in his former life he was their chief persecutor. Paul knows his privilege of ministry is God's undeserved gift to him, the most unlikely beneficiary of such an assignment. On the other hand, we should note that God didn't just randomly choose Paul to exhibit his grace. Paul was uniquely qualified to preach the good news to the Gentiles because no one had greater zeal for Christ or greater knowledge of God's word than this converted Jew, who was an outstanding scholar of the scriptures. Paul's testimony is a powerful affirmation of God's sovereignty, His love, and His redemptive heart. It is an antidote for any of us who think that our past or some other limitation might prevent God from using us to the fullest in serving Him.

Prayer

Lord, Paul once referred to himself as the "chief among sinners" (1 Tim. 1:15), yet You used him mightily to accomplish Your kingdom plan. Throughout the entire Bible, from Genesis to Revelation, You used weak, stubborn, and unbelieving human beings to do Your will on earth. Help us to see ourselves as part of this community of flawed saints, whose very shortcomings can be used to bring You all the more glory. You tell us, "I am the Lord, and there is no other, besides me there is no God; I equip you, though you do not know me, that people may know, from the rising of the sun and from the west, that

▶

there is none besides me"(Isaiah 45:5–6). So let us not insult You by resisting Your calling. It is You and You alone who gives us strength to accomplish Your divine plans. Thank You for bringing beauty from the ashes of our mistakes and purpose to our once hopeless future. You alone deserve all the honor and praise!

AMEN.

What does Paul mean by "the unsearchable riches of Christ?" We think he is saying, in short, that Christ is simply too wonderful, too marvelous, too glorious for even believers to fully comprehend. He is infinite perfection, and our minds can fathom neither the infinite nor the perfect. Yet we are still beneficiaries of His grace and objects of His love. We have His Spirit dwelling within us and even have access to His power, despite being unable to wholly comprehend it. Simply put, Christ is not only too wonderful to wholly comprehend; His greatness cannot be adequately expressed in human language. To say He is too great for words is an indirect way of expressing the inexpressible.

Perhaps Paul's point is analogous to what the prophet Isaiah revealed about God: "For my thoughts are not your thoughts, neither are your ways my ways, declares the Lord. For as the heavens are higher than the earth, so are my ways higher than your ways and my thoughts than your thoughts" (Isaiah 55:8–9). Job delivers a similar message: "Can you find out the deep things of God? Can you find out the limit of the Almighty? It is higher than heaven—what can you do? Deeper than Sheol—what can you know? Its measure is longer than the earth and broader than the sea" (Job 11:7–9). C.f. (Job 26:14; Ps. 145:3). The *Lexham Survey of Theology* provides a useful insight here: "To say that God is incomprehensible is not to say that we can know nothing about God but, rather, that because God is infinite, no creature can ever come to comprehend, understand, grasp, or describe God in a manner that is worthy, adequate, or all-encompassing."[35]

Paul adroitly inserts this truth in these passages because he is highlighting God's immeasurable gift of the gospel, and what better way to stress the value of this gift than to describe it as priceless? He wants his readers—including us—to appreciate the awesomeness of God's gift to us of eternal life.

Paul says that God revealed the mystery of Christ "so that through the church the manifold wisdom of God might now be made known to the rulers and authorities in the heavenly places" (3:10). The revealing of this mystery is also for the benefit of the angels in heaven.[36] "This was according to the eternal purpose that he has realized in Christ Jesus our Lord, in whom we have boldness and access with confidence through our faith in him" (3:11–12). Paul is saying that none of this was an afterthought but all part of God's original plan. Before He created us, He knew we would fall into sin and that the only way—or best way—we could gain eternal life in His presence was for His Son to die sacrificially to expiate our sins.

People sometimes wonder how a perfect God could love imperfect human beings, especially enough to send His only Son to die for them so they could live. But the Bible is quite explicit that God does indeed love us more than we can imagine. Pastor Timothy Keller describes his awe at God's "delight" in creating us. He cites Proverbs 8, which we then reviewed, to *our* delight. Part of this Proverb describes the role of Wisdom in creation. Scholars debate whether Wisdom is actually a reference to the pre-incarnate Christ (which we believe) or just the author's way of personifying God's wisdom. Apart from that question, there is no doubt that the following verses of this proverb affirm God's delight in creation (c.f. Genesis 1:1–31) and especially in the crown jewel of His creation: human beings, whom He made in His image. In the passage, "Wisdom" is speaking:

> The Lord brought me forth as the first of his works,
> before his deeds of old;
> I was formed long ages ago,
> at the very beginning, when the world came to be.
> When there were no watery depths, I was given birth,
> when there were no springs overflowing with water;
> before the mountains were settled in place,
> before the hills, I was given birth,
> before he made the world or its fields
> or any of the dust of the earth.
> I was there when he set the heavens in place,
> when he marked out the horizon on the face of the deep,
> when he established the clouds above
> and fixed securely the fountains of the deep,
> when he gave the sea its boundary
> so the waters would not overstep his command,
> and when he marked out the foundations of the earth.
> Then I was constantly at his side.
> I was filled with delight day after day,
> rejoicing always in his presence,
> rejoicing in his whole world
> and delighting in mankind. (Prov. 8:22–31)

John Phillips enthusiastically expounds on these passages:

> What God has chosen to reveal of Himself in the realms of creation and redemption fills our souls with awe. In these two realms alone He gives us glimpses, bright and brilliant beyond all thought, of His eternal purposes. One such purpose concerns [mankind].... Surely that is why God made man in His image. That is why God did not write

> man off when Adam sinned, but initiated instead a wondrous, infinite, and costly plan of salvation. According to Screwtape, it is a source of astonishment and outrage to the demon world that God actually likes "disgusting little human vermin." Whether or not that is true, God's love for people is a source of wonder and praise in Heaven.[37]

Though we noted that human beings cannot look directly upon the radiance of God and live, the glory of the gospel is that through Christ we do have personal access to the living God of the universe. The Son is "the radiance of the glory of God and the exact imprint of his nature" (Heb. 1:3); He is the image of the invisible God" (Col. 1:15).

In fact, it's even better than having access. We may approach Him in "boldness" and "confidence." That is, this omnipotent, omnibenevolent, and omniscient God not only gives us access but invites and exhorts us to have a personal relationship with Him. And as related in Hebrews, we must enter into His presence through prayer: "Let us then with confidence draw near to the throne of grace, that we may receive mercy and find grace to help in time of need" (Heb. 4:16). Furthermore, "Since we have confidence to enter the holy places by the blood of Jesus, by the new and living way that he opened for us through the curtain, that is, through the flesh, and since we have a great priest over the house of God, let us draw near with a true heart in full assurance of faith, with our hearts sprinkled clean from an evil conscience and our bodies washed with pure water" (Heb. 10:19–22).

PRAYER

Jesus, You told Your disciples, "For truly, I say to you, if you have faith like a grain of mustard seed, you will say to this mountain, 'Move from here to there,' and it will move, and nothing will be impossible for you" (Matt. 17:20). But do we really live out our faith this way? Do we boldly come to Your throne of grace and ask You to move the mountains we face in our day-to-day lives? Do we call upon Your name to cure the sick, break generational cycles of addiction or dysfunction in our families, or radically save the most lost among us? We ask You for increased faith, Lord! We do want to see miracles in our midst. We do want to be used as Your twelve disciples were used to share the gospel, cure the sick, and bring people into Your kingdom family. That is what You have called us to do. Help us to see ourselves as You see us—not just as ordinary people living ordinary lives, but as hidden heavenly beings living on earth who have been given access to the power and authority of the almighty, all-powerful Creator of the universe. One word from You can shift someone's life forever. Help us to partner with You and usher in that type of miraculous change. We believe in Your power and Your word!

AMEN.

God accomplished His "eternal purpose" in Christ's death on the cross. As such, Paul continues, his readers should not "lose heart over what" Paul is suffering for them, which is their glory (3:13). Paul isn't parading his humility here any more than he was in saying he is the least of all the saints. He is simply noting that were it not for his sharing of the gospel with them, they wouldn't have transitioned from spiritual death to the glory of spiritual life. He by no means regrets that he is suffering in prison as a result of his preaching and wouldn't take it back for anything. His readers should rejoice along with him—and should be inspired to similar action by his example.

At last, Paul returns to his introductory phrase "for this reason" and writes, "For this reason I bow my knees before the Father, from whom every family in heaven and on earth is named, that according to the riches of his glory he may grant you to be strengthened with power through his Spirit in your inner being, so that Christ may dwell in your hearts through faith—that you, being rooted and grounded in love, may have strength to comprehend with all the saints what is the breadth and length and height and depth, and to know the love of Christ that surpasses knowledge, that you may be filled with all the fullness of God" (3:14–19).

This is quite a lengthy sentence, but first let's revisit Paul's interruption at the beginning of this chapter and his belated return to the thought. Why did he construct his thought this way? If you believe the Bible is God's word, you surely don't believe this was an afterthought. If you understand Paul's brilliance you surely don't think he lost his place or his train of thought—especially considering that he could review and edit his work. R. C. H. Lenski tackles this directly. The break at verse 2, he says, is "not due to a sudden flood of new thoughts, it is deliberate." The interruption itself, says Lenski, is the best way to get this point through to Paul's readers. He wants to grab their attention, then detail his apostolic mission to the Gentiles, before telling them he was imprisoned for this very mission and his work on their behalf.[38] He wants to jolt them into fully grasping the profound nature of his mission and that they are the direct and intended beneficiaries of that mission by way of God's grace.

In his letter up to this point, Paul has communicated basic Christian doctrine. But in verses 3:14–19, he turns to the practical side.[39] We Christians must not stop at the acquisition of "head knowledge" but live out these principles. I (David) confess that sometimes I get so wrapped up in studying theology that I probably don't think enough about application, so I always have to remind myself to maintain a balance.

Interestingly, Paul frames this part of the message in the form of a prayer because he knows that even regenerated Christians don't live out their faith on their own strength. He prays to the Father to renew believers in their very hearts with the power of the Spirit. For what purpose? So that Christ may dwell in their hearts through their faith. This will ground them in love and give them the strength to understand the limitless and incomprehensible love of Christ and be filled with God's fullness. We love that Paul uses similar language in one of our favorite scriptures to describe God's unfathomable love for us: "For I am sure that neither death nor life, nor angels nor rulers, nor things present nor things to come, nor powers, nor height or depth, nor anything else in all creation, will be able to separate us from the love of God in Christ Jesus our Lord" (Romans 8:38–39).

In the Ephesians passage, Paul is adamant that we fully understand Christ's enormous love for us, which will fill us with God's fullness. Love is central here. But in what way? F. F. Bruce explains that "it is impossible to grasp the divine purpose in all its dimensions without knowing the love of Christ"—and crucially, this can only happen through experiential knowledge. Bruce is insisting we can't fully understand God's fullness with our intellectual power alone. "It requires personal acquaintance with [Christ], whose nature is perfect love."[40] How can we not just adore that revelation?

Paul desperately wants the Ephesians—and all Christians—to be filled with all of God's fullness. Commentators offer different interpretations of this phrase, suggesting, alternatively: filled with God's excellence; filled with the kind of love that fills God; filled with the attributes of Christ, that is, to grow more Christlike; filled with God's moral perfection; filled with his power and wisdom; and so on. Another sensible interpretation is: "that God may fill you to the full measure of his own presence."[41] We see little profit in quibbling over this matter and believe we can all agree that any of these readings conveys the gratifying notion that Paul is petitioning the Father to make all believers increasingly like Himself.

Paul ends the chapter honoring God, "who is able to do far more abundantly than all that we ask or think" (3:20) and giving glory to God in the church and in Christ throughout time (3:21). Paul acknowledges that God can respond to our prayers in ways we can't even imagine, which is a tacit admission that we aren't sufficiently on His level to always understand fully what we are asking Him to do. We tend to ask for our immediate needs, but God, in His omniscience, understands our true needs infinitely more than we do, so we must trust Him to respond to our prayers in ways that He knows best. To us, this seems comparable to the realization that we must always condition our divine requests with, "if it is Your will."

Christ Himself exemplified this at His point of greatest distress when He was suffering in the Garden of Gethsemane before His crucifixion, as we alluded to in a prayer in Chapter 2. Christ was dealing with excruciating spiritual agony as He was separated from the Father and about to receive His full wrath for all the past, present, and future sins of mankind. He implored His Father, "Father, if you are willing, remove this cup from me," then immediately and selflessly qualified His request with this: "Nevertheless, not my will, but yours be done" (Luke 22:24). He expressed His deference in two different ways—"if you are willing," and even more emphatically, "Your will must trump my own." This should be a timeless lesson for us on prayer. We must always pray that God's will be done, and we must do more than pay lip service to that—we must mean it.

PRAYER

Father, it's so difficult not to immediately rush to our personal requests when we sit down to pray. Teach us, through scripture and meeting with other believers, how we can simply worship You with our prayers. The psalmists have many examples of this type of prayer. Psalm 106 begins, "Praise the Lord! Oh give thanks to the

▶

Lord, for he is good, for his steadfast love endures forever! Who can utter the mighty deeds of the Lord, or declare all his praise?" The next time we sit down to pray, help us to pause and remember this. Rather than going straight to our petitions, let us instead declare how wonderful You are, and let us acknowledge and thank You for the personal blessings You've bestowed upon us. This type of prayer is what increases Your presence—when we take the focus off ourselves and instead glorify You with our mouths—for this is the very thing we were designed to do! Let Your will be done, Lord, and may we learn to praise You all of our days.

AMEN.

CHAPTER 4

Paul begins this chapter repeating that he is "a prisoner of the Lord," which we should not interpret as a complaint of victimhood. The thrust of his writing, in this letter and elsewhere, conveys that he accepts his plight as God's will and understands it has enhanced his Christian witness in some ways. In his first sentence, he says that because of what he has laid out in the preceding chapters (what God has done for us), we must live consistently with our Christian calling and do so humbly, patiently, lovingly, and in a manner that promotes and maintains spiritual unity and peace among believers. He makes clear that we are all united: "There is one body and one Spirit—just as you were called to the one hope that belongs to your call—one Lord, one faith, one baptism, one God and Father of all, who is over all and through all and in all" (4:4–6).

Paul's obvious meaning here is that Christians must be humble, love one another patiently, and live in unity and peace because these are all characteristics of Christ. It's as if he is saying, "Be like Christ by adopting His character qualities," or simply, "Imitate Christ." Perhaps we should think of it this way: Because of the fall, man descended into a sinful state, and man's God-like image was marred.

But conversion and regeneration of individual human beings through faith in Christ begins the process of restoring that image as we become more Christlike through the power of the Holy Spirit. It's inspiring to consider that through the practice of the spiritual disciplines we can return to the path of reflecting God's image and glorifying Him.

John Calvin suggests that Paul puts humility at the beginning of his list of virtues because we must first cultivate this quality to achieve the other virtues. Humility, he says, is the first step toward unity. Without humility we will be prone to rudeness, pride, and disagreeable language toward others, which will lead to quarrels and insults. Why? Because "every one carries his love of himself, and his regard to his own interests, to excess. By laying aside haughtiness and a desire of pleasing ourselves, we shall become meek and gentle, and acquire that moderation of temper which will overlook and forgive many things in the conduct of our brethren."[42] It is undeniable that pride, in this sense, is an enemy of these virtues. Being centered on self, it obviously impedes unity. It puts our own interests above others, which is the opposite of the servant's heart we are to model as Christians. Overall, Paul is arguing against the pagan culture of his time in which humility was devalued and pride was lauded.

Prayer

Father, often our pride stems from a place of resentment; forgetting our own unworthiness, we compare our lives to others' whom we feel are less deserving of blessing, and bitterness begins to swell in our hearts. Protect us from ourselves, Lord. We don't want to be like Jonah, who couldn't experience the joy You had prepared for him because his pride blinded him to his own sin. Proverbs reminds

▶

us, "The Lord is watching everywhere, keeping his eye on both the evil and the good" (Prov. 15:3 NLT). Nothing is hidden from You, Lord; You see all things. When we feel we've been wronged or treated unfairly, remind us that judgment belongs solely to You, and that in the end You will make everything right. Until then, we ask the Holy Spirit to replace our seeds of self-righteousness with humility. Replace hardness in our hearts with tenderness and compassion. Thank you, Lord.

AMEN.

As the church is the body of Christ, and since unity in the church and among believers is essential to the healthy development and functioning of the church, God directs that we work toward unity in our own congregations and for the church as a whole.[43] Peace goes hand in hand with unity, and achieving peace is emphasized throughout the Bible. But this peace is not so much about peace treaties between warring nations. Rather, it is part of God's covenant promises to His people and is integral to the message of the gospel as prophesied in the Old Testament. For example, consider these passages:

- ★ "How beautiful upon the mounts are the feet of him who brings good news, who publishes peace, who brings good news of happiness, who publishes salvation, who says to Zion, 'Your God reigns.'" (Isaiah 52:7)
- ★ "'For the mountains may depart and the hills be removed, but my steadfast love shall not depart from you, and my covenant of peace shall not be removed,' says the Lord, who has compassion on you." (Isaiah 54:10)

★ "I will make a covenant of peace with them. It shall be an everlasting covenant with them. And I will set them in their land and multiply them, and will set my sanctuary in their midst forevermore." (Ezek. 37:26)

Here, the prophets are foretelling a peace that can only be achieved through Christ. Christian love is a precondition to both unity and peace.[44] All these virtues are interdependent.

After calling us to unity, Paul shows how that is perfectly logical and fitting as he ticks off a list of "ones"—one body, one Spirit, one hope, one Lord, one faith, one baptism, and one God and Father of all. Notice that these components of unity are grounded in the Triune God—all three persons, the Father, Son, and Holy Spirit. One body refers to the church comprising individual members. One Spirit is, of course, the Holy Spirit who indwells the church corporately and its individual members. We all share a common "hope," which, as we've noted, means an assurance that because of our faith in Christ, we will be with God in eternity (1 Peter 1:3). And one Lord denotes Jesus Christ—the head of the church.[45]

There is some debate over Paul's reference to "one faith." Some commentators believe it means Christian doctrine, as described in the book of Jude: "the faith that was once for all delivered to the saints" (Jude 3). In John MacArthur's view, "God's Word contains many truths, but its individual truths are but harmonious facets of His one truth, which is our one faith."[46] Others, however, believe "one faith" refers to our saving faith in Jesus Christ—trusting in Christ for our personal salvation.[47]

As to "one baptism," some scholars believe Paul is referring to water baptism and others to spiritual baptism. We won't attempt to break down the competing views of the term "spirit baptism." (It is different from water baptism and involves the Holy Spirit's activity in sealing believers into the body of the church.) Besides, most scholars tend to believe Paul is here referring to water baptism. Also beyond the scope of this book is a discussion of the various views on water baptism—infant baptism or adult baptism, whereby the believer publicly proclaims His faith in Jesus. Regardless, Paul is saying that baptism is another element of the unity of believers. Concerning water baptism, Bruce Barton observes that "Paul's inclusion of this one baptism reveals the great importance that baptism held for the early church. Baptism replaced circumcision as the initiation rite of the new order, the new covenant."[48]

Last, but obviously not least, Paul mentions "one God and Father of all who is over all and through all and in all." With his reference to God the Father, Paul completes the three persons of the Trinity, while at the same time emphasizing that there is one God. We are all unified in God—there are no other gods. God is *over* all Christians because we are His spiritual children; He is *through* all in that He works through us; and He is *in* all because God dwells in us through His Holy Spirit (Eph. 2:22).[49]

We note that right after he details our multi-faceted unity, Paul says we are nevertheless individuals who have received certain gifts from Christ to use in the church, and these gifts contribute, and do not detract from, the unity just described. We see a useful analogy in Paul's highlighting the unity and diversity of the church following his mentioning of the three individual persons of the Trinity who comprise the unified Godhead. Elsewhere Paul writes that each member of the church body has gifts with which he serves the whole (Romans 12:5–6).[50] Every individual is important, and the church is not complete without its individual members.

Paul then cites scriptural authority for the spiritual gifts he's describing. "When he ascended on high he led a host of captives, and he gave gifts to men" (Psalms 68:18). This Psalm refers to God's victory over His enemies and His subsequent ascension to His throne. In ancient times the victor would take property from the defeated enemy and divide it among his own people. Paul applies this to Christ's triumphal conquest of death through His resurrection. As head of the church, He distributes spiritual gifts to His people (members of the church), just as a warrior distributes the spoils of victory to his people.

We are a community of believers. It is important that we honor God's will to build one another up (1 Thessalonians 5:11), and we should fully embrace that command. He knows exactly what we need, and we must learn to open our hearts and become vulnerable with trusted fellow believers in order to sharpen and be sharpened by each other.

In much of today's church culture, however, we can become hooked on systems and programs. If we aren't signed up for a Bible study group or serving at church, we can feel as though we're not doing our part. While participating in these groups is important, we should not put ourselves (or God) in a box when we think about our roles as members of the church body. Having a small circle of intimate friends (even one friend) whom you can pray with and pray for on a regular basis can sometimes be as valuable as volunteering your time on a Sunday.

Prayer

Father, we ask that You highlight people in our lives who at this very moment could use our prayer, and who could help pray for us. We want to live in the fullness of all You have for us, and we trust that includes inviting other believers to be part of our journey with You. Help us to honor your will that we be in relationship and community with other believers as you are with Your Son and the Holy Spirit.

Amen.

Paul says that prior to ascending far above all the heavens, so that he might fill all things, Christ descended into the lower regions—the earth. (4:9–10). Christ, the Son of God and living in perfect bliss with the Father and the Holy Spirit in eternity past, voluntarily became a human being, suffered all the indignities attendant thereto, died on the cross, and rose—all so that we could live (Philip. 2:5–11). Scholars disagree as to what Paul means by Christ's descending, but regardless of his precise meaning it should be clear that Christ's descent stands in stark contrast to His ascent "far above all the heavens, that he might fill all things" (4:10). It seems logical to conclude, as Paul does, that Christ descended in order to ascend on our behalf. Were it not for His passion we would die in our sins, so by juxtaposing "descent" and "ascent," Paul expresses the magnitude both of His sacrifice and His victory on our behalf.

British singer and songwriter Graham Kendrick captures the sublime beauty of Christ's dual nature—human and God—by showing the extent of the paradoxical contrast between the two, yet their perfect compatibility in His Person: "Meekness and majesty, Manhood and Deity, In perfect harmony, The Man who is God." Kendrick then expresses awe at the Lord who humbles Himself by dwelling among us and suffers and sacrifices to give us life.[51]

Paul identifies several gifts given to us by the conquering Christ—apostles, prophets, evangelists, and the shepherds (pastors) and teachers—"to equip the saints for the work of ministry, for building up the body of Christ, until we all attain to the unity of the faith and of the knowledge of the Son of God, to mature manhood, to the measure of the stature of the fullness of Christ, so that we may no longer be children, tossed to and fro by the waves and carried about by every wind of doctrine, by human cunning, by craftiness in deceitful schemes" (4:12–14). We love this long sentence because Paul is accentuating the importance of correct doctrine and its indispensability to our spiritual growth and to church unity. He has a method of describing similar ideas in various ways that are not redundant but all add color to his meaning. The apostles and prophets, whom he had previously described as foundational (2:20), laid the groundwork in scripture and in their preaching and prophesying, and the pastors and teachers have built on that foundation to impart this knowledge of Christ and the Bible to all mankind throughout the generations. Thus spiritually fed, we are equipped to become more Christlike and grow in spiritual maturity so that our faith will not falter with the shifting sands of doctrinal uncertainty and the deceitful approaches of false teachers.

Can't you just hear Jesus' words here: "Everyone who hears these words of mine and does them will be like a wise man who built his house on the rock. And the rain fell, and the floods came, and the winds blew and beat on that house, but it did not fall, because it had been founded on the rock. And everyone who hears these words of mine and does not do them will be like a foolish man who built his house on the sand. And the rain fell, and the floods came, and the winds blew and beat against that house, and it fell, and great was the fall of it" (Matt. 7:24–27).

While God doesn't want us to be puffed up in our knowledge of scripture or to understand it intellectually without incorporating it into our daily lives, He does make clear that it is crucial that we understand His word, to better know Him and to become more Christlike. Without mature knowledge of the scriptures we'll be vulnerable to the cultists and pluralists, to those who distort scripture and would lead us toward the path of death rather than life.

I (Christen) have personally experienced God in the most tangible ways when I've been deeply rooted in Bible study. If you've had difficulty in seeing personal messages from God through scripture, we'd encourage you to ask the Holy Spirit to guide you to a chapter of the Bible to study. When we seek Him wholeheartedly, He is faithful to reward us!

Paul now ties it all together, showing that understanding God through the scriptures is not only essential for our individual growth but central to the flourishing of the church. He says that "speaking the truth in love, we are to grow up in every way into him who is the head, into Christ, from whom the whole body, joined and held together by every joint with which it is equipped, when each part is working properly, makes the body grow so that it builds itself up in love" (4:15–16).

We often hear the phrase, "speak the truth in love," and it almost always means "speak the hard truth," as if being brutally honest with people—even if it causes them pain—is noble. That strikes us as a little bit cold and self-serving, or it at least has that potential. We think it's different from just being brutally and insensitively honest. Those trying to impart difficult advice to others should take special care in how they express it.

Admittedly, however, we mustn't candy-coat something to the point that it loses its sincerity and constructiveness to the hearer. As with so many things, we must seek the proper balance in these difficult exchanges. "Love makes truth palatable, while truth makes love practical," writes Warren Wiersbe. "Truth without love could destroy a person by its brutality, while love without truth could destroy a person by its insincerity. Love without truth is sentimentality, feeling without responsibility. Truth without love is powerless to change lives, while love without truth could change them in the wrong direction."[52]

Exactly right. So with that clarification, we believe Paul is saying that we must speak the truth in love and become more like Christ, who lived the perfect human life, speaking truth in love. One poignant example is Christ's interaction with the woman at the well. He responds to her admission that she has no husband truthfully, yet sensitively. He doesn't sugarcoat his statements as would a people-pleaser, nor does he bitterly scold her. He simply states, "You are right in saying, 'I have no husband': for you have had five husbands, and the one you now have is not your husband. What you have said is true" (John 4:17–18). The gentle but firm nature of His words make His voice almost palpable. Jesus loves this woman too much to let her keep living quietly in sin, and He feels the same way about each of His children. As believers, we are members of His body who are all joined together, so the more spiritually equipped each of us is, the better the body will function as a whole—and love drives it all.

Please note how this chapter beautifully illustrates that Paul practices what he preaches—that is, he speaks the truth in love. For as soon as he completes his essay on the necessity of unity in the body of Christ, he turns to reminding us of the importance of purity in the church as well. This is practical advice because we often encounter disagreements over doctrinal points and wrestle with which of those might be theological hills to die on. Here again we must strike a balance. We mustn't achieve unity at the expense of diluting God's word, but we mustn't be so dogmatic about every fine detail of scriptural interpretation that we descend into squabbles, which are often more about our pride than honoring the word.

PRAYER

Lord, there are so many denominations and branches of believers whose opinions differ on aspects of Your word. May we remember Your wise instructions, "Let every person be quick to hear, slow to speak, slow to anger" (James 1:19), and the wisdom of Proverbs 18:2, "A fool takes no pleasure in understanding, but only in expressing his opinion." We marvel at how well You know us. May we learn to care more about showing love to fellow believers than winning arguments, but may we also understand that true love is deeper than making people feel good all the time. Help us to find the balance to speak truth in love as You do. In Your power and love,

AMEN.

So after exhorting his readers to be Christlike, Paul, following his own advice on speaking the truth in love, reinforces the message by warning them of behavior they must avoid to succeed in their effort. And he begins this section by reminding them that he is speaking for God, which clearly indicates the gravity of his admonitions: "Now this I say and testify in the Lord, that you must no longer walk as the Gentiles do, in the futility of their minds. They are darkened in their understanding, alienated from the life of God because of the ignorance that is in them, due to their hardness of heart. They have become callous and have given themselves up to sensuality, greedy to practice every kind of impurity" (4:17–19).

Paul is not referring to Gentile converts to Christ but those who consciously reject God—the arrogant heathens who don't consider repenting because they don't want to abandon their licentious lifestyle. They have hardened their hearts against God—another way of saying they have turned themselves over to the devil—and they aren't ashamed of it. These observations still ring true today, as do all timeless truths revealed in the Bible.

Have you ever encountered a self-professed atheist—not just an agnostic, but full-blown atheist—who condescendingly taunts believers as unthinking rubes? It seems that as long as they harbor that attitude they make themselves unreachable, though hopefully that's not the case in the long run. The *ESV Study Bible* comments on this phenomenon: "Both in antiquity and today, people who reject the knowledge of God think of themselves as 'enlightened' (cf. Heb. 10:32). Their ignorance here is not lack of general education; some are brilliant in their own way, but such brilliance is all wasted and futile in the end when combined with hardness of heart toward the truth of the gospel in Christ."[53]

In responding to the disciples' question of why He speaks in parables, Jesus invokes the words of the prophet Isaiah, who wrote about those with this very hardness of heart. Jesus says,

> This is why I speak to them in parables, because seeing they do not see, and hearing they do not hear, nor do they understand. Indeed, in their case the prophecy of Isaiah is fulfilled that says: "You will indeed hear but never understand, and you will indeed see but never perceive. For this people's heart has grown dull, and with their ears they can barely hear, and their eyes they have closed, lest they should see with their eyes and hear with their ears and understand with their heart and turn, and I would heal them." But blessed are your eyes, for they see, and your ears, for they hear. For truly, I say to you, many prophets and righteous people longed to see what you see, and did not see it, and to hear what you hear, and did not hear it. (Matt. 13:13–17)

Ambrosiaster, the name ascribed to the anonymous author of the earliest complete Latin commentary on Paul's epistles, warns the Ephesians that unless they strive to live the Christian walk and think Godly thoughts, they will "end up like the Gentiles who...have a darkened mind which prevents them from contemplating the truth of divine light. Instead they go after vain things like idolatry, and are restrained by the devil from walking in the way of the one God so that he can make them share in his own damnation."[54]

PRAYER

Lord, You spoke to Your people through the prophet Ezekiel, "And I will give you a new heart, and a new spirit I will put within you. And I will remove the heart of stone from your flesh and give you a heart of flesh" (Ezek. 36:26). We acknowledge that our ability to experience and give any goodness comes directly from You. Thank You for sharing Your overflowing love with us, and for transforming our once hardened hearts to be able to accept the truth of Your word.

AMEN.

Paul reminds them that this Gentile life of sin and impurity is not what they were taught when they learned about Christ (4:20). To live the way of the pagan Gentiles is entirely incompatible with the Christian walk. The truth, says Paul, is in Jesus (4:21). Christianity is not a religion. It is not about rules. It is about the person of Jesus Christ. In Him, ultimate truth resides. He is God. He is Truth. Jesus said, "I am the way and the truth and the life" (John 14:6). This is rightfully emphasized by many Christian commentators. "All real and effective teaching must be in harmony with truth as truth is in Him," writes R. W. Dale.[55] "Truth came once into the world with her divine master, and was a perfect shape most glorious to look upon," proclaims John Milton.[56] "Truth is not finally to be found in abstract notions or theories, but rather in the person of Jesus Christ, the unique Son of God and the living embodiment of truth," writes J. R. Franke. "From this perspective, knowing truth depends on being in proper relationship to this one person who *is* divine truth. Jesus is categorically different from all other prophets, witnesses, and messengers from God. Jesus is all of these things, yet more. Along with the Father and the Spirit, Jesus himself is God."[57]

Paul's message is relevant in today's environment filled with disinformation and competing truth claims. The devil is the author of lies, and it is in his interest to confuse us about what is true, whether truth even exists, and whether Jesus is who He says He is. Just as he told Eve it wouldn't matter if she ate from the tree, the devil tells men today that it doesn't matter if we follow Jesus. He tries to convince us there are multiple paths to eternity, though Jesus Himself said there is no other way to the Father except through Him (John 14:6).

Pilate challenged this claim, mocking Jesus to His face about the very existence of truth. Just as Jesus stood His ground with Pilate, we must not shrink in the face of cultural condemnation of what is true and what we know to be true. If we try to please man by accepting the narrative that it's intolerant to teach that there is no other way to God but through faith in Christ, we are betraying Christ. Will we choose to please man or God? If we dilute the gospel or acquiesce to today's pluralism, which claims it doesn't matter what you believe and that there are many truths ("my truth and your truth"), we do our fellow man no favors either. If we believe what we say we believe—that Jesus is truth, that He is the way, the truth, and the life, and that there is no other way to God but through Him—we better be clear and unwavering about it, as people's eternal destiny depends on how they respond to the gospel.

The Ephesians (and all readers of this epistle) must wake up and recognize these things. They must put off their "old self," which is their "former manner of life and is corrupt through deceitful desires." Instead, they must "be renewed in the spirit of [their] minds," and "put on the new self, created after the likeness of God in true righteousness and holiness" (4:22–24).

The Bible is clear that man is fallen and in a sinful state. The prophet Jeremiah, for example, said, "The heart is deceitful above all things and desperately sick; who can understand it?" (Jer. 17:19). Jesus affirmed this as well, saying, "For from within, out of the heart of man, come evil thoughts, sexual immorality, theft, murder, adultery, coveting, wickedness, deceit, sensuality, envy, slander, pride, foolishness" (Matt. 7:21–22). But as we've noted, upon conversion through faith in Christ, man is regenerated and begins the process of sanctification—becoming holier through the power of the Holy Spirit. It's exciting that God offers to us the means by which to throw off our old self and put on the new self.

In his sermon on Romans 12:2, Pastor Voddie Baucham highlights that in the original wording of this verse, God tells us to be transformed by the "renewing" of our minds, which is an active verb. Our sanctification is exactly that—a daily renewing of our minds, a process of casting off our sinful nature and aligning our hearts with God's.

PRAYER

Father, when we begin to wallow in self-loathing and shame due to backsliding, may we remember that our journey of sanctification is an ongoing process meant to be lived out one day at a time. May we submit to You in all things, that You may make our paths straight.

AMEN.

Having told the Ephesians to discard the old and adopt the new, Paul now provides them particular instructions on how to do it. As they have renounced falsehood, they must speak truth with their neighbors because they are all members of the same church body (4:25). Christians owe this duty to speak truthfully both to fellow believers and to the church as a whole because falsehood is destructive to the body as well as to the individual.[58]

Next, do not allow your anger to lead you into sin, and especially, don't let the sun go down on your anger, which just gives the devil a foot in the door (4:26–27). Scholars say this comes from Psalm 4:4. The *New Living Translation* of that verse is clear: "Don't sin by letting anger control you. Think about it overnight and remain silent." Paul then adds that the thief must not steal any more but should do honest work with his own labor and share with those in need (4:28). It is interesting and entirely commonsensical that Paul at least partially ties stealing to idleness, laziness, and sloth. He is saying that the able-bodied should work and that an added blessing to this practice is that they can share the fruits of their labor with the needy.

As is so often the case, New Testament moral standards call us to a higher duty without being legalistic. "Thou shalt not steal" is one of the Ten Commandments we all know, but here Paul is telling us that we shouldn't just quit taking what is not ours. We should actively get to work and share the fruits of our labor with others. The Book of Acts records Paul as having walked the walk on this lesson: "You yourselves know that these hands ministered to my necessities and to those who were with me. In all things I have shown you that by working hard in this way we must help the weak and remember the words of the Lord Jesus, how he himself said, 'It is more blessed to give than to receive'" (Acts 20:34–35).

Paul says we must not speak profanity but rather use language that builds others up under the circumstances so that it benefits those with whom we're communicating. Silence may be appropriate sometimes, but other times we must use our words to encourage and inspire others.

Paul told the Thessalonians not to quench the Holy Spirit (1 Thes. 5:19), and here he tells the Ephesians not to grieve the Holy Spirit, who seals us for the day of redemption (4:30). As the Holy Spirit indwells us, we are not to disappoint Him by using foul language. We have been saved by grace through faith, and the indwelling Holy Spirit protects and empowers us in our Christian walk from the point of our conversion until we are finally glorified with Christ in eternity. So we must honor Him by living up to the standards He makes possible because we have our new self.

In addition, Paul says we must "let all bitterness and wrath and anger and clamor and slander be put away from [us] along with all malice" (4:31). We must "be kind to one another, tenderhearted, forgiving one another, as God in Christ forgave [us]" (4:32). Remember that Jesus taught there is a relationship between our forgiving others and God's forgiving us: "For if you forgive others their trespasses, your heavenly Father will also forgive you, but if you do not forgive others their trespasses, neither will your Father forgive your trespasses" (Matt. 6:14–15). Jesus also reminded us that before we pray we must get our hearts right with others, saying, "And whenever you stand praying, forgive, if you have anything against anyone, so that your Father also who is in heaven may forgive your trespasses" (Mark 11:25). Similarly, James says, "For judgment is without mercy to one who has shown no mercy. Mercy triumphs over judgment" (James 2:13). Remember that this entire chapter of Ephesians essentially provides a roadmap to Christlike behavior. So it's logical that

Paul tells us to forgive others because forgiveness is at the core of God's being—it is an essential lifeline to eternity with Him.

PRAYER

Heavenly Father, just before You commissioned the prophet Isaiah, You took him up in a vision of Your glory-filled throne room. Isaiah's awe of Your holiness immediately led him to a position of repentance, as he cried out, "Woe is me! For I am lost; for I am a man of unclean lips, and I dwell in the midst of a people of unclean lips; for my eyes have seen the King, the Lord of hosts!" Help us modern-day believers understand the importance of studying Old Testament scriptures such as this because they vividly paint a picture of Your power and majesty.

We thank You for revealing to us that after Isaiah's confession, a seraphim touched his lips with a burning coal, saying, "'Behold, this has touched your lips; your guilt is taken away, and your sin atoned for.' And I heard the voice of the Lord saying, 'Whom shall I send, and who will go for us?' Then I said, 'Here I am! Send me'" (Isaiah 6:7–8). What a dumbfounding, beautiful story. Rather than feeling as though something like this could never happen to us, let us instead be encouraged that we live in the age of the Holy Spirit, who grants us full access to You at all times thanks to Your Son's sacrifice! May we be encouraged to seek out scriptures that describe Your glory so we can have a visual reminder in our minds' eyes of Your perfection and wonder. This imagery can help inspire us, as Isaiah was inspired, to regularly confess our sins in order to purify our hearts and minds. Lord, help us to desire to be holy as You are holy and to make our hearts a godly place for the Holy Spirit to dwell.

AMEN

CHAPTER 5

This chapter begins with another reminder that we must imitate God, as His beloved children. This should make perfect sense to us, as children learn by imitating their parents. That can be good or bad, depending on the parents, but it can only be good in the case of Christians' imitating their Holy Father and His Holy Son. The Apostle Peter left similar instructions. "For to this you have been called, because Christ also suffered for you, leaving you an example, so that you might follow in his steps" (1 Peter 2:21), said Peter, noting that Christ "committed no sin, neither was deceit found in his mouth" (1 Peter 2:22). Significantly, Paul tells us to imitate God as His children, as opposed to, for example, slaves, because the latter would do so out of duty and the former out of intimate love and trust.[59]

Paul adds that we must "walk in love, as Christ loved us and gave himself up for us, a fragrant offering and sacrifice to God" (Eph. 5:2). This metaphor points back to the laws God gave Moses and the Israelites for their burnt offerings in the desert. These sacrifices were temporary and could not bring people to perfection. The law reminded man of his sins, which was necessary because it was impossible for the animal sacrifices to wholly take away sins (Heb. 10:3–4). This is why they had to be repeated year after year. The writer of Hebrews explains, "For since the law has but a shadow of the good things to come instead of the true form of these realities, it can never, by the same sacrifices that are continually offered every year, make perfect those who draw near. Otherwise would they not have ceased to be offered, since the worshipers, having once been cleansed, would no longer have any consciousness of sins? But in these sacrifices there is a reminder of sins every year. For it is impossible for the blood of bulls and goats to take away sins" (Heb. 10:1–4).

As part of these sacrifices, the Israelites were to offer a young male animal without defect to atone for their sins and show their devotion to God (Lev. 1). This burnt offering is described in Leviticus 1:13 as "an aroma pleasing to the Lord." The *NIV Life Application Study*

Bible explains that this "pleasing aroma is a way of saying that God accepted the sacrifice because the people's attitude was pleasing to him."[60] In other words, God's laws for burnt offerings were not about adhering to rules for the sake of it but rather were a physical expression of the Israelites' turning their hearts back to God and acknowledging their need for Him. God expressed this in Hosea 6:6: "For I desire mercy, not sacrifice, and acknowledgment of God rather than burnt offerings."

But again, the Old Testament sacrifices could never fully atone for man's sinfulness and didn't lead to man's salvation. A permanent sacrifice is needed to eradicate sin permanently and redeem mankind. So when Jesus died for our sins, He became the final, perfect sacrifice, as He gave His life in order that we might once again live in God's presence and be saved from the penalty of death—hence Paul's description of Him as the "fragrant offering and sacrifice to God." According to the writer of the Book of Hebrews, "For by a single offering he has perfected for all time those who are being sanctified" (Heb. 10:14). Likewise, the *ESV Study Bible* asserts, "In contrast to the repeated Mosaic animal sacrifices, Jesus came into the world according to God's will in order to eternally sanctify a people through offering himself as a sacrifice once for all."[61]

Paul purposefully couples Christ's sacrificial death for us with his command that we live our lives in love, as Christ did. He is echoing Christ, who said, "This is my commandment, that you love one another as I have loved you. Greater love has no one than this, that someone lay down his life for his friends" (John 15:12–13). Paul also wants to stress that true Christian love is much more than positive feelings and behavior toward others. It involves self-sacrifice—putting others ahead of ourselves. "Given the unbelievable privilege and grace of being his beloved," writes H. C. G. Moule, "they are to respond in showing 'self-forgetting kindness.'"[62]

Having imparted these commands, Paul warns us to avoid like the plague those things that can pervert sacrificial love. We must not even think about engaging in sexual immorality or any other impurity or covetousness (5:3). There must be no filthiness or foolish talk nor crude joking. Rather, there should be thanksgiving (5:4). Paul says that a person who is sexually immoral or impure or covetous, which he identifies as idolatry, "has no inheritance in the kingdom of Christ and God" (5:5).

Concerning sexual sin, the Gnostics, as we've noted earlier, believed that spirit alone is good, and all matter is evil. This is contrary to God's word, which tells us that everything God created is good, and He is pleased with it. But these heretics taught that because only spiritual things matter, man could do what he wanted with his body. To the contrary, Christianity teaches the importance of material things and especially of the human body—after all, Christ inhabited a human body. He is fully God and fully man. As we've also seen, the body is the temple of the Holy Spirit, which further underscores its importance. When believers die they will be resurrected with a glorious body (1 Cor. 15:35–53; Philip. 3:21). We won't just be a bunch of ethereal ghosts floating around in heaven. The body matters, deeply, which is why sins involving the body or against the body are a profoundly serious matter.

Covetousness—a desire to have what others have—is forbidden by the Tenth Commandment. It's worse than envy because a covetous person wants to deprive the owner of something and take it for himself. Paul says this kind of unhealthy obsession amounts to idolatry—a serious charge—because it involves worshiping created things rather than the Creator.[63] Jesus warned, "No one can serve two masters, for either he will hate the one and love the other, or he will be devoted to the one and despise the other. You cannot serve God and money" (Matt. 6:24).

Expressing thanksgiving is not only in contrast to filthy talk; it also proceeds from the opposite motive of covetousness.[64] If you are grateful for what you have—what God has provided you—then you are not going to crave what others have and wish to dispossess them of it. The absence of a grateful heart is failing to appreciate God as the giver of every good gift. As James teaches, "Every good gift and every perfect gift is from above, coming down from the Father of lights, with whom there is no variation or shadow due to change" (James 1:17).[65]

PRAYER

Father, we ask that You take stock of our hearts and reveal the things we have made our idols. Help us to cease worshipping these idols, and show us how You want to bring Your presence and goodness into each area of our lives that we are currently filling with things that are not of You. Holy Spirit, help us to be grateful for what God has provided, and give us the spiritual gift of generosity, which is the antidote to covetousness. Proverbs 19:17 teaches, "Whoever is generous to the poor lends to the Lord, and he will repay him for his deed." May we show generosity to those who need us with our time, money, and focus, and may we remember that in doing so we show You honor.

AMEN.

Does Paul's stern warning in Ephesians 5:5—that "everyone who is sexually immoral or impure, or who is covetous (that is, an idolater), has no inheritance in the kingdom of Christ and God"—mean that the redeemed can lose their salvation by occasional sinning? Most commentators agree Paul means that the regenerated person will not habitually engage in such sins. He has the new nature after having cast off the old. It's not that a saved person will lose his salvation by sinning; it's that if he habitually and intentionally sins, he probably wasn't saved in the first place.[66] "No one born of God makes a practice of sinning, for God's seed abides in him; and he cannot keep on sinning, because he has been born of God" (1 John 3:9).

But believers should be aware of their conduct and try to please God. "We know from the whole teaching of the New Testament that all our sins, and certainly this includes our sexual sins, are forgiven when we trust in Jesus for our salvation," writes Richard Phillips. "So Paul is not saying that sexual sin places us in an unredeemable situation, in which case there would be practically no one in heaven with Jesus. Instead, Paul's point is that habitual, unrepented sexual sin is so incompatible with Christianity that it is impossible that a man or woman willingly and positively immersed in sexual sin possesses a true and living faith in Jesus."[67]

In any event, despite our salvation's being a gift from God and owing to no works of our own, God will never be indifferent to sin. Paul made that clear in writing to the Romans and in his other epistles: "What shall we say then? Are we to continue in sin that grace may abound? By no means! How can we who died to sin still live in it?" (Romans 6:1–2). Furthermore, "We know that our old self was crucified with him in order that the body of sin might be brought to nothing, so that we would no longer be enslaved to sin. For one who has died has been set free from sin" (Romans 6:6–7). In other words, freedom from the bondage of sin does not mean freedom *to* sin.

Paul's next verses further reinforce God's intolerance of sin from the redeemed: "Let no one deceive you with empty words, for because of these things the wrath of God comes upon the sons of disobedience. Therefore, do not become partners with them; for at one time you were darkness, but now you are light in the Lord. Walk as children of light (for the fruit of light is found in all that is good and right and true)" (5:6–9).

Believers must not allow themselves to be deceived by false teachers and other cynical loose-talkers who try to convince them that these things don't matter to God. We dismiss the gravity of sinfulness at our own peril. This is one of Satan's oldest tricks—trying to deceive people into thinking that disobedience is inconsequential. Satan wants to dilute God's moral standards and confuse man, which leads to moral chaos and disobedience. God told Eve that if she ate of the tree or even touched it, she would die. "But the serpent said to the woman, 'You will not surely die'" (Gen. 3:3–4).

Paul warns us not to become partners with people who spread such lies because they are children of darkness, and as believers we are now children of light. He is not saying Christians must avoid all contact with nonbelievers—rather, they should not partner with them in their sinfulness. We mustn't make it a practice to associate with those who pretend to be Christians but practice and promote permissiveness, as if it doesn't matter to God. To join hands with such people is to degrade Christ's sacrifice.[68]

We must cultivate what is good, shun what is evil, and live as people of light—that is, we must imitate God because God is light. As the Apostle John wrote, "God is light, and in him is no darkness at all. If we say we have fellowship with him while we walk in darkness, we lie and do not practice the truth. But if we walk in the light, as he is in the light, we have fellowship with one another, and the blood of Jesus his Son cleanses us from all sin" (1 John 1:5–7). Jesus affirmed this message clearly, declaring, "I am the light of the world. Whoever follows me will not walk in darkness, but will have the light of life" (John 8:12). The prophet Isaiah had spoken these truths hundreds of years earlier: "I will make you as a light for the nations, that my salvation may reach to the end of the earth" (Isaiah 49:6).

We must try to discern what is pleasing to God (5:10). But we aren't always sure what that is; it's not all a matter of instinct. He gave us His holy word as guidance, however, and He exhorts us to stay in the word daily, which will help us to understand His will for our lives.

The entire Bible is instructive, and the book of Proverbs is especially useful in imparting principles for godly living. Paul adds that we mustn't just steer clear of sinful behavior but expose it (5:11). In part, this means we can't just be neutral to sin—we must confront it and condemn it with clearly demarcated lines. We often hear of churches going astray because they avoid the topic of sin. In those instances, congregants must have the courage to identify sin for what it is and avoid trying to please man rather than God. This doesn't mean cultivating a judgmental or superior attitude but staying true to God's word and will—we must be honest about what we know to be sinful behavior and resist cultural temptations to cavalierly dismiss it.

PRAYER

Father, Psalm 147 provides insight on how we can please You: "His delight is not in the strength of the horse, nor his pleasure in the legs of a man, but the Lord takes pleasure in those who fear him, in those who hope in his steadfast love" (10–11). This verse reveals that it is not our efforts or strength that please you; rather, it is our reverence for You—the act of making You Lord over our lives—that brings You delight. May our individual relationships with You develop so that we honestly seek to make You smile, asking ourselves, "What can I do to make God happy today?" And may we have hope that those things are in fact what will bring us the greatest amount of joy, as we know that all true goodness comes from You.

AMEN.

Paul says that "their evil intentions will be exposed when the light shines on them, for the light makes everything visible" (5:13–14). Likewise, Jesus said, "For everyone who does wicked things hates the light, lest his works should be exposed. But whoever does what is true comes to the light, so that it may be clearly seen that his works have been carried out in God" (John 3:20–21). Paul is expanding on his command that we condemn evil, thereby helping ourselves and others discern and distinguish between evil deeds and good ones. "When light exposes evil deeds, they become visible, manifest for what they really are," writes H. W. Hoehner. "Seeing them as evil, a believer then cleanses himself of them (1 John 1:5–7), realizing they are detrimental not only to him but also to other believers."[69]

Paul reminds his readers that we must walk carefully as wise people mindful that we don't have unlimited time, as we live in evil days. So we must not be foolish; rather, we must understand God's will (5:15–17). There are many non-believers in this sinful world, so believers, who have a duty to evangelize, must live their lives wisely. In living their lives, they should set a good example so that non-believers will be attracted, not repelled, by professing Christians. And they must winsomely approach non-believers with the gospel message. God's will, obviously, is that we make good use of our time in advancing His kingdom.

Jesus told His disciples, "I have told you these things so that you will be filled with my joy. Yes, your joy will overflow!" (John 15:11 NLT) As Christians, we should have a tangible joy in our lives, one that is recognizable and dumbfounding to those who are lost in the darkness. This joy doesn't mean we will all look like happy-go-lucky automatons. It is an inner peace that surpasses all understanding, a zest for life that radiates hope, and a sense of compassion that extends even to those we consider our enemies.

Prayer

Jesus, thank You for giving us full access to your overflowing joy! We ask for an increase of this joy in our hearts. We want to live in a way that will attract others to Your light and life. As Paul instructed, "Walk in wisdom toward outsiders, making the best use of the time. Let your speech always be gracious, seasoned with salt so that you may know how you ought to answer each person" (Col. 4:5–6). Help us to live this out with every nonbeliever we encounter.

Amen.

Paul then cautions us not to get drunk, which leads to debauchery. Instead, we must be filled with the Spirit (5:18). To set a good example for non-believers, we want to put our best foot forward, and intoxication can impede that. "Immoderate indulgence makes one rash, passionate, prone to stumbling, anger and severity," writes Chrysostom. "Wine was given to gladden us, not for intoxication."[70] Similarly, Ambrose observes, "One drunk with wine sways and stumbles. But one who is filled with the Spirit has solid footing in Christ. This is a fine drunkenness, which produces even greater sobriety of mind."[71]

God has given us His Holy Spirit and wants us to be filled with it. We should cultivate that through the practice of the spiritual disciplines. For clarification, we want to distinguish between the indwelling of the Holy Spirit and the filling of the Spirit. The Holy Spirit permanently indwells all believers beginning at the moment of their conversion (Eph. 1:13; Gal. 3:2), as Jesus promised, "And I will ask the Father, and he will give you another Helper, to be with you forever, even the Spirit of truth, whom the world cannot receive, because it neither sees him nor knows him. You know him, for he dwells with you and will be in you" (John 14:16–17).

The filling of the Spirit (5:18) is a different matter, which is why Paul commands us to be filled with the Spirit in verse 18, but nowhere in the Bible are we commanded to be indwelt with the Spirit. That is automatic for believers and thus not subject to a command. Non-believers are neither indwelt nor filled with the Spirit. One must be indwelt by the Holy Spirit to be filled with the Spirit.[72]

The filling is neither permanent nor guaranteed but is related to our attitude. If we grieve or "quench" the Holy Spirit, as referenced above, we do not avail ourselves of His full power working within us and through us. We must consciously yield ourselves to Him, inviting Him to be present in every aspect of our lives—guiding and directing us. Sin impedes the filling of the Spirit, and because we are all sinners, we can't be filled all the time. But obedience to God causes it to occur.[73]

Prayer

Holy Spirit, we thank you for indwelling us. We acknowledge that You are a full member of the Holy Trinity, and that You are not to be set aside or neglected. The original Greek word used for "quench" in Paul's letter is "sbennumi," which means, "to extinguish, to quench, thwart or suppress" (*Strong's Greek Lexicon* 4750). Father, may we not be found guilty of suppressing or extinguishing Your Holy Spirit's power in our lives. Open our hearts to being filled with the Holy Spirit, to receive His unique gifts and not be skeptical, cynical, or fearful about receiving them. Remove our pride and reveal steps of faith we can take to invite the Holy Spirit to fill us on a deeper level.

AMEN.

Paul urges believers to speak to one another in psalms, hymns, and spiritual songs and to give thanks to the Father in the name of the Son (5:19–20). Scholars suggest these verses helped lead to the practice of singing hymns in church, whereby spirit-filled believers use music to encourage one another and praise God. Hymns based on scripture can be greatly fulfilling, which is why some people prefer traditional hymns that are loaded with doctrinal truth. "Grounded in God's Word and correct doctrine, music can be an important part of Christian worship and education," writes Bruce Barton.[74] Music is also an opportunity for the Holy Spirit to fill our hearts and minds. God created music as a gift that we can use to worship Him. So when we sing in church, we should never just go through the motions but instead consciously recognize that our heartfelt praises manifest God's presence.

In Chapter One—Colossians—we discussed Paul's instructions concerning wives and husbands, children and parents, and slaves. In the balance of chapter 5 and the beginning of chapter 6 of Ephesians, he addresses the same subjects, though in a bit more detail, and explains why he gives these instructions. He says that the husband is head of the wife just as Christ is head of the church, and wives should submit to their husbands (5:22–24). Here, Paul also explicitly commands husbands to love their wives as Christ loved the church "and gave himself up for her.... Husbands should love their wives as their own bodies. He who loves his wife loves himself" (5:25, 28). As we noted in Chapter One, these teachings have provoked an array of contemporary objections, many of which highlight the wife's duties to her husband while deemphasizing the husband's obligations to his wife.

PRAYER

Father, You reveal in 2 Timothy 3:16, "All Scripture is breathed out by God and profitable for teaching, for reproof, for correction, and for training in righteousness, that the man of God may be complete, equipped for every good work." Help us to remember that every single word of scripture was breathed out by You, and that, if we find any passage hard to understand or accept, we need to dig deeper, rather than sweeping these sections under the rug. Psalm 92 tells us that You are righteous, our Rock, and there is no wickedness whatsoever in You! Therefore, when certain aspects of Your word make us uncomfortable, may we always be mindful that You are an amazingly good Father, and there is not a trace of malice in Your heart—everything You want for us comes from a place of deep affection and love. Take us to new heights of understanding, bring us into Your hiding place of revelation, and let those things the enemy uses to harm our faith be used instead as the very things that will strengthen our trust in You. In Your name let it be done,

AMEN.

CHAPTER 6

Paul shifts now to instructions concerning parents and children, telling kids to obey their parents "in the Lord" and to honor their father and mother, which he says is the first commandment with a promise. They should respect their parents so that "it may go well with you and that you may live long in the land" (6:1–3). Fathers must not provoke their children to anger and must raise them "in the discipline and instruction of the Lord" (6:4).

To obey their parents in the Lord probably means they should do so because it is the right thing to do and pleases the Lord, for Paul had stated in Colossians that the Lord is pleased when children obey their parents in everything (Col. 3:20). This is part of God's intended order for the family. As Luke notes, Jesus Himself honored his parents' authority and obeyed them (Luke 2:51). Children's obedience mirrors the practice of believers' submitting to God's authority, so children's obedience can lead to their submission to God's authority when they become older.[75]

In saying children will live long lives by honoring their parents, Paul is quoting one of the Ten Commandments (Exod. 20:12; Deut. 5:16). But why would obedience to this command lead to a long life? Obedience promotes self-discipline, so it follows that those who live disciplined lives increase their chances of longevity. Obedience to this command also strengthens the family unit, while disobedience weakens it. Thus, when the family unit deteriorates and parental respect decreases, people will not live as long. H. D. M. Spence notes this is a general statement with exceptions, as many people who obey their parents die young and many who disobey live long lives. But it is a reliable general rule. "Where obedience to parents is found," writes Spence, "there is usually found along with it temperance, self-control, industry, regular ways of life, and other habits that tend towards prosperity and longevity."[76]

The biblical injunction against parents' provoking their children has always resonated with me (David) as a parent and in observing other parents. Disciplining your children is clearly necessary, but gratuitously aggravating them or lording your authority over them is neither loving nor healthy. Paul wrote in Colossians that provoking one's children discourages them (Col. 3:21). Moreover, mistreating children could stoke their resentment and cause overall psychological damage. We are told that in the pagan world of Paul's day, fathers had virtually unlimited authority over their families and their slaves—they could even murder them with no accountability. So

Paul's instruction, though uncontroversial today, may have been shocking to nonbelievers at the time.[77]

We found one helpful list of provocative behaviors that parents should avoid in accord with Paul's instructions:

- ★ Refusing to accept there are generational changes—and not all of them are bad—just because you didn't experience them as a child. You must strike a balance between encouraging traditional behaviors you believe are healthy and allowing children to be part of their generation, provided the changes aren't detrimental.
- ★ Over-controlling a child. I (David) have sometimes had to pull myself back as a parent, recognizing that even though I was trying to constructively discipline this or that child, tightening the reins too much could lead to stress and angst.
- ★ Under-controlling a child. We mustn't treat our children like adults, and we can't give them too much freedom, especially at an early age. This could have disastrous consequences in the child's development.
- ★ Living an inconsistent life in front of your children. Telling your kids to behave in a certain way and then violating your own rules can lead to confusion and provocation.[78]

Instead of mistreating or provoking children, properly discipline them and train them according to God's word. One of the surest ways to teach your children obedience is to familiarize them with the Bible and its teachings. "Do you want your son to be obedient?" asks Chrysostom. "Rear him from the outset in the teaching and discipline of the Lord. Never regard it as a small matter that he should be a diligent learner of Scriptures."[79]

PRAYER

Father, help us to understand that our mothers and fathers are only human and that there is no such thing as the perfect earthly parent. However, You are the Perfect Father, and You can mend any wounds or hardness in our hearts we might be harboring toward our earthly parents. Please help us to see them from Your Heavenly perspective; give us the grace we need to obtain the peace which surpasses all understanding when it comes to our familial relationships. For those of us who are parents, may we continually look to the truth held in Proverbs 14:26: "Those who fear the Lord are secure; He will be a refuge for their children." No matter what phase of life our children may be in, help us to see that it's never too late (or early) for You to have Your way in their lives. May we never give up hope for our children. Please help us to make it a regular practice to pray over them and with them, and to speak words of blessing and encouragement over their lives. Give us the direction we need to be the godly leaders of our homes You have created us to be, and may our insecurity not keep us from the riches that await us when we take small leaps of faith in the way we pray and interact with our kids.

AMEN.

Concerning the duties of bondservants, Paul repeats the message he delivered in Colossians. Bondservants are to obey their earthly masters as they would Christ, says Paul, and they must do so all the time, not just when the masters are watching them. He is even more emphatic here than in Colossians that their true master is the Lord, and they will receive rewards from Him every bit as surely as if they were not slaves. In other words, in God's eyes they are not lesser human beings but are told to perform their services while keeping the spiritual realm in perspective. Though they were freed from sin through their faith in Christ, they are still bound to obey their earthly masters.

Telling servants to obey even when their masters aren't looking reinforces that the servants' true master is Christ. It is reminiscent of the well-known quote of UCLA Bruins men's basketball coach John Wooden: "The true test of a man's character is what he does when no one is watching." Read in light of Paul's words, Wooden's words become even more profound, for it could be argued he's implying that if you behave well when no one is looking, you are behaving in a way that pleases God—because God is always looking.

Without repeating our discussion in Colossians, let's say that regardless of how repugnant slavery is, we can draw some comfort from Paul's message that servants are every bit as important to Christ as any other human being and that they are ultimately serving Christ, not their earthly masters. Paul also issues a stern warning to masters not to mistreat their servants, telling them they have a master too, and He's in heaven and doesn't play favorites—meaning they are no greater in His eyes than their servants.

The next section, verses 6:10–20, is one of our favorite sections of scripture because it so clearly tells us we are engaged in a fierce spiritual war and that we cannot afford to regard the spiritual world as some make-believe world of ghosts and goblins. The spiritual realm is real—as is Satan. It's as real as the material world, even though we can't see it—only its effects. It is important that we quote the entire passage here because we want people to understand just how real spiritual warfare is. While Paul describes the battle gear figuratively, he is clearly telling us that the enemies we face are as real as if they were Roman soldiers—except far more powerful:

> Finally, be strong in the Lord and in the strength of his might. Put on the whole armor of God, that you may be able to stand against the schemes of the devil. For we do

> not wrestle against flesh and blood, but against the rulers, against the authorities, against the cosmic powers over this present darkness, against the spiritual forces of evil in the heavenly places. Therefore take up the whole armor of God, that you may be able to withstand in the evil day, and having done all, to stand firm. Stand therefore, having fastened on the belt of truth, and having put on the breastplate of righteousness, and, as shoes for your feet, having put on the readiness given by the gospel of peace. In all circumstances take up the shield of faith, with which you can extinguish all the flaming darts of the evil one; and take the helmet of salvation, and the sword of the Spirit, which is the word of God, praying at all times in the Spirit, with all prayer and supplication. To that end, keep alert with all perseverance, making supplication for all the saints, and also for me, that words may be given to me in opening my mouth boldly to proclaim the mystery of the gospel, for which I am an ambassador in chains, that I may declare it boldly, as I ought to speak. (6:10–20)

Paul first tells his readers to lean on Christ's strength because believers cannot fight spiritual enemies with their power alone. We must draw on Christ's power "that you may be able to stand against the schemes of the devil" (6:11). He commands us to put on the whole armor of God, which is figurative but only insofar as likening our spiritual battle gear to the physical. The enemy and the warfare are real, and the imagery of physical shields and weapons impresses upon us the gravity of the spiritual threats confronting us.

In commanding us to proactively put on the armor of God, it seems he is saying this doesn't happen on its own. We must consciously approach God, constantly praying in the Spirit for our armor and the strength to engage in these battles (6:18). If Paul were only speaking figuratively in describing our enemy, he wouldn't say "for we do not wrestle against flesh and blood" (6:12). No, our real enemies are the rulers, the authorities, the cosmic powers over this spiritual darkness and the spiritual forces of evil in the heavenly realm (6:12). The *NLT* rendering is helpful: "For we are not fighting against flesh-and-blood enemies, but against evil rulers and authorities of the unseen world, against mighty powers in this dark world, and against evil spirits in the heavenly places" (6:12).

Interestingly, Paul reiterates his command that we put on all of God's armor. What could this mean other than that we face real spiritual enemies and that we simply cannot stand up against them on our own? We must be prepared. "We are waging war against the fiercest of enemies," writes Ambrosiaster. "He is skilled in every deceit. We must therefore keep on the lookout, with all circumspection and care, that wherever they test our resistance they will find us protected and ready."[80] If we do put on all of God's armor, we'll be able to stand firm (6:13).

But what are the spiritual weapons believers must employ as they set out for spiritual battle? In addition to relying on God for all of it, Paul says they must fasten on the belt of truth and the breastplate of righteousness, and have their feet fitted with shoes that provide the readiness that comes from the gospel of peace. In all circumstances take up the shield of faith, which will empower you to extinguish all of Satan's flaming darts (6:14–16).

As the father of lies, the devil can't stand up against God's truth. Believers must preach the gospel in truth, overcoming the deceit of false teachers who deny Jesus is fully who He says He is. This also applies to the everyday battles we wage in our own minds. There are many mental struggles we encounter because we believe—whether consciously or subconsciously—lies about our identity, just as Adam and Eve were originally led astray by the devil. When we apply the truth about our identity in Christ, we can face whatever obstacles may come because we will know that because God is for us, nothing can stand against us (Romans 8:31).

By ordering us to put on the breastplate of righteousness, Paul is telling us to live righteously, which will guard our hearts against the devil's assaults.[81] Of course, he does not mean our own righteousness but that conferred on us by the Holy Spirit through our faith in Christ. As we'll see in the next chapter, Paul tells the Philippians that he has no righteousness "but that which comes through faith in Christ, the righteousness from God that depends on faith" (Philip. 3:9).

What does Paul mean by the readiness of peace that comes from the gospel? Theologian Charles Hodge explains, "As the gospel secures our peace with God and gives the assurance of his favor, it produces that joyful alacrity of mind which is essential to success in the spiritual conflict."[82] John MacArthur has a similar take. "The gospel of peace pertains to the good news that, through Christ, believers are at peace with God and He is on their side," writes MacArthur. "It is that confidence of divine support which allows the believer to stand firm, knowing that he is at peace with God, and God is his strength."[83] The shield of faith probably describes the small, round shield Roman soldiers used to block the enemy's sword, arrow, or spear. To don the shield of faith, then, means to reject the temptation to doubt, or to sin, or even to quit. By resting in your faith you'll shield yourself against these assaults.[84]

Continuing with the war imagery, Paul says they must "take the helmet of salvation, and the sword of the Spirit, which is the word of God, praying at all times in the Spirit, with all prayer and supplication" (6:17–18). Since Paul described the helmet as "the hope of salvation" in 1 Thessolonians 5:8, many scholars believe he is referring here to the glorious assurance that we are saved through faith as protection against our spiritual enemies' efforts to discourage us and sow intellectual doubt in our hearts. In likening the Bible to a sword of the Holy Spirit, Paul is probably suggesting that the words of scripture applied to specific situations can defeat the enemy and deliver us from his assaults.

This reminds us of Jesus using that very tactic against Satan's efforts to tempt Him during His period in the wilderness in preparation for His public ministry. In each case Jesus invoked scripture to ward off the devil (Matt. 4:1–11; Mark 1:12–13; Luke 4:1–13). Crucially, the Holy Spirit was with Jesus during this period—He led Jesus into the wilderness to be tempted by the devil. As believers are to imitate Christ's behavior, it follows that His empowerment by the Spirit to protect Himself against Satan and His use of scripture during that period are to serve as models for us as we fight our own spiritual battles.

That is surely what Paul is advising here, and let's also note that it's not just references to the Bible in general but the application of specific passages and principles. This is just one more reason we should be in awe of scripture and realize that among other things it is God's manual to help us fight evil. As such, it's another reason we should regularly read the Bible and memorize specific passages, which we can use as we confront temptations and other spiritual assaults.

Again, Paul commands that through all these struggles, even armed with these various weapons and shields, we must pray constantly in the Spirit. We must remember we can't fight these battles on our own. We must call on the Holy Spirit in every situation and pray ceaselessly in the Spirit. It's important that we understand, however, that prayer is not just one of the weapons we are to use in these spiritual battles as much as it's a practice that accompanies the use of every other spiritual weapon and tool.[85] It is more fundamental than a single weapon; it fuels all the weapons in our spiritual arsenal.

But how does this work as a practical matter? The *Life Application New Testament Commentary* advises us to "make quick, brief prayers your habitual response to every situation you meet throughout the day. Order your life around God's desires and teachings so that your very life becomes a prayer. You can make prayer your life and your life a prayer while living in a world that needs God's powerful influence."[86]

If such advice strikes you as a bit excessive, please understand that the crux of Paul's message in this chapter highlights that so many battles we face here on earth are spiritual battles—that's what God is trying to reveal to us through this scripture. Therefore, even many of those things that manifest themselves as physical struggles can be dealt with in the spiritual realm. That is why Paul writes in Philippians 4:6–7, "Don't worry about anything; instead, pray about everything." Emphasis on *anything* and *everything*! It's true: nothing is too great or too small for our God. So the next time you're struggling with something, whether it's getting your kids to school on time or helping a sick family member, take it to God and ask for His will to be done and for the divine order of His heavenly realm to take over where the enemy is currently causing distress.

Paul closes out this section with a call for his readers to keep alert with all perseverance. While we mustn't be paranoid, we should always be vigilant, watching for spiritual attacks, as we know they often come in subtle and disguised forms. We must pray for discernment and for the spiritual energy to recognize real threats and respond accordingly. Remember, we are not talking about physical warfare here but using these spiritual weapons and shields to keep ourselves on track and to help others.

Paul encourages his readers to pray for all believers and specifically for him so he will have the right words to boldly proclaim the mystery of the gospel. Note that Paul, though commissioned by Christ Himself to be His ambassador to spread the gospel to the Gentiles, and though filled with the Holy Spirit, nevertheless asks his fellow believers to pray for him. This is fascinating considering that Paul had written to the Romans, "Likewise the Spirit helps us in our weakness. For we do not know what to pray for as we ought, but the Spirit himself intercedes for us with groanings too deep for words" (Romans 8:26). Similarly, Jesus promised believers that in certain times of difficulty the Holy Spirit would give them the proper words to say (Luke 12:11–12; Mark 13:11; cf. Matt. 10:19). The point is that Paul is intimately aware that the Holy Spirit would help us on His own initiative, yet he *still* is commanding his readers to proactively pray for him as well to come up with the right words to evangelize and to have the courage to boldly proclaim them.

We also find interesting Paul's use of the word "boldly" twice in this passage. It is a reminder that we must not only preach the gospel to nonbelievers and believers alike but to do so *boldly*. And Paul's plea for their prayers that he preach boldly is encouraging because we ourselves may feel awkward or uncomfortable evangelizing in certain situations. If Paul admits to having difficulties with this, we should see that it's natural to have these feelings, and we should not be ashamed by them. Instead, we must be encouraged that we, too, can lift each other up to gain the strength to overcome any discomfort.

Paul's exhortation to boldness, however, doesn't mean we should be rude or combative. We must always approach our work in spreading the good news winsomely, with a keen awareness of whom we are speaking to and what the most effective ways to communicate with them are. Above all, let's be mindful of Paul's wonderful statement to the Romans: "For I am not ashamed of the gospel, for it is the power of God for salvation to everyone who believes, to Jew first and also to the Greek. For in it the righteousness of God is revealed from faith for faith, as it is written, 'The righteous shall live by faith'" (Romans 1:16–17). We must never be ashamed of the gospel, and we must preach it boldly, for it is the power of God for salvation to everyone who believes.

PRAYER

Father, please give us the heavenly perspective to identify the spiritual warfare being waged by the enemy against us and in our families, jobs, and friendships. Help us to recognize the demonic forces that seek to steal, kill, and destroy all the goodness You have intended for us (John 10:10). Give us the mental awareness and fortitude we need to take up each piece of armor described in Ephesians 6 to stand against these evil forces. And may we not just play defense against this darkness but proactively live out our divine callings for Your kingdom. Help us to see ourselves as instrumental members of Your heavenly ranks chosen to shine light into the darkness and to boldly speak truth against deception. In Your Holy Name,

AMEN.

Paul concludes his letter by assuring the members of the church in Ephesus that he would send his "beloved brother and faithful minister" Tychicus to deliver this letter and "tell them everything" (v 6:21). Since Paul lived in Ephesus for three years and became close with the church there, its congregants are surely interested to know how he is doing. However, this letter is not being delivered solely to the believers in Ephesus; it will also be sent to several other churches in the area, which is why Paul leaves it to Tychicus to share Paul's entire personal-life update when he sees believers in person.

Though these brief portions of Paul's letters might seem relatively trivial, we love that God allows us to see the personal side of Paul, which humanizes him for us. These personal notes of greetings are a reminder that Paul is indeed a man who clearly has real friends, problems, and concerns just like we all do. By allowing us to see into the intimate parts of Paul's life, God gives hope that He can use each of us to carry out His amazing plans.

CHAPTER FOUR

PHILIPPIANS

REJOICE IN CHRIST

This letter "points us to Christ, both for now and forever. Christ is the gospel; Christ is Savior and Lord; thus Christ is our life; Christ is our way of life; Christ is our future; Christ is our joy."

—Gordon D. Fee[1]

Most scholars believe Paul wrote his epistle to the Philippians during his imprisonment in Rome. Full of joy, thanksgiving, and encouragement, the letter is personal, as Paul shares his feelings and his work as Christ's servant and addresses the congregants as his partners in the gospel. He expresses his deep love and kinship for them and his appreciation that they are fellow believers who join with him in defending the gospel. Paul has a special affection for the Christians at Philippi because it was the first church he planted in Europe (Acts 16:6–40).[2] He wants the believers there to grow in Christ, following his example as one who is content with his life despite his imprisonment and suffering. Paul also holds up his colleagues Timothy and Epaphroditus as models of the faith. Paul's model, however, is Christ Himself, the willing suffering servant.

As Paul's life exemplifies, Christians must not rest on their laurels simply because they are saved. While saving faith involves no effort on our part, we do need to work on our spiritual disciplines as we seek to grow in Christ. Our growth will always be empowered by the Holy Spirit, but we must expend effort to "work out" our "salvation with fear and trembling." We are honor bound, as believers, to model Christlike behavior to draw others to the faith. We must sacrificially serve the cause of Christ, and our actions must be fueled by prayer.

Sometimes in this process we will experience personal hardship and suffering. Our struggles are not solitary, however, as we are joined with fellow believers in this common cause. Nor are our struggles overwhelming because the joy of our life in Christ and in our hope (certainty) of eternal life makes any hardships we endure bearable, as shown by Paul's own example. Indeed, Paul reminds us that our "citizenship is in heaven" and that we can be assured that in the future, Jesus—our Savior—will transform our earthly bodies into glorious bodies in eternity. Paul exhorts us, therefore, to be joyful, knowing what awaits us.

Commentators differ about the main theme of this epistle, but few could disagree that a prominent idea is that believers must be joyful while suffering and sacrificing for Christ and the advancement of the gospel. But the Christian's joy is not automatic; otherwise Paul would not instruct us to be joyful. "Joy is not a feeling, it is an activity," writes Gordon Fee. "In keeping with the Psalmists, Paul urges them to 'rejoice in the Lord,' which can only mean to vocalize their joy in song and word. Above everything else, joy is the distinctive mark of the believer in Christ Jesus; and in this letter it comes most often as an imperative. Believers are to 'rejoice in the Lord always' (4:4), because joy has not to do with one's circumstances but one's relationship with the Lord."[3]

Believers must always be humble and grateful for what Christ has done for them. In no letter does Paul more poignantly express Christ's humility and servanthood than Philippians. Christ, who is God, humbled Himself to a degree unimaginable for mere human beings so that we could be saved. The description of Christ emptying Himself in His incarnation makes this epistle unique (2:1–11). Equally invaluable are Paul's words of encouragement and instructions for joyful living in the Lord, which are among our favorite passages in scripture (4:4–8). In this letter as much as any other Paul shows his personal side, and his life and feelings jump from its pages as he shares his hardships as well as his gratitude, friendship, and loving service on behalf of Christ and the spreading of the good news.

Interestingly, Paul mentions four women who played a prominent role in the Philippian church: Lydia and the slave girl, who were the first to be converted there, and Euodia and Syntyche, who both worked with Paul.[4]

CHAPTER 1

Paul opens the letter identifying himself (and Timothy) as author and as a servant of Christ Jesus, surely in part because a significant portion of the letter concerns Christ's exemplary servanthood and the believers' duty to follow his example. Commentators note that he doesn't mention his apostleship, presumably because his readers are quite familiar with him, his commission, and his work.[5] We may also infer that no one at the church questions his apostolic authority, so he sees no need to address it. In identifying himself and Timothy as servants, Paul is emphasizing not his superior calling as an apostle but their equality in Christ and their coequal duty to serve Him and His church. He addresses the believers in the church and its leaders—the overseers and deacons. Paul seems especially to want to commend the leaders' additional responsibilities and services to the church.[6]

He tells his readers he thanks God every time he thinks of them and prays for them joyfully because they have been his partners in spreading the gospel from the time they became believers (about ten years before) until today. As he has told others, he says he is sure God will complete the good work He began in them. They will continue to grow more like Christ until He returns. He confides that the Philippians hold a special place in his heart as they support him even in his imprisonment and share in his work for Christ. Unapologetically wearing his heart on his sleeve, Paul tells them God knows he loves them with the same tender compassion with which Christ loves the church.

Paul is living out his teaching that believers are to love and support one another in harmony and unity. Their love must not remain static, however, but continue growing, and he is fervently praying for that result. He also prays that they will keep growing in "knowledge and understanding." By connecting their growth in love and their growth in knowledge and understanding, Paul conveys that one's Christian love will increase along with his growth in the knowledge of the Bible and God. This makes sense, as the Bible teaches us all about God, and God's essence is love. As we learn more about God, we necessarily learn more about love.

Book knowledge alone, though, isn't enough. As we grow in wisdom, we'll gain spiritual insight into how we should live our lives.[7] The NLT illuminates his meaning clearly: "For I want you to understand what really matters, so that you may live pure and blameless lives until the day of Christ's return" (1:10 NLT). As we learn more about love, our insight will also grow, which will lead us to be more loving toward others.

Paul prays they will "always be filled with the fruit of [their] salvation," which he identifies as "the righteous character produced in your life by Jesus Christ" (1:11 NLT). This, he says, will bring great glory and praise to God. In his letter to the Galatians, Paul describes this fruit as "the fruit of the Spirit," which is the qualities believers begin to exhibit with the process of sanctification—growing in holiness through exercise of the spiritual disciplines. These qualities include "love, joy, peace, patience, kindness, goodness, faithfulness, gentleness, self-control" (Gal 5:22–23). We grow more Christlike through the power of the Holy Spirit, so all praise and glory for it belongs to God.[8]

PRAYER

Lord Jesus, You exemplify every fruit of the Spirit, so in order for us to receive these spiritual gifts, we must first grow in our intimacy with You. We want our lives to reflect Your love, bearing in mind, as *The Message* interpretation puts it, "You need to use your head and test your feelings so that your love is sincere and intelligent, not sentimental gush" (Phil. 1:10). Love without sincerity is meaningless, but love deeply rooted in the realization of who You are will make You "attractive to all, getting everyone involved in the glory and praise of God" (Phil 1:11 The MSG). Jesus, we open our hearts to You and offer a moment of silence. Speak to us through Your word and in our hearts, and give us direction today on how we can take a specific step of faith toward serving You.

AMEN.

Paul assures his readers he is not complaining when he relates his struggles—to the contrary, his imprisonment has helped to advance the gospel. News of Paul's "imprisonment for Christ" has spread throughout the imperial guard and beyond, which has served to embolden fellow believers to evangelize without fear. When the people realize Paul is imprisoned not for being a criminal but for standing by Christ and teaching the gospel, and when believers see that Paul is unafraid to speak boldly for Christ even while imprisoned, they are encouraged to do likewise. What certain people seek to use for evil, God uses for good (Gen. 50:20). Not only is the gospel not impeded during Paul's imprisonments, but its advocates are multiplying. Paul is allowed to continue to preach from his house arrest, and other believers are working the streets where Paul can't.

Paul makes specific reference to Roman soldiers and officials. Had he not been imprisoned and thus in direct contact with some of them, it is unlikely they would have been exposed to the gospel. What an encouragement to the brothers in Philippi, who are receiving direct testimony from their spiritual father Paul, that despite any fears they might have over his imprisonment, the gospel continues to spread through new avenues. We can imagine Roman soldiers speaking among themselves about the bizarre and unfamiliar message Paul is communicating. With its supernatural implications, it must have been of keen interest to Roman soldiers who learned about it from their colleagues who heard Paul's compelling testimony directly. It's unclear whether any Roman guards are immediately converted, but there is no question many of them heard the message. Paul makes that point explicitly (1:13).

Paul reveals that of those who were emboldened by his circumstances to preach the gospel, some do so out of love and others due to selfish ambition, envy, and rivalries (1:15–17). These people are Paul's rivals and perhaps want to show him up, elevating themselves at his expense. Paul isn't overly concerned about their motives, however, because either way, they are proclaiming the good news (1:18). Though Paul sometimes talks about himself and his own circumstances, as is the case here, his heart is always committed to promoting the cause of Christ, not himself. So it matters little to him whether he gets credit for preaching Christ. And while the text is silent about this, we can only assume that even those spreading the gospel for the wrong reasons are accurately conveying the message. Otherwise, Paul would surely have denounced the distortion.

Early church father Theodoret confirms our speculation—that these wrongly motivated people are not preaching a false gospel, only preaching it for the wrong reasons. "Even against their will, Paul shows, the enemies of truth inadvertently cooperate with truth," writes Theodoret. "Some are foolish enough to think that these can also be said about heresies." But no. Paul "does not condemn those people for preaching bad things but for preaching good things poorly, being led not by reverence for God but by partisanship."[9] Augustine makes a similar point. "Even though they were tolerated who proclaimed the truth without purity of mind, they were not praised, as if to assume that they were preaching with a pure mind," writes Augustine. "So Paul says of them that, whether in pretense or in truth, Christ is proclaimed. Yet he certainly does not imply that Christ may now be denied in order to be later proclaimed."[10]

Paul explains he is not licking his wounds but is rejoicing, "for I know that through your prayers and the help of the Spirit of Jesus Christ this will turn out for my deliverance, as it is my eager expectation and hope that I will not be at all ashamed, but with full courage now as always Christ will be honored in my body, whether by life or by death" (1:19–20). Again, Paul follows his own teachings. He knows that joy, as we've noted, is not a fleeting feeling but a state of contentment in Christ. While anything but Pollyannaish, he keeps the long game in mind. He always takes the temporary setbacks, obstacles, and hardships in stride, mindful that he will ultimately be delivered by his Lord. That is the nature of his faith and the faith he urges us to adopt. As the writer of Hebrews so aptly states, "Now faith is the assurance of things hoped for, the conviction of things not seen" (Heb. 11:1). Paul has that very assurance. "That is the way it is in the church," writes Dietrich Bonhoeffer. "It never lives by its deeds, not even by its deeds of love. Rather it lives by what it cannot see and yet believes. It sees affliction and believes deliverance."[11]

Scholars debate what Paul means by his "deliverance," but it seems that sometimes they complicate things when common sense leads to the simple answer. We think it is pretty clear he isn't talking about his own vindication from competing teachers or his anticipated victory in trial because both of those would be more Paul-focused than Christ-focused. Additionally, he isn't sure of the outcome in those two situations, as he later will make clear, at least as to the trial. But he has no question about his personal salvation (deliverance) through his faith in Christ.

The succeeding verses accentuate Paul's Christ-centeredness. He is certain he will not be put to shame because he will always honor Christ, in both life and death. He is adamant that he will put Christ first and honor Him despite any hardships he has to endure. He has already fought the good fight, run the race, and demonstrated his perseverance (2 Tim. 7). That he will buckle now is unthinkable.

Poignantly summarizing his message in these passages, the next verse is another one of our favorites: "For to me to live is Christ, and to die is gain" (1:21). On this side of heaven—as long as Paul has a breath in him—he will be exclusively devoted to Christ, living the Christian walk, growing ever more Christlike, ceaselessly communing with Christ in prayer, and honoring the Great Commission to spread the gospel to the ends of the earth, even if he has to do some of it while in Roman chains.

While in his earthly body Paul will live Christ and only Christ. But after his physical death he will be even more in Christ, for He will be with Him in a literal sense, and upon His resurrection, Paul will acquire his new glorified body and remain permanently in Christ's presence. He spells all this out in the following verses:

> If I am to live in the flesh, that means fruitful labor for me. Yet which I shall choose I cannot tell. I am hard pressed between the two. My desire is to depart and be with Christ, for that is far better. But to remain in the flesh is more necessary on your account. Convinced of this, I know that I will remain and continue with you all, for your progress and joy in the faith, so that in me you may have ample cause to glory in Christ Jesus, because of my coming to you again. (1:22–26)

These straight-forward verses confirm what we explained above: Paul is living not for himself but for Christ and for all those he can help bring to Christ while he is still in his human body. He unequivocally prefers to die physically and be with Christ spiritually—right now—but instead, he will opt for sacrificially remaining "in the flesh" and continuing his unfinished work on earth. He is committed to the Philippians' joy in the faith's progressing, intent that they will continue to grow in their walk for their own Christian development and become better equipped ambassadors for the gospel. The more they grow, the more they will evangelize and the more people will be saved—all to the glory of Christ. Ambrosiaster states it well. "Who would not abandon all the cares of the present out of a desire to go up to the third heaven?" he asks. "Who would not lay aside everything out of a desire for the paradise above?... Who would not have chosen peace and quiet after so many sufferings? But because Paul made love for everyone his priority, he did what would benefit the brethren."[12]

Now Paul gives the Philippians instructions on how they should live, which are both sobering and encouraging: "Above all, you must live as citizens of heaven, conducting yourselves in a manner worthy of the Good News about Christ. Then, whether I come and see you again or only hear about you, I will know that you are standing together with one spirit and one purpose, fighting together for the faith, which is the Good News" (1:27–28 NLT). In other words, it doesn't matter whether Paul can visit them again. They should always conduct themselves in a way that honors Christ. They must be united in spirit and in their goal of fighting for the spread of the gospel. There is strength in the individual but more so in numbers and even more so in those who are unified and working together in a common cause, especially *this* common cause. If they keep their minds and purposes focused on Christ rather than being distracted by disagreements over doctrine or otherwise, they will be immeasurably more effective in accomplishing their work on Christ's behalf.

Believers must not be frightened by their opponents, who will interpret Christians' determination and fearlessness as their own destruction and the believers' salvation. That is, the Philippians must not panic in the face of their adversaries and neither be deterred nor descend into chaos as a result. John Calvin saw that when the gospel was in its incipiency, Satan was working overtime to stop it before it mushroomed. As such, "the most cruel persecutions raged almost everywhere." The more Christ infused believers with "the grace of his Spirit," the "more enraged" Satan became.[13] Aware of this, Paul encouraged his readers to gird themselves against this onslaught and to proceed undaunted.

Opponents of any cause might be angered when encountering the proponents' stubborn persistence, causing the opponents to strive even harder to defeat the cause and discourage their adversaries. Paul's point is that in this case, the believers' opponents are sure to be dispirited if their Christian adversaries don't succumb to their disruptive efforts and instead grow stronger. We can imagine that those opponents who think this new religion is like any other cult will be shocked to discover the believers are undaunted in the face of adversity. It gives them pause about their claims and causes them to reflect on their own spiritual state, realizing they might well be on the road to damnation. In the end, Satan's armies are no match for obedient Christians infused with God's grace and empowered by His Spirit.

It would serve us well to consider just how important the gospel is to God and how much He disfavors anyone who would impede it. There is a special place in hell for scoffers, mockers, and those who would drag others down with them into damnation. It's one thing for unbelievers to go about their business and leave believers and the church alone. It's entirely another for them to become Satan's soldiers and proactively work against the gospel and against believers, and to try to blind seekers or potential believers from the truth and from accepting Christ. Jesus warned that anyone who leads children into a path of sinfulness has sealed his own doom: "It would be better for him to have a great millstone fastened around his neck and to be drowned in the depth of the sea" (Matt. 18:6).

We believe this principle applies beyond children and especially to spiritual children, or seekers. It is especially sinful to lead anyone, not just children, away from salvation. As Paul told the Romans, "Decide never to put a stumbling block or hindrance in the way of a brother" (Romans 14:3). He elaborated the point to the Galatians: "I am astonished that you are so quickly deserting him who called you in the grace of Christ and are turning to a different gospel—not that there is another one, but there are some who trouble you and want to distort the gospel of Christ. But even if we or an angel from heaven should preach to you a gospel contrary to the one we preached to you, let him be accursed. As we have said before, so now I say again: If anyone is preaching to you a gospel contrary to the one you received, let him be accursed" (Gal. 1:6–9).

Moreover, Jesus told His disciples, "Temptations to sin are sure to come, but woe to the one through whom they come!" (Luke 17:1). Indeed, the Bible is replete with warnings against altering God's word (Rev. 22:18–19; Prov. 30:5-6; Heb. 4:12; Deut. 4:2).

As the entirety of God's word points to Jesus Christ, one who attempts to lead people away from Jesus is gravely sinning. Just as it is especially sinful to lead people astray, it is especially noble to stand strong against those who would lead you or others astray. Paul is telling the Philippians that their steadfastness to Christ and God's word in the face of fierce opposition will defeat their opponents like nothing else, alerting them to the futility of their own lives and their evil mission as well as reminding them of their eternal damnation.

We want to emphasize at this juncture how important it is that believers understand they are not exempt from these admonitions. That is, even believers could unwittingly lead people astray if they deviate from God's word. We are stewards of God's word and have a strong duty to respect it, honor it, and to present the gospel to others in a way that is consistent with the word. We dare not change the word of God, and we dare not put stumbling blocks in the way of anyone seeking the truth.

PRAYER

Father, when the Apostles Peter and John faced opposition from spiritual leaders in Acts 4:23, they called upon Your name and asked You to enable them to speak Your word with great boldness and to work through them to heal and perform signs and

▶

wonders in the name of Jesus (4:29–30). Your response to them in verse 31 is astounding: "After they prayed, the place where they were meeting was shaken. And they were all filled with the Holy Spirit and spoke the word of God boldly." Amazing! Lord, help us to seek this same boldness and to call upon Your Name to empower us to work in miraculous ways for Your kingdom. The gospel is not just for our personal growth; it's meant to be shared with all people on earth, and we are part of that, whether we see ourselves this way or not. Help us to follow the instruction to "always be prepared to give an answer to everyone who asks you to give the reason for the hope that you have" (1 Peter 3:15). To do this, we must be deeply rooted in Your word and fitted with the "shoes of readiness" described in Ephesians 6. Please enable, equip, and embolden us!

AMEN.

Paul concludes this chapter by informing his readers they are privileged to have been led to Christ and to suffer for Him: "For it has been granted to you that for the sake of Christ you should not only believe in him but also suffer for his sake, engaged in the same conflict that you saw I had and now hear that I still have" (1:29–30). According to the *ESV Study Bible*, "Paul teaches that both suffering and faith are gifts of God; for both, Paul says, have been granted to you. Suffering for the sake of Jesus is a great privilege."[14] This, of course, is consistent with Jesus' own teachings: "Blessed are those who are persecuted for righteousness' sake, for theirs is the kingdom of heaven. Blessed are you when others revile you and persecute you and utter all kinds of evil against you falsely on my account. Rejoice and be glad, for your reward is great in heaven, for so they persecuted the prophets who were before you" (Matt. 5:10–12).

It might seem counterintuitive to consider suffering a privilege. But the Bible is consistent that we should rejoice in our persecution. When the apostles were helping to launch the gospel, they were subjected to intense persecution from the religious authorities. They were threatened, beaten, arrested, and warned against preaching the word. What was their reaction? "Then they left the presence of the council, rejoicing that they were counted worthy to suffer dishonor for the name. And every day, in the temple and from house to house, they did not cease teaching and preaching that the Christ is Jesus" (Acts 5:41–42).

If it is noble to believe in Christ, how much more so it is to stand strong for Him when being punished for it. Under such circumstances we are necessarily drawn closer to Christ—closer than we otherwise would have been—so of course we should be grateful and rejoice for that privilege. Stated another way, it could be said that our primary purpose in living is to be in Christ and to experience Him to the fullest. If persecution maximizes that experience, then it maximizes our very purpose for existence, and we must rejoice in it.

Moreover, when believers suffer for the sake of Christ, they are imitating Christ Himself, who suffered immeasurably for us. "But if when you do good and suffer for it you endure, this is a gracious thing in the sight of God. For to this you have been called, because Christ also suffered for you, leaving you an example, so that you might follow in his steps" (1 Peter 2:20–21). F. F. Bruce said that while our suffering on His behalf can't possibly compare with His suffering on ours, our suffering "is a participation in his suffering, such as he had warned them to expect."[15] Similarly, D. K. Lowery observes, "One of the many paradoxes of the Christian life is that the grace of God is most keenly experienced not in the best but in what seem to be the worst of times."[16]

James also tells of the joy in suffering for Christ: "Count it all joy, my brothers, when you meet trials of various kinds, for you know that the testing of your faith produces steadfastness. And let steadfastness have its full effect, that you may be perfect and complete, lacking in nothing" (James 1:2–4). Here, James seems to be saying that we should rejoice in our trials because they will lead to our growth in Christ. This is similar to Paul's counsel to the Romans: "We rejoice in our sufferings, knowing that suffering produces endurance, and endurance produces character, and character produces hope, and hope does not put us to shame, because God's love has been poured into our hearts through the Holy Spirit who has been given to us" (Romans 5:3–5).

The irony is that suffering on Christ's behalf does not estrange us from God or cause us to feel abandoned and separated from His love. "For Christians, suffering does not negate the reality of God's love, but provides the occasion to affirm and apply it," writes Barton. "[Perseverance] is one step in a process that eventually strengthens our hope."[17]

Prayer

Jesus, we ask for courage—courage to seek closeness with You even if it comes at the cost of our own suffering or persecution. But we want to be honest with You, Lord. And the truth is, none of us wants to suffer; it goes against everything about us to seek out our own harm. But You know this—You created each of us and formed us in our mothers' wombs and know the very hairs on our heads, so we shouldn't shrink from being completely honest with You about our fears or doubts to follow You even into the face of trouble. Paul himself once spoke of an affliction, and his words draw a beautiful conclusion we can all follow: "Three times I pleaded with the Lord about this, that it should leave me. But he said to me, 'My grace is sufficient for you, for my power is made perfect in weakness'" (2 Cor. 12 8–9). Lord, without You we are completely helpless. Remind us to be honest

▶

with You about our weaknesses, so that in doing so, You can be our strength. Please increase our trust in You, that we might actively seek Your will in every situation, even if it means we will have to suffer here on earth. We close by speaking Your comforting assurance over our lives from 1 Peter 5: "So after you have suffered a little while, he will restore, support, and strengthen you, and he will place you on a firm foundation" (v 10 NLT).

AMEN.

CHAPTER 2

Paul begins, "So if there is any encouragement in Christ, any comfort from love, any participation in the Spirit, any affection and sympathy, complete my joy by being of the same mind, having the same love, being in full accord and of one mind" (2:1–2). Scholars agree that Paul isn't actually questioning whether there is encouragement in Christ or the other qualities he lists but urging his readers to take stock of themselves to see whether these things are present in their lives. He's basically saying, "If these qualities are present in the ordinary Christian experience—and we all know they are—then you should make sure you exhibit them yourselves. So, make me—your spiritual father—happy and show yourselves to be united in purpose and Spirit and above all, by the love of Christ." As Matthew Henry proclaims, "We are of a like mind when we have the same love."[18]

Paul tells the Philippians to avoid selfish ambition or conceit and to be humble to the point that they consider others more important than themselves. Of course they will tend to their own interests, but they must also look to the interests of others (2:3–4). He brings home his point by directing them to Christ's example, in another well-known passage of scripture, which we will print in full:

> Have this mind among yourselves, which is yours in Christ Jesus, who, though he was in the form of God, did not count equality with God a thing to be grasped, but emptied himself, by taking the form of a servant, being born in the likeness of men. And being found in human form, he humbled himself by becoming obedient to the point of death, even death on a cross. Therefore God has highly exalted him and bestowed on him the name that is above every name, so that at the name of Jesus every knee should bow, in heaven and on earth and under the earth, and every tongue confess that Jesus Christ is Lord, to the glory of God the Father. (2:5–11)

This passage speaks for itself, but for emphasis, let's zero in on a few points. To understand the magnitude of Christ's sacrifice we must first contrast the degrading experience of His incarnation with His blissful position in eternity past, prior to His incarnation. Christ, the Son of God, and the second person of the triune Godhead, is equal in essence with God the Father and God the Holy Spirit. He is God. He enjoyed perfect love and joy in the Godhead before God (including Christ) created the physical world—space, matter, and time.

Being omniscient, God knew before He created the universe and mankind that man would fall into sin and that the fall would disrupt His divine plan for man to live with Him in eternity unless other provisions were made. He determined that the only way or best way to restore and redeem mankind would be for the Son to become man; voluntarily surrender some of His divine attributes; endure all the indignities of that existence; live a sinless life; suffer separation from the Father despite committing no wrongs; receive the real wrath of God for all the past, present, and future sins of mankind;

die on the cross in our place; and then be resurrected back to life to be king of all creation and of heaven. We fallen human beings can then individually appropriate His sacrificial death through faith in Him as our Lord, His perfect righteousness will be imputed to us, and we will be legally declared righteous (for salvation purposes), adopted as God's children, and live eternally in God's presence.

Here's the most moving aspect of this divine transaction. The Father, Son, and Holy Spirit all decided to create human beings knowing there would be no point in creating us unless the Son experienced this unbearable pain on our behalf. So God created us knowing full well that the Son would literally sweat blood so that we could live with Him in eternity.

Furthermore, understand that all three persons of the Godhead experienced this pain—Jesus directly in the flesh and in the Spirit, and the Father and the Holy Spirit through their infinite love for the Son. Imagine a parent losing a child, and you can get but a faint glimpse of what God the Father and God the Holy Spirit endured through Christ's incarnation and passion. Christ's redemptive death on the cross is not part of some abstract divine equation that would blot out the sins of those who place their faith in Him. It was real pain and real agony that exceeded what any human being has endured or will ever endure. And it was infinitely exacerbated by the level to which Christ had to descend and demean Himself for this to be possible—from infinite love and bliss to excruciating pain and receipt of God's real wrath. This is incomprehensible to us because we have never experienced such bliss and never experienced such pain. We don't even have the words to adequately describe this contrast. But what we can understand is that this illustrates God's boundless love for us and our boundless debt to Him, though He has marked it paid-in-full as a gift to us because He loves us—all to His eternal glory.

If we conclude our explanation here, we won't fully convey the depth of God's sacrifice in Christ's incarnation and death. Ponder this for a moment. He went as far as to permanently transform His nature from the Son of God—fully divine, an entirely spiritual being—to fully divine *and* fully human. We must explore why such a transformation (on our behalf) was necessary. Why would the Son of God transform His nature for mere human beings? We submit that he did so because it was necessary to save us, and it enabled us to have a personal relationship with a God who could truly understand us and relate to us because He would experience everything we've ever experienced.

So in addition to being necessary for our salvation, the incarnation also makes God personally and forever accessible to us in a way not possible had He not also taken on human form. "Jesus was fully God. Jesus was also fully man," writes theologian Wayne Grudem. "He was fully both at the same time. The eternal Son of God took to himself a truly human nature. His divine and human natures are forever distinct and retain their own properties even though they are eternally and inseparably united together in one person." He continues, "This is probably the most amazing miracle of the entire Bible—the eternal son of God, himself fully God, became fully man and in doing so joined himself to human nature forever. Jesus, a man unlike anyone else the world will ever see again, by eternally bringing together both the infinite and the finite, changed the course of history forever."[19]

Again, Christ had to be fully man and fully God for the salvation plan to make sense and to work. Man is hopelessly sinful and can therefore never satisfy the requirements of God's law. So man sinned and was given a death sentence. His death brought him no closer to reconciliation with God because God cannot look upon sin. He cannot allow sin in His presence. Man, then, on his own, is hopelessly lost, entirely irredeemable. But God cannot die and thereby accept the death sentence on our behalf. He is an eternal, spiritual being. But by taking on human form, Christ, the Son of God, could and did die, not to mention he endured for us many other aspects of pain and suffering. He had to be fully human to die and to feel the full scope of pain He experienced on our behalf.

At the same time, He lived a sinless human life even though subjected to all the temptations any human being could ever confront. By living a sinless life, He satisfied God's standard of righteous perfection, and by dying he accepted our punishment for us. Consider this: Unless Christ was fully human, He would not have experienced temptation. God can't be tempted. But because Christ was also fully human, He could be tempted. "Jesus' temptations speak to the authenticity of the Incarnation," states the *Faith Life Bible*. "Only people can experience temptation."[20] Charles Ryrie observes, "The doctrine of the person of Christ is crucial to the Christian faith. For if our Lord was not what He claimed to be, then His atonement was a deficient, not sufficient, payment for sin."[21]

As Paul wrote to the Romans, "For God has done what the law, weakened by the flesh, could not do. By sending his own Son in the likeness of sinful flesh and for sin, he condemned sin in the flesh, in order that the righteous requirement of the law might be fulfilled in us" (Romans 8:3–4). God directed His wrath at Christ, who stood as our substitute and rendered sin powerless to kill those who receive Christ in faith and appropriate His finished work on the cross.

"Man's sin was so great, God's Holiness so pure, that the gulf between them which must be spanned required an amazing accomplishment on the part of our Lord," write Guy Duffield and Nathaniel Van Cleave. "Through His death, He fully met every need of the sinner relative to sin, enabling him to enjoy eternal fellowship with God. At the same time, Christ fully met every requirement necessary for a righteous and just God to freely forgive sin and receive man back into fellowship. At no time throughout eternity will anyone, man, devil or angel, be able to challenge the perfect and full provision of God's great salvation."[22]

I (David) addressed a related point in *Jesus on Trial*: "If Jesus Christ were not simultaneously fully human and fully divine at the point of His incarnation, He could not have lived a sinless life, and His separation from the Father and His substitutionary endurance of the Father's wrath would not have been possible. He couldn't have truly suffered for us, He couldn't have become sin for us, the cross would have been meaningless, and the entire salvation scheme would become pointless." Millard Erickson explains the point succinctly: "If the redemption accomplished on the cross is to avail for humankind, it must be the work of the human Jesus. But if it is to have the infinite value necessary to atone for the sins of all human beings in relationship to an infinite and perfectly holy God, then it must be the work of the divine Christ as well. If the death of the Savior is not the work of a unified God-man, it will be deficient at one point or the other."[23]

PRAYER

Jesus, it can be difficult to comprehend you are fully human—a real man who physically walked the earth and who will one day return to rule the whole world (Revelation 20). Thank You for lowering yourself to our feeble state, enduring temptation, brutally suffering, and never asking for anything in return. To think of the Creator of the Universe humbling Himself and becoming a helpless baby at one point is unfathomable! We thank You, Jesus—thank You for enduring all these things so that when we come to You with our troubles, You'd be able to say, "I understand, I have been there." Your goodness knows no bounds and we adore You, Our perfect High Priest.

AMEN.

Paul continues, telling the Philippians that because Jesus humbled Himself in the incarnation and His death, God raised Him to life and highly exalted Him, and He gave Him the name that is above every name (2:9). But why did Christ, who was already God, need to be exalted at all? To answer this, we must understand the different functions of the three persons of the Trinity, which do nothing to alter their respective divine essence. They are all equal in essence, as Jesus assured us in declaring, "I and the Father are one" (John 10:30). But Christ was subordinate to the Father and submissive in certain functions, which Christ also corroborated when He said, "The Father is greater than I" (John 14:28). This reference, writes Leon Morris, "is not to Christ's essential being, but to his incarnate state. The incarnation involved the acceptance of a certain subordination, as is insisted upon throughout the New Testament. The words must be understood in the light of 'I and the Father are one.' John was not asserting...that Jesus was a created being. He is talking about the departure of the human Jesus from this earth to be with the Father. In light of this Jesus sees it as a matter for rejoicing that he returns to the Father."[24]

"We must especially avoid the conclusion that God the Father is here portrayed as 'promoting' Jesus by virtue of his self-emptying and self-humbling," argues M. J. Gorman. "Something quite different is happening.... [These verses do] not signal that God has promoted Jesus to a new status, as if divinity...could be manufactured or gained by some act, however noble. Rather, it indicates that God has publicly vindicated and recognized Jesus' self-emptying and self-humbling as the display of true divinity that he already had and that makes the worship of Jesus as Lord (that is YHWH, the God of Israel) perfectly appropriate."[25]

The honor of this new name was bestowed on Christ as a result of His incarnation.[26] Christ was already God, so the Father didn't bestow on Him a status that would increase His already perfect essence or His position in the Trinity. This exaltation, explains MacArthur, concerned Christ's new identity as the God-Man. "Christ's new status as the God-Man meant God gave Him privileges He did not have prior to the Incarnation," writes MacArthur. "If He had not lived among men, He could not have identified with them as the interceding High-Priest. Had He not died on the cross, He could not have been elevated from that lowest degree back to heaven as the substitute for sin.... Christ's new name which further describes His essential nature and places Him above and beyond all comparison is 'Lord.'"[27]

Most commentators agree that Christ's new name is "Lord," but not all agree on the significance of the name. Most also agree that the title refers to Jesus' character as well as his function. Peter said as much in his Pentecost sermon: "Let all the house of Israel therefore know for certain that God has made him both Lord and Christ, this Jesus whom you crucified" (Acts 2:36).[28] This honor was also in answer to Jesus' "high-priestly prayer," which he spoke to the Father after giving His disciples their instructions just before he was betrayed, arrested, and crucified: "And now, Father, glorify me in your own presence with the glory that I had with you before the world existed" (John 17:5). R. P. Lightner notes that Jesus' new name "is not merely a title; it refers to His person and to His position of dignity and honor."[29] The *ESV Study Bible* explains it similarly: "Paul means that the eternal Son of God received a status and authority that had not been his before he became incarnate as both God and man. Jesus' being given this name is a sign that he exercises his messianic authority in the name of Yahweh."[30]

With His elevated status, says Paul, everyone in heaven, on earth, and under the earth will bow at the mention of His name, and every tongue confess that He is Lord, to the glory of God the Father

(2:10–11). Here Paul is paraphrasing Isaiah: "By myself I have sworn; from my mouth has gone out in righteousness a word that shall not return: To me every knee shall bow, every tongue shall swear allegiance" (Isaiah 45:23). Paul is affirming the Old Testament truth that there is only one God and He alone is to be worshipped. Christ, along with the Father and the Spirit, is one of the three persons of the one true God. As Paul is stating that Christ will be worshipped, he is confirming His divinity. And Paul makes clear that this worshipping will be universal—"in heaven, on earth, and under the earth," all shall bow and confess Him as Lord.

The Philippians, writes Paul, need to continue to be obedient when he is with them and especially when he's away, and to continue to "work out" their "own salvation with fear and trembling, for it is God who works in you, both to will and to work for His good pleasure" (2:12–13). Paul is clear in this letter and others that believers are saved by grace through faith in Christ—period. So what is it they must work out and what does obedience have to do with it?

Well, we must always be mindful that our salvation is a gift from God for which we must be eternally grateful, and we must be especially obedient to God and honor His will for our lives. Our salvation gives us a higher duty to live in accordance with our standing in Christ. So we don't earn our salvation, but we work out its implications and significance for our lives. We must strive to grow more Christlike, which involves our personal effort but is mainly accomplished by exercising the Spiritual disciplines, because even here we can't become more Christlike on our own power—the Holy Spirit empowers us. But there is personal effort involved in the sense that we must have the right attitude of obedience and a strong desire to please God—so we place ourselves in a position to be empowered by the Spirit through prayer, Bible reading, worship, and the other disciplines.

The right attitude, as the text makes clear, is one of "fear and trembling," signifying we must treat the matter seriously. We must recognize it matters deeply to God that we live in accordance with our Christian calling and become good witnesses for Christ. If God is so gracious as to indwell us with His Spirit, we better do everything we can to facilitate our own spiritual growth. In short, we must be good stewards of the gift of salvation that God bestowed upon us. "Using a play on words, Paul said they were to 'work out' because God 'works in,'" writes Richard Melick. "God's work in them provided both the motivation and the ability to do his good pleasure.[31]

Contemplating these passages, Augustine asks whether they imply that God has taken away our free will, since the text says it is God who is working in us to accomplish His will. He concludes our free will is not undermined, otherwise Paul would not have commanded that we work out our salvation. "For when he bids them work, it is agreed that they have free will," writes Augustine. "But they are free to work with fear and trembling so that they will not, by attributing the good working to themselves, be elated by his good works as though they were their own."[32]

Paul admonishes the Philippians to do everything without grumbling or arguing so they will stand out as "children of God" and "as lights in the world" against the backdrop of the "crooked and twisted generation" in which they live (2:15). They must "hold firmly to the word of life," so when Christ returns Paul can be proud that he did not work in vain on their behalf (2:16). F. F Bruce teaches that in warning his readers against grumbling or arguing, Paul is recalling the Old Testament descriptions of the ungrateful Israelites complaining in the wilderness (Num. 11:1–6; 14:1–4; 20:2; 21:4, 5). Instead, believers are to be good examples as ambassadors for Christ and "lights in the world" in the same way Christ called us to be "the salt of the earth" (Matt. 5:13).[33] "This 'light' consists not only of representing the gospel in words, but in purity of Christian obedience," says David Chapman.[34]

Paul continues, "Even if I am to be poured out as a drink offering upon the sacrificial offering of your faith, I am glad and rejoice with you all. Likewise you also should be glad and rejoice with me" (2:17–18). Some commentators believe Paul is acknowledging that he might end up being martyred for his faith and for his evangelism on their behalf and for others. Some, however, argue that he wasn't referring to his possible martyrdom but his present imprisonment, which was a result of his sacrificial work in spreading the gospel. Despite his sacrifice, he assures them, he will be happy and rejoice with them because their eternal life would be worth his sacrificial death. In turn, if that should happen, they should be glad and rejoice with him, knowing he's in a better place and that his labors were not in vain but directly benefited them.

John MacArthur raises an interesting point. Most Christians, he notes, would avoid pointing to themselves as examples of faithful servants, feeling it would be presumptuous and prideful. But Paul unabashedly holds himself out as such in this letter and sometimes in others. Does this mean he was afflicted with the sin of pride? MacArthur says no, arguing Paul was Spirit-led and obedient, so he didn't have the "self-conscious sense of inadequacy" that most believers have. "Though he was humble and had a deep sense of his weakness (1 Tim. 1:15), he could still use himself as an example because his motives were pure and his life holy," writes MacArthur. "With both sincerity and genuine humility he therefore could admonish the Corinthians, 'Be imitators of me, just as I also am of Christ' (1 Cor. 11:1; cf. 4:16)."[35]

MacArthur raises another point, which is instructive and somewhat sobering. Some, he suggests, might not comprehend how Paul could feel joy in his suffering—a subject we discussed earlier. These people only experience joy from earthy pleasures or successes. But Christians who strive to do God's will and please Him will view sacrifice for Him with joy. "The reason many believers know little about Paul's kind of joy is that they know little about his kind of sacrifice," says MacArthur.[36] This is a hard lesson and a reminder to us all to keep our godly priorities in order. It's easier said than done, but we are all, to varying degrees, works in progress.

Exemplifying God's instruction to show honor and brotherly affection to fellow believers (Romans 12:10), Paul concludes this portion of his letter to the Philippian church by commending two co-laborers in Christ, each of whom has played a unique role in helping him deliver this message. The first recognition goes to Timothy, whom Paul is sending to the Philippians in his stead despite his own need for companionship while imprisoned in Rome.[37]

Paul likens Timothy to a son, saying he has "no one else like him, who genuinely cares" about the Philippians' welfare (2:20 NLT). "Timothy had a genuine interest in the Philippians," writes Barton, "because he had traveled with Paul on his second missionary journey when the church at Philippi had been begun."[38]

Paul's second commendation goes to Epaphroditus, a congregant who had fallen deeply ill after the Philippian church sent him to deliver a gift to Paul.[39] Despite Epaphroditus's having been incapacitated near the point of death (2:27), Paul calls him his "brother and fellow worker and fellow soldier" (2:25). Epaphroditus had displayed his devotion to Christ through his sacrificial service to Paul, and Paul in turn is sending him back to his peers in Philippi, charging them to "welcome him in the Lord's love" and to give him the honor he deserves (2:29 NLT). "Paul did not set out deliberately to present three examples of the same self-renouncing attitude 'as that of Christ Jesus.'" writes F. F. Bruce. "But in fact this is what he has done. His own readiness to have his martyrdom credited to the spiritual account of his Philippian friends, Timothy's unselfish service to Paul and genuine concern for other Christians, Epaphroditus's devotion to his mission at great risk to his health and (as it might have been) to his life—all these display the unselfconscious care for others enjoined at the beginning of this chapter and reinforced by the powerful example of Christ's self-emptying."[40]

PRAYER

Jesus, when Your disciples were tempted to receive earthly glory, arguing over who would be the greatest among them in heaven, You responded, "In this world the kings and great men lord it over their people, yet they are called 'friends of the people.' But among you it will be different. Those who are the greatest among you should take the lowest rank, and the leader should be like a servant" (Luke 22:25–26). Help us to apply to our own lives this heavenly rule exemplified by Paul and his companions. It's so counter-cultural and against our very nature to practice true selflessness. We ask that You connect us with fellow believers who have incredible testimonies of miracles and joy-filled experiences thanks to their sacrificial devotion to You. We believe these stories will help build our faith and give us the appetite to offer ourselves as living sacrifices to You. We ask for a deep longing for Your miraculous power to be exemplified through our lives and the faith needed to forget ourselves and put the needs of others before our own. In Your Holy Name,

AMEN.

CHAPTER 3

Paul begins this chapter with another call for rejoicing, which shows how important this is to him. "Whatever happens, my dear brothers and sisters, rejoice in the Lord. I never get tired of telling you these things, and I do it to safeguard your faith" (3:1). Some scholars believe his repeated calls for joy are meant to allay his readers' concern over his imprisonment. In this sense, "joy" is a protective condition insulating believers from discouragement from dissension and strife in the church and then backsliding in their faith.

Scholars differ on what things Paul is referring to when he says he never tires of repeating them. Is he referring to his calls for joy or his warnings against traps and pitfalls? Either way, it seems clear he wants to assure them he is unburdened by repeating these pep talks and issuing his warnings. He founded their church, and the last thing he would be complaining about is giving instructions to help maintain its vibrancy. "Despondency and worry deprive the soul of its vitality," writes Chrysostom. "For this reason, Paul comforts the Philippians, who were in great despondency because they did not know how things stood with Paul."[41]

After such a benign introduction, Paul immediately issues his readers a stern warning: "Look out for the dogs, look out for the evildoers, look out for those who mutilate the flesh" (3:2). At that time, "dogs" was an epithet Jews used against Gentiles. But here Paul is applying it to the Judaizers—Jewish converts to Christianity who insisted on retaining Jewish rules and rituals after their conversion.[42] He had railed against such types in other letters, considering them opportunists who had invaded established churches and attempted to poison their doctrine by adding their legalism to Christianity's orthodoxy of salvation by faith alone.

By no means is Paul condemning all those who are circumcised but just the Judaizers who conflate the law with the gospel and teach that physical circumcision is mandatory for all Christians. "What Christ had abrogated they demanded as essential;" writes R. C. H. Lenski, "what now counted as nothing (Gal. 6:15) they counted as everything. To yield to them was to fall from grace, to let Christ become of no effect (Gal. 5:3, 4)."[43] Paul always cautions believers against allowing dissension among them over petty matters, but he is adamant about maintaining the purity of the gospel. As such, nothing is more important than salvation by faith alone because to add anything to faith is tantamount to rendering meaningless Christ's sacrificial work on the cross. "The circumcision of the flesh, as preached by the Judaizers, became for Paul the symbol of a total mindset that is opposed to the Spirit and leads to death (Romans 8:5–8; Gal. 5:16–21)," writes Moises Silva.[44] Thus Paul warns against putting confidence in the flesh. John Calvin says Paul is defining "flesh" as everything that is apart from Christ: "He thus reproves, and in no slight manner, the perverse zealots of the law, because, not satisfied with Christ, they have recourse to grounds of glorying apart from him."[45]

Paul elaborates on his warnings: "For we are the circumcision, who worship by the Spirit of God and glory in Christ Jesus and put no confidence in the flesh—though I myself have reason for confidence in the flesh also. If anyone thinks he has reason for confidence in the flesh, I have more: circumcised on the eighth day, of the people of Israel, of the tribe of Benjamin, a Hebrew of Hebrews; as to the law, a Pharisee; as to zeal, a persecutor of the church; as to righteousness under the law, blameless" (3:3–6).

We find this fascinating—though stressing that circumcision is unnecessary for believers, Paul does not dispense with the word. Rather, he teaches that circumcision was always a spiritual matter, as we discuss in our chapter on Colossians. In Old Testament times circumcision was a physical sign that set apart God's chosen people. Indeed, God made it mandatory for all Jewish males. It was a sign of the covenant between God and His chosen people (Gen. 17:9–14). But now that God has unveiled his mystery—that both Jews and Gentiles would be united as part of His spiritual family through faith in Christ—circumcision has become moot. The true "circumcision" are the uncircumcised Gentiles and the circumcised Jews. "Circumcision is no longer merely a bodily mark;" writes Bruce Barton, "instead, it has new spiritual meaning and is symbolized by baptism.[46] As Paul wrote to the Colossians, 'In him also you were circumcised with a circumcision made without hands, by putting off the body of the flesh, by the circumcision of Christ, having been buried with him in baptism, in which you were also raised with him through faith in the powerful working of God, who raised him from the dead'" (Col. 2:11–12).

After condemning an attitude of "confidence in the flesh," Paul notes that if "confidence in the flesh" were legitimate, he would be the most confident of all because he had been the quintessential Hebrew and Pharisee. If anyone could be lifted up for such external matters, it was he. If anyone was qualified to speak to these matters, it was he. Again, he isn't boasting. We don't think he's proud of the qualifications he is spouting off because they led him to persecute his Lord and Savior Jesus Christ and persecute and even murder His followers. But these credentials do qualify him as an expert on the law, on following the wrong path, and on rejecting Christ. His point is that if achievements of the flesh did anyone any good, he of all people would not have needed Christ. But as it turns out, he needed Him more than anyone. By his own admission, he was the worst of sinners (1 Tim. 1:15) and hopelessly lost until Christ confronted him on the road to Damascus. If anyone has credibility to point to the error of hyper-legalism, it is Paul.

There is an extraordinarily positive message in this passage: if such a sinner, such a Christ-denier, can be saved, anyone can—if he will repent and place his faith in Christ. Paul's elaboration on this point is worth quoting in full:

> But whatever gain I had, I counted as loss for the sake of Christ. Indeed, I count everything as loss because of the surpassing worth of knowing Christ Jesus my Lord. For his sake I have suffered the loss of all things and count them as rubbish, in order that I may gain Christ and be found in him, not having a righteousness that comes from the law, but that which comes through faith in Christ, the righteousness from God that depends on faith—that I may know him and the power of his resurrection, and may share his sufferings, becoming like him in his death, that by any means possible I may attain the resurrection from the dead. (3:7–11)

As his words make clear, none of these signature qualifications did him any good at all. Though he once thought they were valuable, he now considers them worthless in view of what Christ has done for him.

Thomas Hale offers a helpful analogy to explain Paul's argument. Imagine that a boat filled with valuable cargo starts to sink in a violent storm. Throwing the heavy cargo overboard is the only way the sailors can save themselves and prevent the boat from sinking. "In the same way, Paul has had to 'throw overboard' all his old religious 'goods'—such as his Jewish background, his circumcision, his legalistic righteousness. Paul has lost all these things so that he may gain Christ—so that he might be saved."[47]

This comparison might not be perfect because in terms of salvation none of Paul's qualifications had any value at all. The metaphor is helpful, however, to illustrate that we sometimes must part with valuable things to preserve more valuable things. Further illustrating his point, Hale cites Jesus' two parables of men who sold everything they had so they could acquire something of infinitely greater value—Christ. These were the parable of the hidden treasure and the parable of the pearl of great value (Matt. 13:44–45). Hale summarizes Jesus' and Paul's lesson: "There is nothing on this earth more valuable than knowing Jesus Christ personally. Nothing else can give a person salvation and eternal life. Only by knowing and accepting Christ as our personal Savior can we obtain salvation."[48]

What the Pharisees don't understand is that you can't become righteous through following the law, even if it were possible to perfectly follow the law as Paul claims to have done. That is because true righteousness is not something you achieve by following rules or even by behaving a certain way. It is internal, a matter of the heart. That's why Jesus said in the Sermon on the Mount, "For I tell you, unless your righteousness exceeds that of the scribes and the Pharisees, you will never enter the kingdom of heaven" (Matt. 5:20).

I (David) remember early in my Christian walk discussing this passage with friends in a Bible study group. I told them I had great difficulty with this because I understood that the scribes and Pharisees rigidly followed the law. How could I ever be more righteous than they were? I fundamentally misunderstood the entire concept of righteousness, assuming, without a lot of reflection at that point, that it was something we achieved on our own. Note, I'm not talking about the issue of salvation here, though it's obviously related. I wrongly assumed that Jesus was being hyperbolic because there is no way we ordinary mortals could live up to the standards of the Pharisees who devoted their very lives to following the law.

I have since learned that righteousness is not a matter of outward behavior or of following rules, even perfectly, but of the heart. Even the Old Testament teaches this: "But the Lord said to Samuel, 'Do not look on his appearance or on the height of his stature, because I have rejected him. For the Lord sees not as man sees: man looks on the outward appearance, but the Lord looks on the heart'" (1 Samuel 16:7). This is the truth behind Jesus' saying, "You have heard that it was said, 'You shall not commit adultery.' But I say to you that everyone who looks at a woman with lustful intent has already committed adultery with her in his heart" (Matt. 5:27–28). The Pharisees may well have obeyed every jot and tittle of the law but for the wrong reasons. It may have been based on pride or something else. But was love at the center of it, even love of God?

Apparently, Jesus didn't believe so, or He wouldn't have constantly criticized the Pharisees for going through the motions of following the law without any internal transformation. This was the point of His response to them when they condemned Him for healing a man with a withered hand on the Sabbath (Matt. 12:9–14)—their rigid adherence to the rules would have prevented the compassionate healing of the man. As Jesus told them, they simply didn't understand the Old Testament principle that God prefers love to sacrifice: "For I desire steadfast love and not sacrifice, the knowledge of God rather than burnt offerings" (Hosea 6:6). So Jesus told them, "And if you had known what this means, 'I desire mercy, and not sacrifice,' you would not have condemned the guiltless. For the Son of Man is lord of the Sabbath" (Matt. 12:7–8).

We see that just as the Pharisees flawlessly followed the law while not grasping the spirit behind it, they knew the Old Testament backward and forward but were blind to its ultimate message. So Paul hammers home the lesson in these passages that we aren't—and can't be—righteous on our own. We must get our righteousness from God, through faith in His Son. Through faith in Christ we are legally declared righteous and saved from our sins, but we also thereby become empowered by the Holy Spirit to grow in true righteousness—a righteousness that comes from within, from the heart, where the Holy Spirit resides in believers. Paul also informs his readers that through faith he can come to know God and the power of His resurrection, share in His sufferings, and ultimately be physically resurrected with Him (3:10–11). The congregation must be heartened, knowing that eternal life with Christ awaits them, which makes any suffering they endure on Christ's behalf an honor and a privilege.

PRAYER

Lord Jesus, we ask You to help us understand the true meaning of righteousness, which comes solely from our faith in You. We ask that through our relationship with You, we will come to know the heart of Father God, who loves and adores us as His children. Some of us might read parts of the Old Testament out of context and come to view the Father as harsh or judgmental, and this can affect our view of the term "righteousness." It's important for us to look deeper in order to understand God's reasoning behind judgment. You explained to Your disciples in John 14:9, "Anyone who has seen me has seen the Father," and You also said in John 5:19, "I tell you the truth, the Son can do nothing by himself. He does only what he sees the Father doing. Whatever the Father does, the Son also does." When this revelation clicks in our hearts, we will be able to approach the Father in an entirely new way compared to when we lived bogged down by shame and fear by looking at righteousness through our own efforts. As God told Moses and His people, "Yahweh! The Lord! The God of

▶

compassion and mercy! I am slow to anger and filled with unfailing love and faithfulness. I lavish unfailing love to a thousand generations. I forgive iniquity, rebellion, and sin" (Deut 34:6–7 NLT). The greatest evidence of the Father's love for us is the most commonly known, yet overlooked verse: "For God so loved the world, that he gave his only Son" (John 3:16 ESV). So we respond and say, thank You, Father! Thank You for loving us through our sin and giving Your perfect Son, Jesus, as a sacrifice so that we too can be counted as righteous. We love You and stand awestruck in Your presence. Blessed be Your Name,

AMEN.

Paul isn't claiming to be perfectly righteous himself—he openly admits he has not attained moral perfection. But he presses on, aiming toward that perfection that he will only finally achieve when he is reunited with Jesus in eternity. In the meantime, he doesn't beat himself up over his past transgressions. He has been forgiven, and he is "straining forward to what lies ahead," continuing "toward the goal for the prize of the upward call of God in Christ Jesus" (3:13–14). Ambrosiaster comments that one reason Paul here admits his imperfection is that he is "concerned that they, like all who are subject to human conceits, might become elated as though they were already worthy."[49] If he is still striving toward perfection, how much more should they do so in humility?

Some Christians seem to have a superior attitude, believing they've arrived morally and are somehow insulated from temptation and sin. But John clearly warned, "If we say we have no sin, we deceive ourselves, and the truth is not in us. If we confess our sins, he is faithful and just to forgive our sins and to cleanse us from all unrighteousness. If we say we have not sinned, we make him a liar, and his word is not in us" (1 John 1:8–10).

Believers still sin, and when we do, we must ask forgiveness, even though we are saved. Otherwise, why would the Lord's prayer instruct us to ask for forgiveness?[50] Keep in mind, we are not talking about our salvation, which we receive as a gift from our faith in Christ. For salvation purposes, as we've noted, our sins are forgiven. But when we sin following our salvation, we still must ask forgiveness. That's why John made a distinction. In verse 7, preceding the verse we just quoted on the need to confess sins, John said, "But if we walk in the light, as he is in the light, we have fellowship with one another, and the blood of Jesus his Son cleanses us from all sin" (1 John 1:7). John didn't contradict himself within the same paragraph—he's saying that believers have been legally declared righteous but thereafter will still sin. Verse 7, explains H. D. M. Spence, concerns freeing us from the penalties of sin, which we call justification—that legal declaration of righteousness previously discussed. Verse 9 refers to seeking forgiveness for our daily sins following our salvation—freeing us from the contamination of sin as we pursue our personal sanctification (holiness).[51]

Paul's words should be comforting to us, for isn't it natural to wonder why we still are as sinful as we are despite our salvation? We believe so, and it's at least mildly reassuring that no less a saint than Paul acknowledged his own sinful nature. Don't misunderstand. We are not saying we can rationalize away our sins because Paul sinned too. To the contrary, Paul is clear that he is still working toward perfection, and we should as well, mindful that it is through the grace and power of the Spirit that we engage in this pursuit and further mindful that moral perfection is an unattainable goal this side of eternity.

Paul continues, "Let those of us who are mature think this way, and if in anything you think otherwise, God will reveal that also to you. Only let us hold true to what we have attained" (Phil. 3:15–16). These verses are straightforward. Paul's readers should take heed of what he says and believe it. If not, God will show them the error of their ways. Mature Christians are humble and will realize their own imperfections, whereas prideful Christians who might believe they're above petty sins are immature, and God will reveal this to them in time.

Christians also need to walk the walk by putting into practice what they've learned. In the words of the NLT, "We must hold on to the progress we have already made" (Phil. 3:16). They have already been saved through their faith in Christ and been declared righteous. They should not squander that gift but do everything they can to retain the righteousness that has been given to them and build on it through the process of sanctification. Don't be satisfied with the righteousness you have, but strive every day to advance toward perfection. A hymn by Johnson Oatman Jr. captures it well: "I'm pressing on the upward way, New heights I'm gaining every day; Still praying as I'm onward bound, Lord, plant my feet on higher ground. Lord, lift me up and let me stand, By Faith, on heaven's tableland. A higher plane that I have found; Lord, plant my feet on higher ground."[52]

Prayer

Lord, we want to be lifted up on higher ground with You, as Oatman's hymn beautifully describes. Part of maturing in our walk alongside You is learning to repent regularly. But in order for repentance to be sincere, we can't simply confess our sins; our hearts must be convicted enough to seek true change in these areas. So where we have failed to die to ourselves and submit to You, please show us the root causes of these areas of sin in our lives. Help us to get to the true source of our sin rather than focusing solely on the surface-level issues. The Bible tells us that Jesus' blood can break any chain in our lives. That even includes struggles we may have inherited from patterns of dysfunction stretching back generations in our families and communities. May we believe in faith that You can and will heal our brokenness and seek to have more of Your goodness in every aspect of our lives. Come, Holy Spirit, and have Your way.

AMEN.

Continuing his call for the Philippians to live in Christ as he taught them when he imparted the gospel to them, Paul tells them to join in imitating him and to keep their eyes on those who likewise follow his example of Christian living. Paul's earnest desire is that all those he has brought to Christ become as zealous for the Lord as he is—that they devote their lives to advancing the gospel and serving Christ sacrificially. Again, Paul is not boasting but setting himself up as an example of one who has turned his life over to his Savior. By pointing to himself, he is showing that to live for Christ is not an unattainable goal, and they will realize that by observing him. "For Christianity," writes Ralph Martin, "the pattern of ethical teaching is embodied not in a written code of precepts and maxims covering every possible contingency of life, but in a life—pre-eminently the life of the Lord Jesus, and secondarily in the lives of his earliest and closest followers."[53]

Paul next issues a stern warning about the enemies of Christ whose destiny is ruination: "For many, of whom I have often told you and now tell you even with tears, walk as enemies of the cross of Christ. Their end is destruction, their god is their belly, and they glory in their shame, with minds set on earthly things" (3:18–19). Most scholars believe Paul is here, once again, warning his readers to steer clear of false teachers whose evil ways may be difficult to discern and whose subtle advances difficult to avoid. These people claim to be Christian, but their hearts and minds are not on God but on earthly things. They are focused on self-aggrandizement rather than giving God all the glory. "To 'glory in their shame' means to take pride in what they ought to conceal," writes Chrysostom. "For it is bad enough to do shameful things. But if the doer is ashamed, it is only half so terrible. When, however, someone preens himself on his own shame, that is the extreme of shamelessness."[54] People shall reveal themselves by their works. As John Calvin said. "Faith alone saves, but the faith that saves is not alone."[55]

Paul closes the chapter contrasting the false teachers with himself and the true believers in Philippi. "But our citizenship is in heaven, and from it we await a Savior, the Lord Jesus Christ, who will transform our lowly body to be like his glorious body, by the power that enables him even to subject all things to himself" (3:20–21). The Philippians are mostly proud Roman citizens, but Paul seeks to turn their eyes to their heavenly home, which is far superior. Just as their city belongs to a wider political entity, their church is part of a spiritual entity whose capital is heaven. They await their Savior, who will transform their earthly bodies into glorious heavenly bodies like His own, by the power He has over all of creation.

As citizens of Rome the Philippians would normally associate power with the conquering force of the Roman emperor, but Paul is talking about a different kind of power—the ability to transform them and their bodies. Only Christ possessed such power.[56] "Behold!" he exclaimed to the Corinthians, "I tell you a mystery. We shall not all sleep, but we shall all be changed, in a moment, in the twinkling of an eye, at the last trumpet. For the trumpet will sound, and the dead will be raised imperishable, and we shall be changed. For this perishable body must put on the imperishable, and this mortal body must put on immortality" (1 Cor. 15:51–53). Church father Marius Victorinus explains, "When we rise and are changed...the body in which we have been humbled will be raised. It will be of the same and an equal form to the body of Christ's own glory."[57]

By informing his readers that Christ will transform them by the power that allows Him to subject everyone and everything to Himself, Paul is putting the final exclamation point on this chapter and its message. Bible scholar Gordon Fee summarizes this beautifully:

> This passage reminds us that, despite appearances often to the contrary, God is in control, that our salvation is not just for today but forever, that Christ is coming again, and that

at his coming we inherit the final glory that belongs to Christ alone—and to those who are his. It means the final subjugation of all the "powers" to him as well, especially those responsible for the present affliction of God's people. With Paul we would do well not merely to "await" the end, but eagerly to press on toward the goal, since the final prize is but the consummation of what God has already accomplished through the death and resurrection of our Savior, Jesus Christ the Lord.[58]

PRAYER

Lord, we come to You in reverence and awe, pondering the fact that as new creations in Christ, we are now considered "citizens of heaven." This glorious reality means that no matter what trials we face here on earth, we know that our true home is with You in paradise. Therefore, the ultimate battle has been won. Help us to truly look forward to what awaits us in heaven. There have been many portrayals in modern culture depicting heaven as a vast white void, where people float around without much purpose. But the Bible shows us that heaven is anything but a void! The Book of Revelation tells us there will be no more death, mourning, crying or pain in heaven (21:4), and it also beautifully describes how "the angel showed me a river with the water of life, clear as crystal, flowing from the throne of God and of the Lamb. It flowed down the center of the main street. On each side of the river grew a tree of life, bearing twelve crops of fruit, with a fresh crop each month. The leaves were used for medicine to heal the nations" (Rev. 22:1–2). We believe that heaven will be infinitely more "real" than our reality here on earth. Help us Lord to see glimpses of heaven on earth and for those glimpses to inspire us to bring more of heaven and Your presence into the world.

AMEN.

CHAPTER 4

Paul opens by encouraging his beloved Philippians, who bring great joy to him, to stay strong in the Lord. He fervently wants them to experience love, joy, and peace, and that is only possible if they make Christ the center of their lives.[59] He strongly encourages unity in the church, which might be especially on his mind because of apparent dissension between church members Euodia and Syntyche, whom he singles out by name, encouraging them to come together in the Lord. He asks an unnamed companion of his to help reconcile these women, who formerly worked side by side with Paul in spreading the gospel, along with others, all of whom are saved by virtue of their faith in Christ.

After these greetings Paul pens some of the most uplifting verses in the Bible (4:4–9), words that have provided much encouragement to us and that we have shared with others who needed reassurance and a little boost for their faith. If you're ever down, open up your Bible to these verses: "Rejoice in the Lord always; again I will say, rejoice. Let your reasonableness be known to everyone. The Lord is at hand; do not be anxious about anything, but in everything by prayer and supplication with thanksgiving let your requests be made known to God. And the peace of God, which surpasses all understanding, will guard your hearts and your minds in Christ Jesus" (4:4–7).

No matter what difficulties we face in life, we can always turn to Jesus and rejoice in Him because we know our final destination is with Him. Paul is not playing mind games or asking his readers to pretend they won't experience hardship and suffering. In fact, we have seen that he assures them of the opposite. Rather, he's saying that if they are in Christ they can enjoy an abiding happiness internally that will transcend whatever external troubles they encounter. John MacArthur refers to it as "the inward tranquility of soul granted by God."[60] While our circumstances in life will constantly change, sometimes bringing hurt and heartache, the one thing that will never change is God's consistent, effusive love and our permanent access to Him. If we are content in God through faith in His Son, we will have the strength to face and endure any problems life may throw our way.

Paul tells them, "Let your reasonableness (or gentleness) be known to everyone" (4:5). Paul is implying they will face difficulties and trying situations, but they should retain their equanimity through it all, as a consoling witness to others. Think of Christ, who always remained calm and of good cheer and never became defensive despite the insults hurled at him and the abuse he experienced. As Peter, an apostle and eyewitness to Christ's life, explained, Christ "committed no sin, neither was deceit found in his mouth. When he was reviled, he did not revile in return; when he suffered, he did not threaten, but continued entrusting himself to him who judges justly" (1 Peter 2:22–23). Paul likewise confirmed Christ's demeanor to the Corinthians: "I, Paul, entreat you, by the meekness and gentleness of Christ" (2 Cor. 10:1).

As Peter points out, Christ was untroubled by his abusers because He knew his true judge was God. When we are treated unjustly, we should keep Christ's example in mind, remembering that God is our judge. Indeed, Paul reminds us that God is our true judge in the next clause, declaring, "The Lord is at hand" (4:5). Some think those words introduce the succeeding verses that instruct readers not to be anxious and always thankfully present their requests to God, but they could work either way: "Always rejoice and be gentle because God, who is at hand, is your true Judge," or "because God is coming, don't be anxious about anything, but in everything by prayer and supplication with thanksgiving let your requests be made known to God. And the peace of God, which surpasses all understanding, will guard your hearts and your minds in Christ Jesus."

As we've noted all along, our God is different from the false gods devised by man. Our God, though perfect and infinitely superior to us, is always available for us. What's more, we are encouraged to avail ourselves of that accessibility, to proactively cultivate a personal relationship with Him, to learn about Him, His thoughts, and His will in the God-breathed words of scripture and in direct prayer. We are to express our gratitude to God as we approach Him in prayer—but approach Him we must. He wants us to. Through Paul and through Jesus, He is telling us to. We must approach the Father, the Son, and the Holy Spirit in prayer, together or separately, though they are never separated.

Paul promises us that if we obey his command to pray and make our requests known to God, God's peace—the type of peace that surpasses our very ability to understand it—will flow over us and guard our hearts and minds in Christ. Note that these aren't speculations by Paul but God's *promises* that Paul is simply delivering as His messenger. No matter what difficulties we are facing, we can go to Him in prayer and find peace.

Again, let's not fool ourselves. Paul does not guarantee we can avoid all hurt, pain, and suffering in our lives by turning on a divine spigot in prayer. We will always be human, and on this side of eternity will never be immune from suffering. Things happen to people that they simply cannot understand, horrors so unimaginable they can barely go on. God is not promising us that those will be entirely eliminated through prayer. But he is saying that He will give us a peace to enable us to get through it and a perspective that will remind us that in the end, everything will be better and that "He will wipe away every tear from their eyes, and death shall be no more, neither shall there be mourning, nor crying, nor pain anymore, for the former things have passed away" (Rev. 21:4). I-Jin Loh and Eugene A. Nida explain that peace, as described in the Bible, is never just the absence of trouble. "Rather, this term stands for a total well-being associated with the state of salvation (Isaiah 52:7)," they write. "It follows from the right relationship with God made possible through Jesus Christ (Romans 5:1) and the resultant friendly relationship with one's fellow man (Eph. 2:14)."[61]

We know from personal experience that without God we cannot always be free of anxiety. We cannot always have peace of mind. The Psalmist ponders why wicked people enjoy a life of ease while their riches multiply: "Did I keep my heart pure for nothing? Did I keep myself innocent for no reason? I get nothing but trouble all day long; every morning brings me pain" (Psalm 73:13–14 NLT). Then he admits he is incapable of comprehending this on his own due to the limitations of his human mind: "So I tried to understand why the wicked prosper. But what a difficult task it is!" (Psalm 73:16 NLT)

Watch what comes next, however: "Then I went into your sanctuary, O God, and I finally understood the destiny of the wicked. Truly, you put them on a slippery path and send them sliding over the cliff to destruction" (Psalm 73:17–18 NLT). You see, we can only grasp these incomprehensible things if we are in God's sanctuary. As the Psalmist continues, his epiphany becomes even clearer: "Then I realized that my heart was bitter, and I was all torn up inside. I was so foolish and ignorant—I must have seemed like a senseless animal to you. Yet I still belong to you; you hold my right hand. You guide me with your counsel, leading me to a glorious destiny. Whom have I in heaven but you? I desire you more than anything on earth. My health may fail, and my spirit may grow weak, but God remains the strength of my heart; he is mine forever" (Psalm 73:21–26 NLT). Then he closes with this elevating verse, which illuminates Paul's message that God is our refuge and our peace: "But as for me, how good it is to be near God! I have made the Sovereign Lord my shelter, and I will tell everyone about the wonderful things you do" (Psalm 73:28 NLT).

Perhaps we can think of it this way. If we are in Christ, we are at peace, for Christ is peace. So if we could always be in Christ—having the eternal perspective 100 percent of the time—we would be bathed in a calm beyond our understanding. This calm will "guard our hearts" and keep us from anxiety. Jacobus Muller captures the essence:

> The peace of God will keep watch over and guard hearts and minds—the world of affection and thought—against worries and temptations towards anxiety; will keep watch over heart and mind so that nothing can cause unrest and discord, because everything is placed trustingly in the hands of God by the prayer of faith. This, however, takes place only *in Christ Jesus*, in our attachment to Him and fellowship with Him. Apart from Him there is no surety or guarantee for peace of mind, but whosoever is in Christ, is entrusted to the infallible safekeeping of the peace of God.[62]

PRAYER

Jesus, we want to be enveloped in Your life-giving peace through intimacy with You. But for this to happen, we must become sincerely familiar with You, talking with You as we would a friend or brother. That means we must push past our misplaced fears of what You'll think of us if we show You the ugly side of ourselves. The very frustrations and doubts we avoid bringing to You, fearing You'll be disappointed in us for having such thoughts, are actually the keys to growing closer with You. In our earthly relationships, when someone ▶

shows us love and understanding when we are at our worst, it creates a bond stronger than other surface-level friendships. It is the same with You. The more real and raw we allow ourselves to be with You, the more we will come to discover just how deep Your love is and how much peace You can bring into any circumstance. Lord, help us to call on Your name when we find ourselves in the darkest valleys, not keeping any fear, frustration, or question hidden from You. Of course, You can handle us at our worst, and when we put our hope in You, our strength is renewed. Holy Spirit, we offer our hearts to You in this moment—please reveal something we've been keeping from You with which You'd like to help us.

AMEN.

Now Paul exhorts his readers to worthwhile thinking, not just empty platitudes. He takes us to a higher plane, a plane of beauty and elevated morality: "Finally, brothers, whatever is true, whatever is honorable, whatever is just, whatever is pure, whatever is lovely, whatever is commendable, if there is any excellence, if there is anything worthy of praise, think about these things. What you have learned and received and heard and seen in me—practice these things, and the God of peace will be with you" (4:8–9). In short, Paul is saying we should be loving people and consummate imitators of Christ, which will bring us peace. While he doesn't say this directly, he seems to be arguing that while joy and peace are states of mind and not activities, as we've noted, we can take action that will influence our mindset in that direction. He tells us to "practice these things."

Fascinatingly, Paul is implicitly rejecting the victimhood mentality, telling us to focus our minds on the wonderful things in life and not to succumb to the temptation to be mired in negative and critical thoughts. We should strive, then, for Christian perfection, even though we know we can't completely attain it. It's as if engaging in this practice of arranging our minds toward wonderful thoughts is itself a spiritual discipline of sorts. We should focus our thoughts on these things until they begin to shape our behavior. "It is a law of life that, if a man thinks of something often enough and long enough, he will come to the stage when he cannot stop thinking about it," writes William Barclay. "His thoughts will be quite literally in a groove out of which he cannot jerk them."[63]

We don't think it's any accident that Paul begins his list of virtuous thoughts with "truth." Truth is eminently important in our lives, especially in our spiritual lives. In the words of Pilate, however, "What is truth?" Contrary to the understanding of today's culture, truth is not relative or subjective. This talk of "your truth" differing from "my truth" is morally reckless. Truth is that which corresponds with reality. This definition is sometimes called the correspondence view of truth.[64] We do people no favors, especially children, when we try to pacify them with the lie that the truth is whatever they *consider* to be true, for objective truth does not depend on what we think about it.

All truth starts with God. Jesus is the Truth. The fundamental truth that must organize our lives is that Jesus Christ is the Son of God who died on the cross for our sins so that human beings, by placing their faith in Him, will have their sins forgiven and gain eternal life. The gospel is the starting place for all truth. Theologian Norman Geisler demonstrates that the Bible repeatedly affirms the correspondence view of truth. The ninth commandment is based on it: "You shall not give false testimony against your neighbor" (Exodus 20:16). This commandment, says Geisler, "depends for its very meaning and effectiveness on correspondence, implying that a statement is false if it does not correspond to reality."[65]

Not only is Jesus the Truth, but Satan is the father of lies. Jesus rebukes those who don't understand His words precisely because His words are true. "Why do you not understand what I say?" (John 8:43), he asks. "It is because you cannot bear to hear my word. You are of your father the devil, and your will is to do your father's desires. He was a murderer from the beginning, and does not stand in the truth, because there is no truth in him. When he lies, he speaks out of his own character, for he is a liar and the father of lies" (John 8:43–44).

The devil lies and promotes lying with the goal of leading people away from God—who is truth—and away from eternal life. He also deceives people into believing there is no such thing as truth, which is itself a damnable lie that negates the very measuring rod of truth, thus preventing us from even establishing moral standards. This lie is terribly pernicious and destructive to all people and cultures, so we must resist it and stand up for the truth. To do anything less is disobedient toward Christ.

Geisler cites several other examples where the Bible validates the correspondence view of truth:

- ★ Satan told Eve that she would not surely die (Gen. 3:4), which contradicted God's actual words, "You will surely die" (Gen. 2:17).
- ★ Ananias and Sapphira were severely punished for lying about their finances (Acts 5:1–4). They were not given a pass based on the logical absurdity of "their truth."
- ★ Joseph tested his brothers to see if they were being truthful (Gen. 42:16).
- ★ Moses taught that the way to test if a prophet is authentic is to see whether his statements come true (Deut. 18:22).

- ★ At the dedication of the temple, Solomon prayed that God's promise to David concerning the temple would come true (1 Kings 8:26).
- ★ The Psalmist proclaimed that God hates falsehood, and things were false if they didn't correspond to God's law (Ps. 119:163).
- ★ Jesus said, "You have sent to John and he has testified to the truth" (John 5:33).[66]

There are many other examples. Suffice it to say that if we are to get our mind and spirit right with God, we must think of things that are true.

Next, according to Paul's list, we must think of whatever is honorable. Honorable things are those worthy of respect. Proverbs also ties together the speaking of truth and of noble things: "Hear, for I will speak noble things, and from my lips will come what is right" (Prov. 8:6).[67] Paul says we must also think of whatever is right, which means what is true but also what is righteous, as God has defined it.[68] We must think, additionally, of things that are pure. "Purity of thought and purpose is a precondition of purity in word and action," writes F. F. Bruce.[69] Think of pure thoughts as those that are wholesome.[70]

Paul also instructs his readers to think of things that are lovely, meaning those things that inspire love and those that are pleasing and attractive,[71] as well as those things that are beloved by God and pleasing to Christlike people.[72] Commentators caution us not to misunderstand what we mean by "pleasing."[73] People can please themselves with perverse thoughts, which is apparently why Paul uses a term that is better translated as "lovely"—the only time the term is used in the New Testament.[74] So to grasp Paul's meaning, scholars recommend that we think of it as things that are lovely or beautiful—and pleasing—provided they are not thoughts of which God would disapprove.

Paul also urges believers to think about whatever is commendable, which means things that are admirable. Here, Paul has in mind things that people generally consider good, such as kindness, courtesy, and respect for other people.[75]

Finally Paul says his readers must think of any excellence and anything worthy of praise, which is a catchall phrase to cover worthy thoughts not otherwise mentioned in his list. Scholars suggest that "excellence" refers to moral excellence or, as some translations use, "virtue." And "praiseworthy" means those things God deems worthy and deserving of praise.

PRAYER

Heavenly Father, thank You for giving us such practical instruction for living our lives to the fullest. You understand how easily we become fixated on things that are not of You; we are the wandering sheep who so quickly lose sight of what's most important in Your eyes. You tell us to "look straight ahead, and fix your eyes on what lies before you. Mark out a straight path for your feet; stay on the safe path. Don't get sidetracked, keep your feet from following evil" (Prov. 4:25–27 NLT). Paul's charge to focus our thoughts on what is "true, and honorable, and right, and pure, and lovely, and commendable" (Philip. 4:8) is the perfect antidote to being led astray by our fleshly desires. May we memorize this verse in our hearts so that when we feel ourselves slipping, we can recalibrate our attention to You. In Jesus's Name,

AMEN.

Paul closes out his paragraph telling his readers to practice the things they have learned and witnessed from him, which will lead to God's peace for them. Again, this is not an egotistical pronouncement but a way to complete Paul's description of good thoughts—covering all those areas he couldn't cover with words—by pointing to his own behavior, with which they would be familiar. "He sees that it is impossible to give precise instructions about everything—their going out, their coming in, their words, their inner condition and their company," says Chrysostom. "All of these a Christian must think about in context. He says concisely and as it were in a nutshell, 'Just do what you have heard and seen me do.'"[76]

In the last section of this letter prior to his final greetings, Paul thanks the Philippians for their financial aid during his imprisonment. They helped him before but had not had an opportunity to do so again until now. He stresses, however, that he is not in dire straits because he has learned how to be content through good times and bad, as he has repeatedly said: "Not that I am speaking of being in need, for I have learned in whatever situation I am to be content. I know how to be brought low, and I know how to abound. In any and every circumstance, I have learned the secret of facing plenty and hunger, abundance and need" (4:11–12).

Paul is not concerned about how he looks to the Philippians for his own sake but for the sake of all his readers. He doesn't want anyone to come away from the letter thinking he desperately needs the church's help, which would undermine his dominant message that he is content in Christ and that such contentment transcends his material circumstances. He accentuates his point with this familiar declaration: "I can do all things through him who strengthens me." Paul is clarifying that his inner contentment is not self-empowered but made possible through his faith in Christ. In his letter to the Colossians he described this internal strength as the "energy that he [Christ] powerfully works within [him]" (Col. 1:29).

These passages in Philippians have been associated with English statesman Oliver Cromwell, who found comfort in them following the death of his eldest son. Cromwell reportedly said, "The Scripture did once save my life; when my eldest Son died; which went as a dagger to my heart, indeed it did." Cromwell then read verses 4:10–11 concerning Paul's professed contentment in Christ no matter the circumstances. Those alone, however, weren't enough to move Cromwell, and he still felt empty. He said, "It's true, Paul, *you* have learned this, and attained to this measure of grace: but what shall *I* do? Ah poor creature, it is a hard lesson for me to take out! I find it so!" Then Cromwell continued reading through verse 13: "I can do all things through him who strengthens me." At that point his faith kicked in, and he was comforted in his heart. He then said to himself, "He that was Paul's Christ is my Christ too!"[77]

Prayer

Dear Jesus, thank You for Your strength, for Your everlasting goodness, Your provision, Your promises, and Your faithfulness. You assured us that though in this world we would have trouble, we are never to lose heart, because You have overcome the world (John 16:33). You know better than anyone that life can be so crushingly painful. Help us to know with increasing depth that when we grieve, You are alongside us, grieving with us through Your abiding compassion. You comfort us in Psalm 34, assuring us that You hear us when we cry to You for help, and You draw near to us when our hearts become broken (17–18). You go on in verse 19 to say, "The righteous person faces many troubles, but the Lord comes to the rescue each time" (NLT). The worship group Maverick City Music has a beautiful

▶

song titled, "God Will Work It Out." The chorus states, "God will work it out, one thing I know, one thing I've found, is God will work it out." If this is something we don't fully accept yet, we ask that You would enlighten us, draw us into Your loving presence and help us to search for promises in Your Word and to speak those Words confidently over our every-day struggles. In faith we hold on to You. For we can do all things with You!

AMEN.

After stressing his contentment despite his circumstances, Paul thanks the Philippians for consistently coming to his aid in times of trouble. He acknowledges that when he left Macedonia, theirs was the only church that entered into partnership with him in giving and receiving. As such he isn't looking for another gift from them but expressing his hope that they will be rewarded for their kindness. He declares that right now he has all he needs and more through their gifts that Epaphroditus delivered to him (4:15–18). He describes these gifts as "a fragrant offering, a sacrifice acceptable and pleasing to God" (4:18).

This shows that the money they gave to help Paul during his imprisonment, during which he was still actively preaching the gospel, was in fact a gift to God because it advanced His work. Paul assures them that in turn God will supply every need of theirs—both material needs and the necessary qualities Paul instructs them to cultivate in verses 4:8–9, as well all other qualities he encourages throughout the letter such as joy and steadfastness in Christ, humility, and spiritual harmony in the church.[78]

Paul closes the letter with a doxology giving glory to God and with his final greetings to all believers in Christ, ending with this: "The grace of the Lord Jesus Christ be with your spirit" (4:23).

Marius Victorinus explains that Paul is confident that the Philippians, unlike those addressed in his other epistles, "had not been seduced by false apostles. He is here writing only a short letter of exhortation," writes Victorinus. "He prays that 'the grace of our Lord Jesus Christ be with your spirit.' For if the Spirit dwells within them, they will respond rightly."[79] Paul, being a man of ceaseless prayer, is essentially praying that his letter will be read and received in the right spirit and made effective by the power of Christ working within each of its readers.

CHAPTER FIVE

1 TIMOTHY
SOUND DOCTRINE AND CHRISTIAN LIVING

Timothy is one of the most likable and devoted Christians of the entire New Testament. From a human standpoint, his greatest honor was to be chosen as an assistant to the church's foremost missionary leader Paul. He was Paul's closest friend to the very end, but the apostle recognized his higher worth and relationship when he called him a "man of God" (Tim. 6:11).

—Irving Jensen[1]

1 Timothy is one of the three pastoral epistles addressed to either of Paul's entrusted and beloved colleagues, Timothy and Titus. The pair occupy important positions in the church and serve as Paul's representatives to churches in their regions.[2] These letters, however, are hardly meant for the two recipients alone. One reason they're called "pastoral epistles"—though neither Timothy nor Titus are pastors of local churches—is that they deal largely with issues of church organization and discipline, even if they also have other useful information. Personal in tone, the letters can serve as practical guides for pastors and all other believers working to advance the gospel.

The three pastoral letters are probably the last epistles Paul writes, so they reflect the concerns that plague him toward the end of his life. Having seen or heard how the early churches are progressing and the problems they are encountering, he wants to address issues of church structure and discipline, and leave a written record of instructions that will survive his passing.[3]

In 1 Timothy, Paul wants to advise Timothy on his oversight of the churches. Born of a Greek father and Jewish mother (Acts 16:1), Timothy is one of Paul's dearest colleagues in the faith. In this letter, Paul delegates to him the critical task of confronting and correcting the false teachers and their erroneous doctrines. In fact, scholars conclude that a primary goal of the standards for church leadership set out by Paul is to root out heresies. As we have been stressing, there is only one true gospel, one God, and one Christ. And there is only one way to God, which is through faith in Jesus Christ. So those who teach otherwise must be refuted and defeated, for they are accursed (Gal. 1:8). Christ's servants, and particularly those charged with preaching and teaching the word, have a special duty to correctly present the gospel and to safeguard God's word jealously and zealously.[4]

As another means to combat false teachers, Paul instructs church members to live in unity as part of God's household (3:15), which would bolster the credibility of the church and diminish that of self-promoting false teachers. He insists, as always, that members model Christlike behavior.[5] Paul cites the destructive behavior of Hymenaeus and Alexander (1:18–20) as examples Timothy should avoid as he models the Christian life. He also urges prayer for all church members, especially the leaders, because such prayer is pleasing in God's sight, and He wants everyone to be saved and to learn the truth (2:1–4). As always, Paul strongly emphasizes prayer, insisting that men should pray in every place (2:8).

CHAPTER 1

In his greeting Paul identifies Timothy as the recipient and himself as the author, calling himself Christ's apostle by command of God. As false teachers and others had challenged his authority in other churches, he puts the subject to rest here at the beginning of his letter. He had nothing to do with his own appointment as an apostle, which was not only God's will but His command. He affectionately calls Timothy "my true child in the faith"—there couldn't be a more ringing endorsement from Christianity's premiere evangelist. At this point, Paul has entrusted vital tasks to Timothy, and he has not disappointed. Those reluctant to delegate authority should consider Paul's selection of Timothy for the most important task imaginable—spreading the gospel—and his vindication by the wonderful work Timothy accomplishes.

Some commentators note that Paul dispenses with his usual expressions of gratitude at the beginning of his letters. That's because he's unhappy with the church's progress due to false teachings.[6] So after offering God's grace, mercy, and peace, Paul turns immediately to false teachers: "As I urged you when I was going to Macedonia, remain at Ephesus so that you may charge certain persons not to teach any different doctrine, or to devote themselves to myths and endless genealogies, which promote speculations rather than the stewardship from God that is by faith" (1:3–4).

Earlier, Paul left Timothy in Ephesus to guard the church against the false teachers. As the threat remains, he urges Timothy to continue with that task. Note that Paul commands him to directly confront these error merchants. As much as he elsewhere stresses unity in Christ's body, Paul obviously believes that the promotion of a false gospel warrants conflict. Without proper doctrine all the harmony in the world won't save people.

Let this, too, be a lesson to us. While we mustn't mire ourselves in petty quarrels, we cannot compromise in the battle against poisonous false teaching. "Be not afraid of men," cautions seventeenth century Scottish Presbyterian pastor Samuel Rutherford. "Your Master can mow down His enemies, and make withered hay of fair flowers. Your time will not be long; after your afternoon will come your evening, and after evening night. Serve Christ.... Let His cause be your cause; give not an hair-breadth of truth away; for it is not yours, but God's. Then, since ye are going, take Christ's testificate with you out of this life—'Well done, good and faithful servant!' His 'well done' is worth a shipful of 'good-days' and earthly honours."[7] And on his deathbed Rutherford exclaimed, "My Lord and Master is the Chief of ten thousand of thousands; none is comparable to Him in heaven or in earth. Dear brethren, do all for Him: Pray for Christ. Preach for Christ. Feed the flock committed to your charge for Christ. Do all for Christ. Beware of men pleasing. There is too much of it. The Chief Shepherd will shortly appear."[8]

Though Paul does not precisely identify the false teachers, they clearly focus on myths and genealogies, which foster conjecture about the meaning of scripture rather than focusing on the correct doctrine that is centered on faith in Christ. Taking pride in their intellect, they philosophize over esoteric points rather than dwelling on Christ crucified. Such teaching is anathema to authentic Christian faith, for it puffs men up with personal pride instead of promoting humility and trust in Christ. "'The myths and endless genealogies' only served to promote speculation and lead to discussion about ideas that did not come from Scripture but from the minds of the false teachers," writes Bruce Barton. By encouraging such idle thinking instead of focusing on the gospel, these heretics distract believers from studying the word.[9] These false teachers, like the Gnostics who will come later, falsely tout a special spiritual knowledge that is only accessible to the spiritually elite.

Paul assures Timothy and all eventual readers of this letter that his instructions aren't meant to be harsh. Rather, he is motivated by love—"a pure heart and a good conscience and a sincere faith" (1:5). By contrast, the false teachers primarily want to be recognized as venerable experts in the law. But they delude themselves, for they don't understand what they are so confidently preaching. They aren't dedicated to honoring God but to dishonoring His word and honoring themselves.[10]

PRAYER

Lord, protect us from our pride and self-importance; may our study of Your word never be motivated by intellectual elitism or moral superiority. The devil is constantly setting cunning traps to divide the body of Christ. Without Your wisdom and love, we will fail to discern the things that are most important to You. Help us to know when and how to correct fellow believers who are being deceived by false doctrine, putting You at the center so our words are inspired by Your Holy Spirit rather than our flawed emotions. Holy Spirit, have Your way in our hearts, that we may have grace in abundance and patience for our brothers and sisters in Christ. We are helpless to correct and sharpen one another without You.

AMEN.

Paul assures us he isn't denigrating the law, which comes from God: "Now we know that the law is good, if one uses it lawfully" (1:8). According to Douglas Milne, "This means that people must understand the true intention of the law, and recognize its limitations too. It was never meant to provide a means by which people can justify or ingratiate themselves with God. Its standards are far too high and pure for sinful human beings even to begin to accomplish that."[11] In his other writings Paul affirms the moral perfection of the law. "So the law is holy, and the commandment is holy and righteous and good" (Romans 7:12). Likewise, David wrote, "The law of the Lord is perfect" (Psalm 19:7).

The law sets out God's perfect standards, but human beings, unaided by the Spirit, cannot consistently live up to it. The law shows man his sinfulness and his inability to save himself, thus leading him to Christ. Numerous passages in Galatians make this clear: "So then, the law was our guardian until Christ came, in order that we might be justified by faith" (Gal. 3:24); "Now it is evident that no one is justified before God by the law, for 'The righteous shall live by faith'" (Gal. 3:11); and, "Yet we know that a person is not justified by works of the law but through faith in Jesus Christ, so we also have believed in Christ Jesus, in order to be justified by faith in Christ and not by works of the law, because by works of the law no one will be justified" (Gal. 2:16). John MacArthur cogently captures the difference between the law and the gospel: "The law is morally right and good, but the law alone is not good news."[12]

Paul specifies to whom the law applies: "The law is not laid down for the just but for the lawless and disobedient, for the ungodly and sinners, for the unholy and profane, for those who strike their fathers and mothers, for murderers, the sexually immoral, men who practice homosexuality, enslavers, liars, perjurers, and whatever else is contrary to sound doctrine, in accordance with the gospel of the glory of the blessed God with which I have been entrusted" (1:9–11).

In his epistle to the Romans Paul repeatedly invoked his initial guidance here—that the law is not for "the just," meaning believers who have been justified and saved by faith in Christ:

- ★ "... because you are no longer under the law but under grace." (Romans 6:14)
- ★ "But now we are released from the law, having died to that which held us captive, so that we serve in the new way of the Spirit and not in the old way of the written code." (Romans 7:5)
- ★ "There is therefore now no condemnation for those who are in Christ Jesus. For the law of the Spirit of life has set you free in Christ Jesus from the law of sin and death." (Romans 8:1–2)
- ★ "For God has done what the law, weakened by the flesh, could not do. By sending his own Son in the likeness of sinful flesh and for sin, he condemned sin in the flesh, in order that the righteous requirement of the law might be fulfilled in us, who walk not according to the flesh but according to the Spirit." (Romans 8:3–4)

Warren Wiersbe sums it up beautifully: "You have been made free from the law of sin and death. You now have life in the Spirit. You have moved into a whole new sphere of life in Christ.... The Law no longer has any jurisdiction over you: you are dead to the Law and free from the Law."[13] Wiersbe explains that the law has no jurisdiction over us because Christ already suffered condemnation for us—He stood in our place and took God's wrath for all of mankind's sins. The law could only condemn and could not save. But it can no longer do either for believers. They are immune from its penalty and have already been saved because Christ's righteousness is imputed to them by their faith. Importantly, Milne reminds us that Paul is not denying that the law has positive uses for the believer—it's one of the moral authorities that shows Christians the way to live.[14] God's moral code will always remain perfect and helps us to better understand God's will and his moral standards for our lives.

But why does Paul go on to say that while the law is not for believers, it is for the lawless and disobedient? Of course, the law is critically important for non-believers because it still functions to show them their woeful inadequacy and sinfulness apart from faith in Christ. While they are still lost, it can lead them to faith in Christ. As for the types of sinners for whom the law is still useful, a brief comparison with Exodus 20 shows Paul included most of the Ten Commandments in his list.[15]

PRAYER

Father, we thank You for Your perfect law, which You lovingly established to create boundaries for us. The Old Testament gives account after account of Your chosen people, Israel, disobeying Your laws and suffering tragic consequences. Yet with every failure, You always gave them the opportunity to repent and return to the good purposes You had for them. One heart-melting instance of this is found in Isaiah 49, where God says to Israel, "Jerusalem says, 'The Lord has deserted us; the Lord has forgotten us.' 'Never! Can a mother forget her nursing child? Can she feel no love for the child she has borne? But even if that were possible, I would not forget you! See, I have written your name on the palms of my hands. Always in my mind is a picture of Jerusalem's walls in ruins. Soon your descendants will come back, and all who are trying to destroy you will go away'" (14–17 NLT). Thank You for Your unconditional love, for creating standards for us to live by that dignify us and help us to aspire to become better versions of ourselves, and for correcting us when we go astray and head toward paths that will end in destruction.

AMEN.

Asserting that Christ appointed him to serve on Christ's behalf, Paul thanks Christ for this privilege despite his initial virulent opposition to Christ:

> I thank him who has given me strength, Christ Jesus our Lord, because he judged me faithful, appointing me to his service, though formerly I was a blasphemer, persecutor, and insolent opponent. But I received mercy because I had acted ignorantly in unbelief, and the grace of our Lord overflowed for me with the faith and love that are in Christ Jesus. The saying is trustworthy and deserving of full acceptance, that Christ Jesus came into the world to save sinners, of whom I am the foremost. But I received mercy for this reason, that in me, as the foremost, Jesus Christ might display his perfect patience as an example to those who were to believe in him for eternal life. (1:12–16)

Thus, Christ not only forgave Paul for persecuting Him but anointed him as His special evangelist.

Paul clearly remains incredulous but exceedingly grateful that Christ chose Him as an apostle. He offers one factor, however, that makes it less difficult to grasp: he had acted ignorantly and in unbelief. We don't believe Paul is arguing that ignorance and unbelief excuse us from our sinfulness, for he describes himself as the foremost sinner (1:15). Ignorance of the law is no excuse. But if one continues flagrantly sinning while one is aware he is doing so, he is behaving worse than one who does so in ignorance.

Paul has always had a heart for God. He worshipped the God of the Bible, for the God of the Old Testament—Yahweh—is indeed the God of the New Testament. God never changes (James 1:17; Psalm 102:27; 1 Samuel 15:29; Heb. 13:8). But like the majority of his people, Paul didn't recognize Jesus as God, the Messiah, the Savior. Jews were expecting a military and political conqueror, and Christ was anything but that in His first coming. He thought Jesus and those promoting Him were imposters, so he thought he was serving the God of the Bible in opposing them. He did so with unparalleled passion and zeal, which might be an additional reason Christ chose him to become his special apostle—he would need such passion and fearlessness as the lead evangelist to a world initially hostile to the gospel. Paul does not get off the hook for being wrong about Christ. But Christ did forgive him because he responded when Christ opened his eyes, and he turned to Christ in faith. He wasn't forgiven because of his ignorance but because of his repentance and trust in Christ.

Paul might also be mentioning his ignorance and unbelief to contrast his circumstances with those of the heretics he is criticizing. "Most likely Paul is contrasting himself with the false teachers," says the *ESV Study Bible*. "When Paul so opposed Christ, he had not yet professed faith. These men profess to follow Christ and still live in an evil manner. In so doing, they are coming dangerously close to being cut off from the possibility of God's mercy."[16]

Chrysostom sheds additional light on the difference between Paul, who acted out of ignorance, and other Jews who were otherwise motivated. "Paul did not act, as some other Jews did, from the love of power, but from zeal," writes Chrysostom. "For what was the motive of his journey to Damascus? He thought the doctrine pernicious and was afraid that the preaching of it would spread everywhere."[17] Paul genuinely believed he was acting on behalf of the true God. He was not self-motivated but zealous to protect the God he had always known. Paul considered the preaching of Christ to be destructive to the law, but that was before he came to understand that Christ came not to destroy the law but to fulfill it (Matt. 5:17).[18]

That's no excuse in the end, however, as there are no second-place prizes: "For there is no distinction: for all have sinned and fall short of the glory of God, and are justified by his grace as a gift, through the redemption that is in Christ Jesus, whom God put forward as a propitiation by his blood, to be received by faith" (Romans 3:23–25). You either eventually find Jesus Christ or you do not. No matter how sincerely you may follow other "gods," your sincerity won't lead to your salvation. But Paul's distinct motivation from that of his fellow Jews made him a better choice for conversion. The others—inflated with their own pride and quest for power, fame, and respect—not so much.

Paul suggests another reason why Christ extended him mercy—to demonstrate His perfect patience as an example for other sinners (1:1–16). If Paul, the foremost sinner, can be saved, there is hope for everyone. "This was so that others could all say to themselves, 'if Paul was cured, why should I despair?'" says Augustine. "'If such a desperately sick man was cured by such a great physician, who am I, not to fit those hands to my wounds, not to hasten to the care of those hands?'"[19] Christ's decision to forgive Paul was thoroughly vindicated. Thereafter, Paul conducted himself with the highest moral standards and was dedicated to spreading the gospel for the rest of his life on earth, which he did better than anyone else in history.

Indeed, Christ chose Paul to be an integral figure in spreading the good news and in launching His church. In one of His resurrection appearances he told His disciples they would receive power from the Holy Spirit, and they would be His witnesses in Jerusalem and in all Judea and Samaria and to the ends of the earth (Acts 1:8). And during His earthly ministry He told His disciples, "Truly, truly, I say to you, whoever believes in me will also do the works that I do; and greater works than these will he do, because I am going to the Father" (John 14:12).

Some people question how Christ could say mere human beings could do works greater than He did. We find this plausible because:

- ★ He is God, and the Holy Spirit is God, and if they choose to empower other human beings to perform greater works, then that's the end of the matter. Their will be done.
- ★ He probably meant this in the sense that, because of their numbers and the people they would influence and evangelize, they would spread the gospel farther and wider than Jesus did during His earthly ministry since He was just one person whose travels were limited to a relatively small area.
- ★ We must also keep in mind that the Holy Spirit indwells those who believe and follow Christ, so it is actually Christ and His power that works through us to evangelize, heal the sick, cast out demons, and perform other miracles (Mark 16:17–18, Matthew 10:19–20). Therefore, we are simply the vessels Christ now uses to manifest His presence and carry out His will upon the earth.

It is moving that Christ entrusted human beings with the most important task ever to be undertaken on earth—the stewardship and spread of the gospel in Jerusalem and to the entire world. "The story of Paul illustrates that Christ's activity continues beyond his historical coming into the world," writes George Wieland. "Paul was empowered by Christ (12); the love that is in Christ was poured out upon him (14); and through showing mercy to Paul Christ demonstrated his patience, which he will continue to exercise for those who will believe in him (16)."[20]

It is sobering to reflect on these passages of scripture—in Acts, John, and 1 Timothy—and realize the profound importance of the charge Christ gave Paul, the apostles, and every believer and foot soldier in the army of His church. Most of us don't hold this divine responsibility close enough to our hearts and don't serve with the diligence and consistency of Paul. Who could? Without beating ourselves up, though, we should consider how these passages specify our role in serving Christ and our duty to spread the word with the goal of bringing the unsaved to Christ.

PRAYER

Jesus, give us hearts that burn for You, as the men on the road to Emmaus described after meeting you (Luke 24:32). The passion that motivated Paul and the other disciples came from being close to You; the disciples knew You firsthand, and Paul had an encounter with You on the road to Damascus. Though our encounters with You may not present themselves in physical manifestations, the more we seek to experience You in tangible ways, the more You will provide these encounters! "For everyone who asks, receives. Everyone who seeks, finds. And to everyone who knocks, the door will be opened" (Matthew 7:8 NLT). If we feel as though we could never be bold enough to spread Your word, if miracles seem completely out of the realm of possibility, please plant seeds of hope and desire in our hearts. May it not be said of us that we did not have because we did not ask (James 4:2). And help us also to remember that You never called us to do these things in our own strength. At the end of Your Great Commission to the disciples, You said, "And be sure of this: I am with you always, even to the end of the age" (Matthew 28:20). We want to know You deeply and see You perform great wonders through our lives. Use us, Lord!

AMEN.

Paul now turns back to Timothy and his task of resisting the false teachers. "This charge I entrust to you, Timothy, my child, in accordance with the prophecies previously made about you, that by them you may wage the good warfare, holding faith and a good conscience. By rejecting this, some have made shipwreck of their faith, among whom are Hymenaeus and Alexander, whom I have handed over to Satan that they may learn not to blaspheme" (1:18–20). While Timothy is Paul's favorite and his son in the faith, he isn't choosing him solely for this reason—he is acting in accordance with prophecies earlier made about him.

Paul distinguishes Timothy from Hymenaeus and Alexander in that Timothy holds to his faith and lives by it, resulting in a good conscience. That is, authentic faith produces righteous behavior, which leads to a good conscience. Granted, you can have a hardened heart and have no pangs of conscience, as one's conscience is a function of the moral standards it evaluates. Paul is talking about a faith-driven conscience grounded in biblical principles and fueled by the Holy Spirit. As he warned us in Romans, "Do not be conformed to this world, but be transformed by the renewal of your mind, that by testing you may discern what is the will of God, what is good and acceptable and perfect" (Romans 12:2). Douglas Moo notes, "When a believer has a renewed mind, his conscience testifies 'by means of' the Holy Spirit."[21] And as Paul told the Romans, "I am speaking the truth in Christ—I am not lying; my conscience bears me witness in the Holy Spirit" (Romans 9:1).

There is always cultural pressure to conform to the customs and standards of the world. We must reject that while proactively placing ourselves before God and allowing ourselves to be transformed from within, with a renewed mind.[22] Our sanctification through the Holy Spirit is an ongoing process, so if we are pursuing the Holy Spirit, we will constantly be transforming toward developing the mind of Christ.

As we mature in the faith we will better understand the mind of the Lord (1 Cor. 2:16).[23] "As a Christian is transformed in his mind and is made more like Christ, he comes to approve and desire God's will, not his own will for his life," writes J. A. Witmer. "Then he discovers that God's will is what is good for him, and that it pleases God, and is complete in every way. It is all he needs. But only by being renewed spiritually can a believer ascertain, do, and enjoy the will of God."[24]

If you hold fast to your faith—practice the spiritual disciplines and keep God close to your heart in prayer, in Bible reading and study, in meditating, and in sitting silent in God's presence and listening to Him—you will be better equipped to resist temptation and spiritual misconduct. By neglecting these things you'll have a more difficult time against the constant wiles of the enemy. But if you affirmatively reject the path of faith, as did Hymenaeus and Alexander, your faith will become shipwrecked and disintegrate. In "handing them over to Satan," Paul expelled them from church—not to permanently cast them out but to open their eyes to their own sinfulness and seek repentance. It was more corrective than a punitive measure.[25]

PRAYER

Lord, may we never be deceived into believing that we have "arrived" in our faith walk with you. Every single day we are faced with unique trials that test our faith, judgment, and dependence on You. If we trick ourselves into thinking that we've read the Bible enough times, prayed enough, or have come to a full understanding of a spiritual matter, correct us. Give us humility. Help us to understand that You ALWAYS have more to teach us and more goodness to provide through continual communion with You.

AMEN.

I (Christen) once heard a sermon wherein the pastor made a profound statement about reading God's word daily. He was correcting those of us who might be discouraged when we read a passage of scripture and fail to receive some type of divine revelation. He said, "If I asked you what you had for dinner three months ago, I bet you wouldn't be able to remember—but that doesn't mean that food didn't nourish you that day." He referenced Ephesians 5:25–26, where Paul explains that Jesus died to make His church holy by "cleansing them through the word." You see, reading the Bible actually cleanses our spirits by connecting us directly with the Father, whether we feel it in the moment or not. Therefore, let us not neglect meeting daily with God by reading His word and communicating with Him in prayer. We need constant connection with Him for our hearts to be at peace and aligned with His will.

CHAPTER 2

Paul urges believers to pray for all people, including those who are in authority, which will help us to live peaceful, quiet, godly, and dignified lives (2:1–2). He mentions different types of prayers—petitions, intercessions, and thanksgivings—all of which should be used. Petitions are requests to God for various things; intercession usually means to pray on someone else's behalf; and thanksgiving is a prayer of gratitude.[26] These verses urge us to pray for all kinds of things using all kinds of prayers, consistent with Paul's teaching to the Thessalonians to pray without ceasing (1 Thess. 5:17). He follows that verse with a command to "give thanks in all circumstances; for this is the will of God in Christ Jesus for you" (1 Thess. 5:18). God wants us to pray constantly and to have thankful hearts. From personal experience we all know the difference between grateful and ungrateful hearts and instinctively know that the former exhibits godly behavior and the latter the opposite.

It may seem odd that Paul would urge us to pray for our leaders, especially in the case of authoritarian governments, such as the Roman Empire he was living under. But praying for those in authority doesn't mean praying for tyranny or for autocratic leaders to succeed in oppressing their citizens. Let's remember that Jesus said, "But I say to you, Love your enemies and pray for those who persecute you" (Matt. 5:44).

We can petition God for an atmosphere that is conducive to evangelism and even to Christian liberty. As Christians we must pray for everyone, including bad authority figures, as no one is beyond God's reach. Indeed, Paul goes on to say in the next verse, "This is good, and it is pleasing in the sight of God our Savior, who desires all people to be saved and to come to the knowledge of the truth" (2:3–4). As God wants all people to be saved, it's only natural that we should pray for everyone, with particular emphasis on salvation for the unsaved.

Prayer

Heavenly Father, when we are under duress or experiencing persecution for our faith, please lift our minds above our circumstances and endow us with the faith described in Hebrews 11:1—to hope for things that are not yet seen and believe that You are working in every situation for Your good purposes, even if we're not seeing evidence of that in the natural realm within the time frame we had envisioned. If we can trust in You with all our hearts and lean not on our own understanding (Prov 3:5–6), we can sincerely give thanks in every situation. In faith we declare, "Let Your will be done, Lord!"

Amen.

We won't exhaustively discuss the differing views of Calvinists and Arminians on this point, which always seems divisive. But we should acknowledge there is a debate over the extent of God's atonement. Neither Calvinists nor Arminians believe that everyone will be saved (universalism), and scripture is clear that some will not be saved (among others, Matt. 25:30, 41, 46; Rev. 14:9–11). The *ESV Study Bible* states that Arminians believe God's strong desire is to preserve genuine human freedom (without which there cannot be true love), so He allows people to accept or reject His offer of salvation. Calvinists believe that God's greater desire is to display his glory, and that salvation depends on His sovereign election rather than human choice.[27]

This may be an oversimplification, and we'll leave this debate to the theologians, but we are comforted by Paul's straightforward, unambiguous, and God-breathed assurance that God wants all people to be saved and to come to the knowledge of the truth. This, to us, is consistent with the omnibenevolent God described in scripture and with Peter's inspired words, "The Lord is not slow to fulfill his promise as some count slowness, but is patient toward you, not wishing that any should perish, but that all should reach repentance" (2 Peter 3:9). Despite this disagreement, both Calvinists and Arminians believe that the gospel message has universal scope in the sense that it's not directed to people based on their race, sex, or national background.[28]

Paul continues, "For there is one God, and there is one mediator between God and men, the man Christ Jesus, who gave himself as a ransom for all, which is the testimony given at the proper time. For this I was appointed a preacher and an apostle (I am telling the truth, I am not lying), a teacher of the Gentiles in faith and truth" (1 Tim. 2:5–7). This passage takes us back to our earlier point: there is but one God, and there is but one way—not just the best way but the only way—to God, and that is through Jesus Christ. Some can wish away these words; they can, in their human error, claim this is an intolerant view. But the fact is, it's not a view at all. It is a divine declaration. Paul reinforces the authoritativeness of his assertion by citing his calling as a preacher and apostle. God chose Him, not the other way around. You better believe he is deadly serious about faith in Jesus Christ's being the exclusive path to the one God. There is no intolerance here; everyone is invited, but you have to come through Jesus, for there is no other avenue, religion, philosophy, or religious or secular figure in whom you can place your faith and be saved.

You can, of course, reject this declaration, but you cannot say the Bible is equivocal on the matter. To say there are other ways to God cannot be squared with scripture, so ignore or distort its words at your peril. There is nothing unloving or egotistical about it, either in human or divine terms. If you understand God's message to us in the Bible—and we've been rehearsing this point throughout these pages—you see there is no other way for sinful man to bridge the gap to God than by appropriating through faith the sacrificial death of His Son. No other religion or belief system can compete with this truth. This is not a hard saying. It is a loving statement because all believers, in accordance with God's will, should desire that all come to salvation in Christ.

For a believer to pretend that other religions are equally valid and offer other ways to salvation is to deny scripture, spit on the finished work of Christ, and voluntarily lead other people astray for the sake of pleasing man rather than God. Loving people means telling them the truth, not telling them what they want to hear, especially when the matter at hand involves eternal consequences. Yes, speak the truth winsomely, lovingly, and sensitively, but don't alter the truth, for that is the opposite of loving and is the height of selfishness.

PRAYER

The new age ideas touted rampantly in our era brand Christianity as exclusive, intolerant, and unloving. Most of us will at some point encounter people deceived by the spirit of this age. Therefore, we should not discount ourselves, no matter how underqualified we may feel, to rise to the calling God has placed on each of us to resist the devil and take a stand against his lies (James 4:7; Ephesians 6:13). While we are all given this command, God has also gifted each of us with unique traits. Jesus, we ask that You work in our hearts, allowing us to see how You intend to use our individual personalities to speak the true gospel to the people we meet. We recognize we are all created differently, so You will use us differently. For some of us, sharing the gospel will be a bold proclamation; for others, our witness may be displayed through the subtlety of a gentle spirit and a humble heart. But we trust that if we surrender ourselves to You and offer ourselves to be used as vessels for Your truth to shine through, nothing will be wasted. So we surrender in Your Blessed Name, Jesus,

AMEN.

Paul now turns to matters that are controversial to many modern readers. "I desire then that in every place the men should pray, lifting holy hands without anger or quarreling; likewise also that women should adorn themselves in respectable apparel, with modesty and self-control, not with braided hair and gold or pearls or costly attire, but with what is proper for women who profess godliness—with good works" (2:10). First, we notice that Paul is addressing men and women along gender lines. He first says men should pray in every place with holiness and in good spirits. He has already said that all should pray everywhere, so he isn't saying only men should pray. But he teaches here and elsewhere that men are the head of the household (and the church), and perhaps here he is simply saying that as such, they should set an example for the household and the church by leading them in prayer.

Doesn't it go without saying that prayer is holy? So why say it? Maybe it's because he wants us to be intentional about our prayer and not just go through the motions. He wants us to be mindful of the holiness of prayer, recognizing that in prayer we're not simply talking to a friend, brother, or parent, but to the God of the universe in whom complete holiness resides. We should be mindful of God's awesomeness while we are praying. This attitude will not deter intimacy with God. In fact, the rote, automatic prayer some engage in is more likely to lack intimacy.[29]

Paul forbids quarrelsome men from leading prayer because conflict and strained relationships distract from our ability to pray. Difficulty in our human relationships will interfere with our communications with God. Peter warned us about this in the context of our relationship with our spouses, saying we should show women honor and be understanding toward them "so that your prayers may not be hindered" (1 Peter 3:7). Jesus was also clear on the interconnection between our human relationships and our relationship with God, telling His disciples, "And whenever you stand praying, forgive, if you have anything against anyone, so that your Father also who is in heaven may forgive you your trespasses" (Mark 11:25). Likewise, James warned us about the toxic effect of anger: "Know this my beloved brothers: let every person be quick to hear, slow to speak, slow to anger; for the anger of man does not produce the righteousness of God" (James 1:19–20).

Paul says women should adorn themselves modestly. "As the men were to show their right attitudes with 'holy hands,' so the women in the Ephesian congregation were to show their holy attitudes with a modest outward appearance," writes Bruce Barton. "Paul emphasized that their internal character was far more important than their outward adornment." Barton insists Paul is not suggesting any extreme modesty but merely for women to dress in a way that is consistent with their culture and not to dress seductively or ostentatiously at church, which would detract from the worship service.[30]

Paul continues, "Let a woman learn quietly with all submissiveness. I do not permit a woman to teach or to exercise authority over a man; rather she is to remain quiet. For Adam was formed first, then Eve; and Adam was not deceived, but the woman was deceived and became a transgressor. Yet she will be saved through childbearing—if they continue in faith and love and holiness, with self-control" (2:11–15).

We must read these verses in the context of the entirety of scripture. Whereas society in those days treated women as less valuable than men, Jesus rejected that distinction, treating women as human beings of equal worth and dignity. While Paul teaches that women should have a submissive role in the church and the household, he is nevertheless respectful of women and alludes to their acceptable practices of prayer and prophecy (1 Cor. 11:5). For example, Paul commends Phoebe as a servant (the NLT describes her as a deacon) of the church at Cenchreae and tells the Romans to "welcome her in the Lord in a way worthy of the saints, and help her in whatever she may need from you, for she has been a patron of many and of myself as well" (Romans 16:1–2). Paul also respectfully describes Prisca, Nympha, Mary, and Lydia as heads of house churches (Romans 16:3, 6, 12; Acts 16:4, 15, 40), and Paul's friend Priscilla taught Apollos (Acts 18:26). "Paul's churches, then, had men and women leading, teaching, and making decisions in the church," writes Lynn Cohick.[31]

"While setting certain limits to the speaking and leadership role of women in the church, for reasons that are creation-based and historical, Paul recognizes everywhere the intrinsic worth of women

(1 Cor. 7:2ff; 11:11f; Gal 4:4), their equal status with men in the common salvation in Christ (Gal. 3:28), and praises their supportive ministries (e.g., Rom. 16:1–16; Phil 4:3)," writes Milne.[32] Additionally, as we noted in earlier chapters, Paul is talking about the differences between men and women in functional roles, not any difference in their essence. Men and women are of equal dignity as being born in God's image (Gen. 1:27).

Some commentators believe Paul is addressing women in the church at Ephesus who are trying to draw attention to themselves through their beauty rather than behaving in a Christlike manner. Christians faced many challenges in the pagan culture of Ephesus, where Artemis (or Diana) was celebrated as the goddess of fertility in erotic, carved representations. Wild orgies were even commonplace during the festival of Artemis.[33] Paul may have these influences in mind when he issues admonitions to the women of the Ephesian church.

Scholars debate whether Paul's further limitations on women—to learn quietly and submissively and not to teach or exercise authority over men—should be universally applied or limited to the cultural context in which Paul was writing. Those who argue for universal application point to Paul's reference to Adam and Eve, which suggests he wasn't merely talking about Ephesian women in the first century A.D. but saying that such functional hierarchies are inherent in God's creation plan.[34] Others disagree, saying Paul was not dealing with the social realities of twenty-first century Western life but a uniquely complicated situation in Ephesus.[35] Grant Osborne provides an interesting take, arguing that in Paul's time, for women to teach men would have been seen as their "lording" it over men. As our modern society doesn't accord teachers that degree of authority, women serving as teachers today would not violate the submissiveness Paul demands.[36]

Paul's final verse in this chapter, that women will be saved through childbearing, has given commentators fits. No fair reader of the text in the context of scripture as a whole can infer Paul is suggesting that salvation by faith does not apply to women, and no serious Bible interpreter reads it this way.[37] The New Testament also uses the term "saved" to describe the spiritual growth that occurs following salvation—the sanctification process. John MacArthur comments that Paul invokes childbearing and salvation in a different sense, not that of saving faith. Rather, since a woman precipitated the Fall, women may reverse that stigma through childbearing and raising godly children, as mothers in general spend much more time with their children than fathers. If they raise godly children and continue to live in faith, love, holiness, and self-restraint, they reverse the blight that has befallen them in the Fall.[38]

Walter Kaiser tackles this verse emphatically. "If there is one truth which Paul spent his entire ministry driving home to his listeners and readers, it is this: that salvation is not gained by the performance of functions and duties or the exercise of specific roles, but by faith in Jesus Christ," writes Kaiser. "It is therefore impossible to conclude that Paul is speaking about personal salvation. That is, women are not saved by any other means than men."

Kaiser believes we must read this difficult verse in light of the heretical teaching of the false teachers undermining the institution of marriage (1 Cor. 7). These teachers devalue the physical and material world, so it is fair to conclude they devalue marriage (and childbearing) and believe they are unworthy of saved people. Paul, Kaiser explains, rejects this heretical teaching, insisting that childbearing is a natural, necessary, and life-giving function and as such does not keep women "from full participation in the community of the saved." Had Paul not corrected this error, heretical teachers would have deceived women into believing they needed to reject their domestic and maternal roles to demonstrate they are among the saved. Therefore, Paul has to refute this viewpoint, which fundamentally misunderstands the gospel.[39] Furthermore, we might add, it also conflicts with God's command to go forth and multiply.

I (Christen) would further note that since giving birth to my first child—a son—the confidence I have in my faith has never been richer. I believe God (through Paul) is emphasizing the unique opportunity women have in experiencing the miracle of motherhood. Remember, God always has our best interest at heart. Whether naturally or by adoption, becoming a mother is one of the most profound demonstrations of God's love for us in that, through motherhood, our own capacity for love exponentially multiplies, and we see how much of our children's lives (and thus our own) are sustained purely by God's hand (Isaiah 46:4). Though strong fathers are equally as important in a child's life, most can agree that a mother's bond with her child is a precious gift that cannot be replicated. It is a role God uniquely bestowed on women, and those who have the ability and call to embrace this assignment will be immeasurably blessed by it. Thanks be to God!

PRAYER

Lord, we ask for divine discernment and patience while we read passages of scripture that are difficult for us to understand and might not sit well with us on our first reading. When the enemy tries to wage war in our minds and turn our hearts away from You, help us to remember the most crucial part of Your character: You sent Your one and only Son Jesus to die for us while we were still sinners. You are inherently upright and good, and there is no wickedness in You (Psalm 92:15). Rather than sweeping our feelings of

▶

confusion under the rug, please encourage us to dig deeper in our quest to understand You. Despite our fears of Your disapproval, You actually welcome our questions, concerns, and doubts. In fact, it is often these types of conundrums that draw us into a deeper relationship with You. May we humbly come before You to search these matters out and uncover more of Your perfect character in our pursuits.

AMEN.

CHAPTER 3

After addressing the conduct of public worship Paul sets out the qualifications for church officials. He delegates the task of church organization to Timothy, thus establishing the standards for his guidance—and for the direction of all who will read this letter in perpetuity. He specifies the requirements for overseers (3:1–7) and then deacons (3:8–12). By "overseers" Paul means pastors, elders, or others in a supervisory position. Paul uses the terms "pastor" and "elder" interchangeably to describe church officials, primarily teachers, who lead specific congregations. Deacons handle the administrative duties, including finances.[40] Paul is not here setting up a new position, as we see in Acts 14:23; 20:17, 28. Overseers already work in the churches. He is just intent on ensuring the proper people fill these positions.

He says that seeking these positions is a noble pursuit, which signals the importance he attaches to these roles. But the person seeking leadership must be of high caliber and want it for the right reasons—not out of ambition but to serve the Lord: "Therefore an overseer must be above reproach, the husband of one wife, sober-minded, self-controlled, respectable, hospitable, able to teach, not a drunkard, not violent but gentle, not quarrelsome, not a lover of money. He must manage his household well, with all dignity keeping his children submissive, for if someone does not know how to manage his own household, how will he care for God's church?" (3:1–5).

These qualifications are straightforward, but we should note that Paul is concerned both with the person's good character and his reputation in the community. It's important that all Christians are good witnesses for Christ, but it is especially so for church leaders. They must be moderate, respectable, committed, and obedient. They must prudently manage their own affairs before they can be trusted to manage those of others. Their performance as parents and heads of the household will also reflect on their ability to manage church affairs and their leadership abilities. If a father's children respect him, it's a good indication he commands respect. The converse is also true: if your children don't respect you, church members may not either. This entire section strikes us as another divine endorsement of the family unit and of marriage, both institutions having been established by God (Gen. 2:20–25, 4:1).

Paul continues, "He must not be a recent convert, or he may become puffed up with conceit and fall into the condemnation of the devil. Moreover, he must be well thought of by outsiders, so that he may not fall into disgrace, into a snare of the devil" (3:6–7). When people are first saved, they lack spiritual maturity and judgment. We all remember the enthusiasm we initially had and possibly the tendency to believe we knew more about the Bible than we actually did. It would not have been wise for us to have been placed in leadership positions in our spiritual infancy—not good for the congregation or for us. For if one is rapidly elevated into leadership he might succumb to the temptation of pride—power has a tendency to corrupt, which opens one up to all kinds of mischief. While we are still experiencing spiritual growing pains, it's better to make our mistakes outside the view of witnesses than to reflect poorly on our position and thus on our faith.

Furthermore, Augustine asks, "What does Paul mean by saying 'or he may be puffed up with conceit and fall into the condemnation of the devil'?" He suggests "it doesn't mean he is to be judged by the devil but that he is to be condemned with the devil. The devil, after all, won't be our judge. He himself fell through pride."[41] We must realize why pride is such an egregious sin—it's mainly because it is the opposite mindset of faith. To be puffed up with pride is to make yourself an idol. The mere flirtation with this sin is dangerous because it places you on your own, seemingly self-sufficient and with no need to trust God—the perfect place for the devil to snatch you up and close the deal.

Paul points out another pitfall that plays into the devil's hands: falling into disgrace and losing respect among those outside the church. Good witnesses for Christ will attract others to the faith, while poor witnesses assist the devil in deterring others who may be looking for any excuse not to become believers. Many nonbelievers mistakenly believe that following Christ demands that we all become boring scolds and that our lives involve little more than rigorously following religious rules and regulations. If church leaders (or members) behave poorly, they provide the devil fodder to turn people further away from the church. Surely you've seen this in your own life, where a non-churchgoer displays contempt for "hypocritical" Christians. "Christians must realize that unbelievers scrutinize their actions with a searchlight of fault-finding investigation," writes Thomas Lea. So Paul is appealing to church leaders not to give Satan an opening by making it easier for unbelievers to find fault in them.[42]

Turning to deacons, Paul says they "likewise must be dignified, not double-tongued, not addicted to much wine, not greedy for dishonest gain" (3:8). The deacons have a lesser position than overseers but still perform important tasks in the public eye. Because of their public profile, they must be as upright as the overseers. They must be men of dignity and respect and be honest and sincere. Additionally, Paul adds, "They must hold the mystery of the faith with a clear conscience" (3:9). That is, they must have spiritual depth, pursue biblical knowledge, and act consistently with their beliefs. Just like the overseers, they must have some spiritual maturity and not be entirely new to the faith, which is what Paul means by saying they must be tested and show themselves qualified before serving in the position (3:10). Their wives must also be "dignified, not slanderers, but sober-minded, faithful in all things" (3:11). Some commentators believe the text refers only to male deacons' wives, while others say it means women generally. Either way, prominent women in the church are held to the same general high behavioral and reputational standards as men.

Paul instructs that deacons must "be the husband of one wife, managing their children and their own houses well" (3:12). That is, they must be faithful to their wives and be good household stewards, just as is required of the overseers. Paul adds that "those who serve well as deacons gain a good standing for themselves and also great confidence in the faith that is in Christ Jesus" (3:13). Thus, deacons who perform their role competently are rewarded with a good reputation among believers and a comforting assurance in their saving faith. It's one thing to have baseless pride in one's standing before God, but assurance from faithful service is another. This assurance "results from putting faith into practice in the service of the congregation, and finding Christ faithful in giving strength to those who humbly depend on him," writes Milne, who appropriately cites Philippians 4:13: "I can do all things through him who strengthens me."[43]

In closing this chapter, Paul reinforces his reasons for writing to Timothy. He wants to ensure that if he is delayed in coming to Timothy, Timothy will understand and teach to others proper behavior in God's church, which is "a pillar and buttress of the truth" (3:14–16). Paul is commissioning and enlightening Timothy to impart the message of this epistle to all the churches. These instructions are not just about church leadership and management, however, but have a broader application for all Christians, whom Paul urges to grow spiritually and conduct themselves in a Christ-like manner.[44]

Prayer

Lord, we pray for spiritual leaders throughout the global church; taking on the responsibilities Paul details in this chapter comes with a tremendous amount of responsibility and all kinds of spiritual attacks. We thank You for creating men and women who have dedicated their lives to serving You wholeheartedly, and we ask You to protect these heads of the faith from temptation, sickness, spiritual warfare, persecution, depression, and pride. Reveal to us areas involving our leaders in which we need to repent—perhaps we have harshly critiqued them or have only taken when You've called us to give. Many of us fail to see our pastors and deacons as ordinary human beings who have the same needs as the rest of us—if we have done this in any way, show us how we can be better. In Your Name, Jesus,

Amen.

The final verse of the chapter contains what many believe was an early church creed or hymn. Paul says, "Great indeed, we confess, is the mystery of godliness: He was manifested in the flesh, vindicated by the Spirit, seen by angels, proclaimed among the nations, believed on in the world, taken up in glory" (3:16). Walter Kaiser shares a helpful explanation of this creed by R. A. Falconer. Falconer writes:

> In 1 Tim. the Church, the house in which God dwells, takes a place of great importance as the organized body which guarantees the truth. This truth is a healthy doctrine, but in 1. Tim. 3:16 it is also equivalent of "the mystery of godliness," and is set forth in a hymn which contains the salient features of the historic manifestation of Jesus Christ, what we might term an outline "gospel." The hymn seems most simply interpreted as referring to the Incarnation; the recognition of Divine Sonship in the Baptism, Temptation, Transfiguration; the revelation of the historic Jesus to the heavenly world, as e.g. to the celestial choir at His birth, the Transfiguration, Gethsemane (Lk 22:43), the Resurrection (Lk 24:4, 5);...the preaching to the Gentiles; the founding of the Church in the world; and the culmination of His triumph in the Ascension.[45]

We believe Paul includes this hymn, in part, to further impress on Timothy the esteemed content of the message of this epistle and the gravity of the task Paul is entrusting to him. He is talking about God's revelations about the very Son of God. Timothy always must be mindful of this as he spreads the gospel and instructs pastors and other church leaders. This will ensure, in the words of John Calvin, that they will discharge their duties with "greater conscientiousness and deeper reverence."[46]

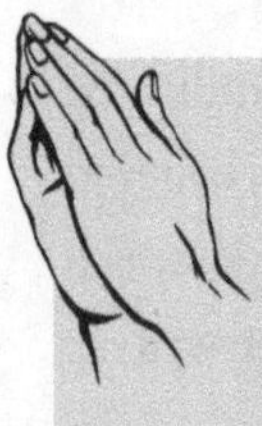

PRAYER

Psalm 84 exemplifies the type of dedication and reverence we should look to as a standard for our individual relationships with God:

> How lovely is your dwelling place,
> O Lord of Heaven's Armies.
> I long, yes, I faint with longing
> to enter the courts of the Lord (1–2 NLT).

Jesus, we praise and thank You for dying for our sins so that we might be saved and have intimacy with You. We ask that as we come to know You personally, our veneration for You would increase. As we come to know You on a deeper level, our eyes are opened to just how majestic, holy, and worthy of praise You truly are. The depth of Your goodness has no bounds. We come to You and ask for more of Your presence, more of Your wisdom, and more of the strength we need to pursue You in ways we have not yet experienced or imagined. Blessed be Your Name, Jesus,

AMEN.

CHAPTER 4

Paul opens this chapter by exclaiming, "Now the Spirit expressly says that in later times some will depart from the faith by devoting themselves to deceitful spirits and teachings of demons, through the insincerity of liars whose consciences are seared, who forbid marriage and require abstinence from foods that God created to be received with thanksgiving by those who believe and know the truth. For everything created by God is good, and nothing is to be rejected if it is received with thanksgiving, for it is made holy by the word of God and prayer" (4:1–5).

Paul here attributes the false teachers' betrayal of the faith to the designs and allures of demons and deceitful spirits. Most scholars agree that "in later times" means the period from Christ's resurrection to His return,[47] and indeed, people have been tricked unwittingly into following evil spirits throughout Christian history. Often masquerading as anything but evil, the spirits lure people away from the true teachings of the Bible and thus away from the Christian faith. Jesus issued similar warnings (Mark 13:21–23), as did Peter (2 Peter 3:1–18) and Jude (Jude 17–19). Paul clearly warns that these people, steeped in evil spirits and with seared consciences, will confuse them about correct Christian doctrine. Notice, too, that idolatry is involved in the mix, for the misguided will "devot[e] themselves to deceitful spirits and teachings of demons." You can't worship the true God if you are devoted to false ones or those teaching lies and undermining scripture.

Some commentators argue that "deceitful spirits" and "demons" don't refer to actual demons, but most believe they do, and we think it's the reasonable interpretation. As we covered in Chapter Three on Ephesians, Paul unmistakably reveals that "we do not wrestle against flesh and blood, but against the rulers, against the authorities, against the cosmic powers over this present darkness, against the spiritual forces of evil in the heavenly places" (Eph. 6:12). We also recognize, however, that these evil spirits usually don't manifest themselves in spiritual form but through human agents doing their evil work for them.

These people are ripe targets because their consciences are seared, and they readily deceive anyone who will succumb to their lies. As Satan disguises himself as an angel of light, it is fitting that his agents would use the same tactic: "For such men are false apostles, deceitful workmen, disguising themselves as apostles of Christ. And no wonder, for even Satan disguises himself as an angel of light.

So it is no surprise if his servants, also, disguise themselves as servants of righteousness" (2 Cor. 11:13–15). It is bad enough when people follow their own cultish religions and lead people away from the one true God, but it is particularly pernicious for these false teachers to slither into Christ's church and attempt to corrupt it from within, which is more damaging to the gospel by orders of magnitude. Paul knows the church will be destroyed before it fully takes off if he doesn't ensure these heresies are forcefully rejected.

The deceivers pretend to be faithful authorities on scripture while leading people away from its teachings, such as forbidding marriage and requiring abstinence from foods that God wants people to eat with gratitude. By establishing strict rules about certain aspects of eating and drinking, these false teachers present themselves as superior moral authorities and impose a kind of legalism that contradicts the gospel; for we cannot attain our salvation through strict discipline but only through faith in Christ. While we must proactively avoid sin in our lives (including even avoiding overindulgence in material pleasures), we know that we'll never achieve perfect sinlessness. We should be even more vigilant against false ideas such as the notion that what we do is more important than in whom we place our trust.

Paul further objects to false teaching because it originates from the false premise that the material world is evil, which is a direct affront to God—His word is clear that everything He created is good (Gen. 1). So, as we saw above, Paul affirms Genesis when he tells Timothy, "For everything created by God is good, and nothing is to be rejected if it is received with thanksgiving, for it is made holy by the word of God and prayer" (4:4–5). Paul here reminds us that we must give thanks to God for our nourishment and dedicate the food to His glory (1 Cor. 10:31). "The food we eat is sanctified (set apart, devoted to God) when we pray and give thanks; so the Word of God and prayer turn even an ordinary meal into a spiritual service for God's glory," writes Warren Wiersbe.[48] Blessing food in prayer does not make it more sanctified; God already created it to be good. But it does properly focus our minds on its sacredness and God's provision for us.[49]

PRAYER

In his novel *The Screwtape Letters*, C. S. Lewis uses a fictional character, Screwtape, to depict how Satan and his underlings work in the lives of human beings to lead us to death through deception. He writes, "Indeed the safest road to Hell is the gradual one—the gentle slope, soft underfoot, without sudden turnings, without milestones, without signposts." Perhaps his inspiration came from 1 Peter 5:8: "Be sober, be vigilant; because your adversary the devil, as a roaring lion, walketh about, seeking whom he may devour" (KJV). Jesus, help us to follow Your instructions to be vigilant, alert, and prepared to stand against the devil's schemes to lead us astray through subtle and gradual deception. Lead us to come to You regularly, seeking knowledge that is firmly rooted in Your word. You instructed us in Matthew 7, "Enter through the narrow gate. For wide is the gate and broad is the road that leads to destruction, and many enter through it. But small is the gate and narrow the road that leads to life, and only a few find it" (13–14 NLT). We recognize how profoundly important it is for us to stay in line with Your will and Your word, and we ask that when we start to wander off the narrow path, You pull us back to it swiftly. In Your Name we lift these requests,

AMEN.

As you'll remember, Paul is even more detailed in his criticism of false teachings about food and drink in his letter to the Colossians:

"If with Christ you died to the elemental spirits of the world, why, as if you were still alive in the world, do you submit to regulations—'Do not handle, Do not taste, Do not touch' (referring to things that all perish as they are used)—according to human precepts and teachings? These have indeed an appearance of wisdom in promoting self-made religion and asceticism and severity to the body, but they are of no value in stopping the indulgence of the flesh" (Col. 2:20–23).

We should be clear, however, that while everything God created is good, created things are not themselves divine and must not be worshipped. Other religions and philosophies through the years have worshipped physical idols and celestial bodies such as the sun and the moon. In so doing, notes Augustine, they "deny that God created those things which the apostle [Paul] plainly declares to the creatures of God, when he says of good, 'Every creature of God is good, and nothing to be refused, if it is received with thanksgiving.' This is sound doctrine.... The apostle praises the creature of God but forbids the worship of it. And in the same way Moses gives due praise to the sun and moon, while at the same time he states the fact of their having been made by God. They have been placed by him in their courses—the sun to rule the day, and the moon to rule the night."[50]

Paul now encourages Timothy directly to put these teachings into practice: "If you put these things before the brothers, you will be a good servant of Christ Jesus, being trained in the words of the faith and of the good doctrine that you have followed" (4:6). Again and again, Paul stresses the importance of studying and rightly handling scripture. It is essential that preachers and teachers of the word correctly understand it and pass on good doctrine to others because it will have a reverberating effect. If teachers dilute the word, it will become even more corrupted down the line. If they insist on purity—staying true to correct doctrine—that purity will be passed on by their students to those they teach. Even a gifted preacher or teacher can't rely solely on his knowledge or memory. He must stay in the word and treat it as his true north. Our minds and memories are fallible. The word of God is not.

PRAYER

Father, may Your holy word be the first place we run when we are seeking wisdom, insight, and connection with You. You describe the wisdom found in Your word in Proverbs 8 in great detail. Verses 5–8 of *The Passion Translation* declare,

> *I'm calling to you, sons of Adam,*
> *yes, and to you daughters as well.*
> *Listen to me and you will be prudent and wise.*
> *For even the foolish and feeble can receive an understanding heart*
> *that will change their inner being.*
> *The meaning of my words will release within you revelation*
> *for you to reign in life.*
> *My lyrics will empower you to live by what is right.*
> *For everything I say is unquestionably true,*
> *and I refuse to endure the lies of lawlessness—*
> *my words will never lead you astray.*
> *All the declarations of my mouth can be trusted;*
> *they contain no twisted logic or perversion of the truth.*
> *All my words are clear and straightforward to everyone*
> *who possesses spiritual understanding.*
> *If you have an open mind, you will receive revelation-knowledge.*

We want to know Your word like the back of our hands. Please increase our spiritual understanding and illuminate scriptures to us that You'd like us to memorize and hold in our hearts, and help us to come to You daily by reading Your word.

AMEN.

Elaborating on this theme, Paul tells Timothy to avoid "irreverent, silly myths" (4:7). He is simply stating that while correct doctrine promotes individual and corporate spiritual growth and unity, frivolous and mythical teaching will degrade the spiritual health of individuals and the church as a whole. Paul also tells Timothy he must train himself for godliness. Physical training is useful (Paul said he disciplines his body and keeps it under control in 1 Corinthians 9:26), but it's nothing compared to spiritual training, which provides incalculable value both for this life and the life to come.

Spiritual training, or "godliness," is profitable for all things. It enhances all aspects of temporal and eternal life and blesses everything.[51] Therefore, says Paul, we toil and strive toward this goal "because we have our hope set on the living God, who is the Savior of all people, especially of those who believe" (4:10). As we've seen, Paul often uses athletic terms and those implying physical exertion in describing the effort Christians must expend in honoring God's will that they stay in the word and spread the gospel. He doesn't tell us it will be easy. In fact, he guarantees us it will be difficult and that we'll experience hardship and persecution along the way.

No one demonstrated that more than Christ Himself. So Paul tells us we must "toil and struggle," "run with endurance," "run the race" in pursuit of "the heavenly prize," and "fight the good fight." Worthwhile things—and nothing is more worthwhile than learning and teaching correct doctrine and spreading the gospel—are worth fighting and expending effort for. And we have the best possible incentive to expend this effort—honoring the living God, who gives us our salvation through faith in His Son. "To suffer persecution for the hope which is in God is something which is perfectly worthy and must be endured, because in the present life hope leads nowhere, but in the promise of God it is firm and certain," writes Ambrosiaster. ".... God has promised that after this life, which ends in death, he will give another one, which lasts forever, to those who know him."[52]

Commentators generally agree that when Paul says God is the savior of all people, he isn't teaching universalism—that everyone will be saved—for throughout his writings he stresses that salvation is by faith alone. He means here that salvation is offered to everyone but only attained by those who trust in Christ. Church Father Origen interprets Paul's language this way: "According to our preaching, Jesus who is called the Christ of God...has come on behalf of sinners in all places, that they may forsake their sin and entrust themselves to God." Likewise, Augustine observes, "You see, if Christ is the Savior of all, especially of the faithful—it is the apostle's [Paul's] judgment, and a true one, that Christ is the Savior of all—then nobody may say, 'I have no need of a savior.' If you say this, you are not bowing humbly to the doctor's orders but perishing in your disease."[53] A succinct way of expressing this is, "Christ is the Savior for all, but his salvation becomes effective only for those who trust Him."[54] Paul is addressing Timothy and other believers here, so by telling them God's salvation applies to them—because they have appropriated the finished work of Christ and attained eternal life—he is reminding them that their hope in God is not in vain but has already paid them incalculable dividends.

Paul continues with his pep-talk to Timothy, telling him again that he must "command and teach these things" that he has set out in the letter. He must not be discouraged by those who would dismiss him and undervalue his authority because he is young. Rather, he must dispel any doubt by setting an example in his speech, conduct, love, faith, and purity. Paul has chosen Timothy as his spiritual son and delegated to him the weighty task of being the primary evangelist to the Gentiles in Paul's absence (due to his imprisonment.) Timothy, whose talents led Paul to choose him, must recognize his gifts and rise to the occasion, delivering the gospel message boldly and authoritatively, not tentatively as might typify someone of Timothy's age. If Timothy doesn't speak with authority, his listeners won't find him credible. A confident and authoritative demeanor will enhance his effectiveness, but so will his walking the Christian walk, showing himself worthy of Paul's trust because he reflects Christlike behavior and spiritual maturity. Paul is certain Timothy is up to the task, but he wants to make sure Timothy himself shares Paul's confidence in him.

Paul adds that until he returns to Timothy, Timothy must devote himself "to the public reading of Scripture, to exhortation, to teaching" (4:13). Some commentators suggest Paul is presenting a model here for public worship. But Gordon Fee says we know from historical sources that public worship also includes "prayers, singing, charismatic utterances, and the Lord's Supper," so public reading, preaching, and teaching are too limited to be a template for public worship. Rather, says Fee, these three commands essentially refer to the same thing—the reading, exhortation, and exposition of scripture. In this way Paul is dovetailing his message throughout this letter, as he is telling Timothy to focus on scripture to counter the false teachers. Paul is saying that Timothy should read, preach, and teach scripture—including the current letter—to the church body.[55]

We find this analogous to Paul's teaching that Christians must put on the whole armor of God to engage in inevitable spiritual battles (Eph. 6:10–18). False teachers are no less than spiritual enemies, and they come armed for battle with their lies. They must be countered with the truth—the inerrant word of God—and Timothy is to steep himself in the word and to bathe his congregation and other believers in it, to insulate them against the onslaught of the devil.

Paul tells Timothy not to neglect his spiritual gift that he was given through prophecy when the council of elders laid their hands on him. Every believer is given spiritual gifts, and Timothy is abundantly endowed with them, but the passage does not specify the precise gift Paul has in mind here. Some scholars infer that the gift must be related to Timothy's position as minister and leader of the church. In any event, Paul is reminding Timothy that he has the requisite credentials to perform his important functions, and he must not squander his gift but use it to the fullest for God's glory. Now is not the time for Timothy to go wobbly. Despite his youth, he needs to graciously accept his gift and maximize it.

PRAYER

Jesus, in Your earthly ministry You demonstrated such empathy for all people, from the most prestigious members of society to the outcasts and gravest sinners. You have always called people to be the best versions of themselves—the people You created them to be. May we not neglect building one another up as You did and as Paul exemplifies in his encouragement to young Timothy. You call us not just to treat one another with dignity and respect but to take our interactions one step further, speaking life and light into our fellow man. One way we can do this is by calling out the goodness we see in others—the impact of this type of encouragement is immeasurable. Make us more like You, Lord, and give us the confidence to make this a habit in our lives, even if we initially feel awkward in doing it. The more we practice this type of grace, seasoning our speech with salt, the easier it will be. Thank You for being such an incredibly loving Savior and friend, Jesus. We love You!

AMEN.

Paul closes the chapter with this word of encouragement and support: "Practice these things, immerse yourself in them, so that all may see your progress. Keep a close watch on yourself and on the teaching. Persist in this, for by so doing you will save both yourself and your hearers" (4:15–16). Common sense principles and practices haven't changed in two thousand years. Perhaps that's because our principles primarily derive from biblical teachings such as these. It's as if Paul is telling Timothy to memorize the instructions in this letter and make them part of his makeup. If he learns these lessons and then diligently applies them, believers will see his progress and the church will thrive. Success in practice speaks louder than words and professions of self-confidence. If Timothy obediently follows Paul's commands the church will respect him, and any question about his age and inexperience will be put to bed.

In telling Timothy to keep a close watch on himself and on his teaching, Paul is reiterating that his deportment matters—that is, how he lives his life matters. He must set a Christlike example, for if church leaders don't exhibit such conduct, how can we expect regular church members to do so? In addition, Timothy must be careful in his teaching. He has been assigned stewardship over God's word, and there is no graver responsibility. "Moral and doctrinal rectitude are the inseparable twins of the Christian life," writes Thomas Lea.[56]

Finally, Paul tells Timothy to persist—to persevere in following his instructions and thereby save himself and his hearers. Again, Paul is not suggesting that Timothy will earn his salvation but that through his obedience he will grow spiritually. His perseverance in sound doctrine and Christian living will enhance his faith and give him further assurance of salvation.[57] And while only God can save sinners, He often does so through evangelizing human agents. Thus, correct doctrinal teaching of the gospel is essential in bringing others to an authentic saving faith. Remember the words of James: "My brothers, if anyone among you wanders from the truth and someone brings him back, let him know that whoever brings back a sinner from his wandering will save his soul from death and will cover a multitude of sins" (James 5:19–20).

PRAYER

Holy Spirit, fill our hearts with compassion for the people in our lives whom we find most difficult. Help us to see them as Your children whom we are called to love despite their behavior and resistance to You and Your will. May our frustration be replaced with fortitude to share the gospel by any means You show us. Thank You for the opportunity to share Your gospel with all people.

AMEN.

CHAPTER 5

Paul's instructions now become more specific. Prior to this point his letter addresses Timothy and the entire church, but now he shifts into advice for certain groups who might need more care, such as widows, slaves, and the elderly. "Do not rebuke an older man," says Paul, "but encourage him as you would a father, younger men as brothers, older women as mothers, younger women as sisters, in all purity" (5:1–2). Paul is giving instructions to Timothy and all future pastors and church leaders on basic pastoral relationships with people in the church. To some extent he particularizes his advice to Timothy as a young pastor, as he has not had as much experience in human relationships as an older leader would have. It might be awkward for any younger man in a position of leadership to exercise authority over an older man, as the natural inclination is to defer to elders, out of respect and because of their greater life experience.

So Paul succinctly instructs Timothy not to rebuke an older man but to encourage him as you would a father. This analogy saves Paul hundreds of words because Timothy will instantly understand in general how to treat a father. In short, he is telling Timothy and other leaders to treat elder gentlemen lovingly and respectfully—as they would their fathers—and to correct them, when necessary, with grace and charity.[58] Paul's teaching is in line with Old Testament scripture concerning respect for the elderly: "You shall stand up before the gray head and honor the face of an old man, and you shall fear your God: I am the Lord" (Lev. 19:32).

We all recognize that it's difficult to correct anyone tactfully, especially an older person. But we can imagine situations where it's necessary, such as when doctrine or church discipline is involved. "It is possible to correct without offense, if one will only make a point of this: it requires great discretion, but it may be done," writes Chrysostom.[59] Indeed, Paul wouldn't bother giving this advice if elders never needed to be corrected.

Continuing the family analogy, Paul tells Timothy to treat younger men as brothers, which means he shouldn't lord his age and position over them but treat them as equals. Paul logically makes his relationship advice gender specific, because again, it saves hundreds of words, and one doesn't treat his mother and sisters quite the same way he treats his father and brothers. But the same principle is conveyed—treat them respectfully, gently, and with charity and grace. By adding that he is to treat younger women as sisters in all purity, he is reminding Timothy he must treat younger women protectively and never cross any sexual boundaries.

Paul next moves to widows, who are typically treated as objects of God's mercy (Deut. 10:18; 14:29; 24:17–21; Acts 6:1–7; James 1:27). The early church charitably assisted widows, but after several decades this practice is taking a big financial toll. This is why Paul distinguishes between truly needy widows and others. He says that if widows have children or grandchildren, they should step up first, which is pleasing to God.[60] But the church should also assist widows without such descendants. Such widows characteristically put their hope in God and pray night and day.

Paul notes, however, that some self-indulgent widows are already spiritually dead. John Calvin interprets this as women who abuse their widowhood to lead easy and luxurious lives.[61] Some commentators, but not all, believe Paul is implying sensuality. Regardless, they are not needy in the sense that other widows are and thus not to be subsidized in the same way. So, simply put, Paul is saying that because church assets are limited, support for widows must be reserved for the truly needy ones, not those whose families can support them or those who exploit their position.

Paul continues, "Command these things as well, so that they may be without reproach" (5:7), meaning Timothy should provide all the foregoing instructions concerning widows and their families to the church congregants so that no one will be blamed. There is no consensus as to whom Paul is referring when he says "they may be without reproach," and translators aren't even aligned here. John MacArthur's interpretation is helpful: "The goal of Paul's teaching is that all involved, widows, families, and the church be above reproach so that no one can find fault with their conduct in this matter."[62] This will protect all individuals involved and the church from criticism. Paul next emphatically asserts that anyone who doesn't provide for his relatives, especially members of his own household, has denied the faith and is worse than an unbeliever (5:8). Thus, if you don't take care of your family, you are so outside the gospel experience that you are effectively denying the faith. Even many unbelievers support their families.

Paul then offers more details on support for widows: "Let a widow be enrolled if she is not less than sixty years of age, having been the wife of one husband, and having a reputation for good works: if she has brought up children, has shown hospitality, has washed the feet of the saints, has cared for the afflicted, and has devoted herself to every good work" (5:9–10). So a qualifying widow must be at least sixty years old, have been faithful to her husband, and be known for her Christian behavior.

On the other hand, younger widows should not be supported because "when their passions draw them away from Christ, they desire to marry and so incur condemnation for having abandoned their former faith" (5:11–12). These types also learn to be idlers, gossips, and busybodies (5:13). Paul's advice, then, is that younger widows should marry, have children, and manage their households, which will insulate them from criticism (5:14). "For some have already strayed after Satan," he argues. "If any believing woman has relatives who are widows, let her care for them. Let the church not be burdened, so that it may care for those who are truly widows" (5:15–16).

This is a challenging verse because it feels out of place in the narrative and because Paul seems to excuse male relatives from supporting these widows. Some scholars don't believe men are excluded here but that Paul is just emphasizing that well-to-do women should also do their part so as to reduce the church's financial burdens. The thrust of the entire section is to limit the church's support only to truly needy widows.[63] So Paul seems to provide a means-test for widows' support while insisting that people must not seek aid due to situations arising from their own selfishness, licentiousness, or faithlessness. No institution, government, church, or private entity can long afford to indiscriminately offer support for everyone. Attempts to do so are unwarranted, often counterproductive, and damaging to the institutions, in this case, the church.

Prayer

Lord, we come to You seeking peace and generosity in our relationships. While we can't control the actions of others, we do have the ability to demonstrate grace when it comes to our own decisions. Paul's instructions in this chapter require a higher level of self-control than what we often feel we are capable of living out. The key to following many of these instructions is generosity—with our finances, our time, and our attentiveness to the needs of others. So we come to You, Holy Spirit, and ask You to increase the spirit of generosity in our hearts. When sinful, territorial feelings start to creep in, remind us of Your promise in Proverbs 11:25: "the generous will prosper; those who refresh others will themselves be refreshed" (NLT). Show us people in our lives, both young and old, whom we can love better. And help us to remember that it is not up to us as individuals to change the entire world; as the *Life Application Bible* highlights, "The church has always had limited resources, and it has always had to balance financial responsibility with generosity.... When church members are both responsible and generous, everyone's needs will be met." When we all follow Your whispers and play our part, You will meet our needs. Please instill in us Your spirit of generosity so that, in keeping with Your will, people of material abundance will graciously provide for the needs of the poor. Thank You for Your intimate care for all of us.

Amen.

Having insisted on honoring legitimate widows earlier in the chapter, Paul now says that elders—especially those who preach and teach—are worthy of double honor (5:17). Some interpreters believe Paul is talking about double the respect, while others believe he's talking about twice the compensation. Regardless, his command underscores the importance Paul attaches to church leadership and even more to preaching and teaching, consistent with his repeated theme of learning and teaching correct doctrine.

Some Christians criticize "book knowledge" (the intellectual aspects of Christianity), as if it is inferior to other facets of the faith. But Paul's continued emphasis on Bible study, preaching, and teaching, and his fervor for correct teaching and against false teaching, make it clear that he highly values the study and exposition of scripture. Other biblical passages convey the same message: "Remember your leaders, those who spoke to you the word of God. Consider the outcome of their way of life, and imitate their faith" (Heb. 13:7); and "Jesus Christ is the same yesterday and today and forever. Do not be led away by diverse and strange teachings" (Heb. 13:8–9).

In support of his command, Paul cites two verses: "You shall not muzzle an ox when it treads out the grain," and, "The laborer deserves his wages" (5:18). The first verse, from Deuteronomy 25:4, means those expecting work from an ox shouldn't muzzle it and prevent it from eating while it is working. That is, Christian service is something we all owe the Lord, but those who engage in it professionally should still be able to earn a living. The second verse—a saying by Jesus as recorded in Matthew 10:10 and Luke 10:7—is self-explanatory. Granted, Paul himself declines payment for his services, but it's not because he believes church congregations shouldn't pay for their leaders' services. Rather, he knows how instrumental his teaching is, and he doesn't want any questioning of his motives to undermine his message (1 Cor. 9:15–23; 1 Thes. 2:9). He feels completely honor-bound to preach the gospel but is not recommending that other Christian servants forego their just compensation or that the church should expect their services for free (1 Cor. 9:4–10; Gal. 6:6).

Just as Paul is acutely aware of false teachers attempting to corrupt the church, he also realizes that others will oppose the ministry of the churches. Because this could lead to false charges against the leaders, he adds safeguards against spurious allegations: "Do not admit a charge against an elder except on the evidence of two or three witnesses" (5:19). This is consistent with Old Testament (Deut. 19:15) and New Testament teachings (Matt. 18:16; John 8:17; 2 Cor. 13:1). But he doesn't want to immunize leaders from legitimate charges of misconduct, so he instructs, "As for those who persist in sin, rebuke them in the presence of all, so that the rest may stand in fear" (5:20).[64] To permit leaders' sins to go unpunished is dangerous enough to the church that it warrants public rebuke.

Given the gravity of this punitive action, Paul insists that Timothy and other church administrators safeguard the process against any prejudice. Those today who believe biblical-era thinking and practices were unsophisticated do not appreciate the maturity of these teachings. Paul says, "In the presence of God and of Christ Jesus and of the elect angels I charge you to keep these rules without prejudging, doing nothing from partiality" (5:21). He conveys here that these matters are so important that God, Christ, and the angels will be monitoring them. And recognizing human nature, he admonishes them not to allow bias to enter into their judicial process.

Next, Paul instructs caution in ordaining new elders, teaching that this must be a deliberative process to ensure qualified leaders—again signaling the importance of church leadership positions. He says Timothy (and the church) should not take part in the sins of others and must keep himself pure (5:22). Scholars interpret this instruction as bolstering Paul's command that the church be deliberative in selecting and ordaining leaders, noting that if they hastily select a sinful leader, they will be joining in that "sin." Chrysostom explains it clearly: "One who authorizes evil is blameworthy. It is just as in the case of anyone entrusting into the hands of a raging and insane person a sharply pointed sword, with which the madman commits murder, that one who gave the sword incurs the blame. So anyone that gives the authority that arises from this office to a man living in evil, draws down on his own head all the fire of that man's sins and audacity."[65]

Paul next throws in some personal advice to Timothy, who apparently suffers frequent illnesses presumably related to his digestion: "No longer drink only water but use a little wine for the sake of your stomach and your frequent ailments" (5:23). Some commentators infer that Paul is cautioning against the asceticism of false teachers because some ascetics (those who are severely disciplined and frequently abstain) only drink water.[66]

Paul now returns to the sins of church leaders: "The sins of some people are conspicuous, going before them to judgment, but the sins of others appear later" (5:24). Because it is sometimes difficult to tell immediately whether someone is sinning, it is important not to be hasty in ordaining leaders. This recognizes that as human beings are fallible, human judges will be as well. There will be mistakes in church administration and in the appointment of leaders, so the church should regard these duties seriously and implement them deliberately and prudently. Ideally, the church should be well acquainted with potential leaders before selecting them because it sometimes takes time to discern the unfitness of certain people.

Paul closes the chapter by declaring, "So also good works are conspicuous, and even those that are not cannot remain hidden" (5:25), meaning that good works are generally readily apparent, but some are not, though they will be evident in time. This is yet one more reason not to rush the leadership selection process. With time, even inconspicuous good works will shine through, and the patient church that avoids the precipitous selection of leaders will be blessed with better leadership.

PRAYER

Father, we take time now to lift up the leaders of Your churches all over the world. We specifically lift up the leaders of our individual churches and ask You to grant them wisdom, discernment, and especially joy. Even if we don't always agree with our pastors and elders, we recognize they have been chosen and called by You for their positions, and by honoring them we are ultimately honoring You. Illuminate how we can pray for these individuals and their families; even if we do not know them personally, we want them to be blessed with all the fullness that You have for them and their earthly missions. If there are issues in our hearts concerning our leaders that we feel need to be addressed, we ask You to provide the perfect words, time, and place for these matters to be conveyed. We resist the devil and ask You to help us from stumbling into any trap he may be using to create discord within our churches. May we be used only for Your glory and rest knowing that submitting all our concerns to You is the best way to handle any and every situation. We surrender these things to You in Jesus' Name,

AMEN.

CHAPTER 6

Paul now turns his attention to bondservants who had been converted to Christianity. Thomas Lea notes they may be confused by their new freedom in Christ while remaining under their masters' authority. Paul encourages them to honor Christ and be good witnesses for Him.[67] Cautioning against rebellion, Paul tells them to regard their masters as honorable and not be disrespectful to believing masters, as they are "brothers." Instead, they should serve even more willingly, as this would benefit other Christians and glorify God by presenting a good impression of Christianity to unbelievers.

As we'll recall, Paul had instructed masters to show reciprocal respect to their servants, as both serve the same Master in heaven (Eph. 6:5–9). All Christians, regardless of economic or political status, are called to servanthood—it is the essence of Christlike behavior. Contrary to arguments by modern critics, Paul is not endorsing slavery. To the contrary, Paul's admonition to masters to treat servants respectfully and as brothers is somewhat revolutionary. In fact, without disrupting society and giving unbelievers yet another reason to oppose Christianity in its infancy, Paul is laying the foundation for the ultimate erosion and eradication of slavery. "[Paul's] way toward a solution commends itself by reason of its evident wisdom," William Hendriksen explains. "It avoids extremes which would result in much harm both to the slave and to his master and would reflect dishonor upon the cause of the Christian religion. He advocated neither outright revolt by the slaves nor the continuation of the status quo." Instead of recommending either of these, says Hendriksen, "he aimed by the law of indirection to destroy the very essence of slavery with all its attendant evils!"[68]

Paul now returns to a matter that is obviously important to him: false teachers. "Teach and urge these things. If anyone teaches a different doctrine and does not agree with the sound words of our Lord Jesus Christ and the teaching that accords with godliness, he is puffed up with conceit and understands nothing. He has an unhealthy craving for controversy and for quarrels about words, which produce envy, dissension, slander, evil suspicions, and constant friction among people who are depraved in mind and deprived of the truth, imagining that godliness is a means of gain" (6:2–5). Paul is zeroing in on the type of false teachers who aren't just passing on factually incorrect information—these are not people who are merely making mistakes. Rather, these are spiritually dark people who willfully reject God's word, as seen in Paul's description of their malicious and quarrelsome mindset. They have an unhealthy craving for controversy that leads to disharmony and ill will among members of the congregation.

Paul is not addressing innocent errors but deliberate acts of disobedience aimed at undermining the body of Christ. They are "depraved in mind and deprived of the truth," and their mental deprivation blinds them to the truth. Their teaching, on its face, is contrary to godliness and the words of Christ. Their ungodly actions and their un-Christian attitudes betray their un-Christian hearts and motives. They not only cause controversy, they thrive on it, which is despicable. They even believe "that godliness is a means of gain," meaning financial gain. "They were motivated by money," writes Bruce Barton. "Their ultimate goal was to enrich themselves! How completely opposite this is from Old Testament teaching, from the teaching of the Lord Jesus and from the apostles, and from the generous and caring attitude of the early church."[69]

All these wicked behaviors should have been evident to those familiar with and in accord with the word. Christians should recognize such people miles away. But it is especially important to Paul that Timothy be on high alert for these saboteurs and to strongly confront them to thwart their evil schemes as soon as they rear their heads. Paul might have had this scripture in mind as he described these puffed-up troublemakers: "A worthless person, a wicked man, goes about with crooked speech, winks with his eyes, signals with his feet, points with his finger, with perverted heart devises evil, continually sowing discord" (Prov. 6:12–14).

Paul then contrasts true godliness with the schemers' greed: "But godliness with contentment is great gain, for we brought nothing into the world, and we cannot take anything out of the world. But if we have food and clothing, with these we will be content. But those who desire to be rich fall into temptation, into a snare, into many senseless and harmful desires that plunge people into ruin and destruction. For the love of money is a root of all kinds of evils. It is through this craving that some have wandered away from the faith and pierced themselves with many pangs" (6:6–10). The pride-gorged false teachers distort the concept of godliness, exploiting it as a means to financial gain. Their "godliness" is not godliness at all. True godliness brings contentment and peace. An authentic faith will produce a contentment that transcends financial status. "Godliness is not about acquiring better and more material things;" writes Philip Towner, "it is instead an active life of faith, a living out of covenant faithfulness in relation to God, that finds sufficiency and contentment in Christ alone whatever one's outward circumstances might be."[70]

These are hard sayings and difficult for us to live out, but we know if we focus on money to the exclusion of God, we are engaging in idolatry. We become slaves to our material pursuits. Jesus was clear on this point as well: "Do not lay up for yourselves treasures on earth, where moth and rust destroy and where thieves break in and steal, but lay up for yourselves treasures in heaven, where neither moth nor rust destroys, and where thieves do not break in or steal" (Matt. 6:19–20). No amount of riches can provide spiritual security, which is why Jesus also said, "For what does it profit a man to gain the whole world, and forfeit his own soul?" (Mark 8:36). Other biblical passages stress the same point: "Whoever trusts in his riches will fall, but the righteous will flourish like a green leaf" (Prov. 11:28); "For where your treasure is, there will your heart be also" (Luke 12:34); "Keep your life free from love of money, and be content with what you have, for he has said, 'I will never leave you nor forsake you.' So we can confidently say, 'The Lord is my helper; I will not fear; what can man do to me?'" (Heb 13:5–6).

Like Paul, we should learn to be content regardless of our financial circumstances (Phil. 4:11). We should note that the Bible does not condemn wealth categorically, but it repeatedly warns it is a snare that can lead people away from God.[71]

Paul elaborates on true contentment, stressing that material things cannot be too important because the Christian life is eternal while our material things are confined to our life on earth. Materially speaking, we start with a zero-slate and end the same way. Job acknowledged this truth: "Naked I came from my mother's womb, and naked I shall return" (Job 1:21). Even regarding things he lost, he said, "The Lord gave, and the Lord has taken away; blessed be the name of the Lord" (Job 1:21). And he resigned himself to this reality without a hint of objection: "In all this Job did not sin or charge God with wrong" (Job 1:22).

Christians must understand, then, that everything they acquire belongs to God—their ownership is not just transitory but subject to God's superior claim to it. God is our benefactor, even if we acquire goods through our own labors. As regarding the human economy, this is no rejection of the concept of private property, which is clearly endorsed scripturally, including in the Ten Commandments, which forbid stealing and coveting. All we really need for physical contentment is food and clothing (6:8). This is obviously easier said than done, but ideally, if we can fulfill the basics of life—our needs, as distinguished from our wants—we should be content.

By contrast, the desire to be wealthy is a pitfall because it can lead us into temptation that will destroy us. If we obsess over the acquisition of wealth, that desire will compete with our focus on God. Some people believe wealth alone will bring them happiness, but a short conversation with many wealthy people will prove that false. Wealth cannot bring contentment, and in fact it can bring great harm, which is why the wealthy must constantly check their hearts and their spiritual condition to ensure their eyes are on eternity more than on material possessions.

The next verse has often been misquoted and misunderstood. Paul writes, "For the love of money is a root of all kinds of evils. It is through this craving that some have wandered away from the faith and pierced themselves with many pangs" (6:10). People mistakenly paraphrase the first part of this verse as, "Money is the root of all evil." This is wrong in three significant ways. First, it's not money alone that Paul is talking about, but the love of money. Second, it is not *the* root, but *a* root. Third, it is not *all* evil, but *all kinds of* evil.

So, while too much money can be a temptation to evil, it is the love of money that you must guard against. As we have said, everything God created is good. And as money is just a representation of value and God created everything of value, he created money. But he did not create temptation, unhealthy desires, or love for the wrong things.

Money itself can be used for good purposes. Money and assets are used to advance God's kingdom, to build His church, and to help the needy. Generous people can use their wealth for all these godly purposes. Financially blessed people are able to give because they control their money. "The problem happens when money controls people," writes Bruce Barton.[72] Augustine also expressed this principle. "Do without greed; don't do without concern for others," he writes. "There's something you can do with gold, if you're its master, and not its slave. If you're the master of gold, you can do good with it; if you're its slave, it can do evil with you."[73] John Wesley, noting the beneficial uses of wealth, puts it in perspective. "Having, first, gained all you can, and secondly, saved all you can, then give all you can," he writes.[74]

Moreover, there are many sources of evil, and the love of money is just one, thus it is *a* root. Furthermore, the love of money is not a root of *all* evil but of various kinds of evil. There are other evils unconnected to money, such as sexual lust and pride-fueled ambition.[75] It is the love of money that is a problem. Love is a strong word, so just wistfully longing for money—as in, "It would be nice to have more money"—is not condemned by this verse. But when you focus too much on it and it becomes such a priority that you could be fairly said to love it, then you have a problem. This unhealthy desire to acquire wealth can lead you onto a path of corruption and destruction. Even worse, it can lead you away from the faith and into a life of misery.

Matthew tells an interesting story about Jesus and wealth: "While he was eating, a woman came in with a beautiful alabaster jar of expensive perfume and poured it over his head. The disciples were indignant when they saw this. 'What a waste!' they said. 'It could have been sold for a high price and the money given to the poor.' But Jesus, aware of this, replied, 'Why criticize this woman for doing such a good thing to me? You will always have the poor among you, but you will not always have me.'" (Matt. 26:7–11 NLT). Bruce Barton notes that this perfume was likely worth an entire year's wages, and that even though the disciples thought this money should have gone to the poor, "Jesus wanted them to understand that even concern for the poor must never be elevated over devotion to him."[76] We love this example because it reveals God's heart in an unexpected way regarding our finances.

Prayer

Lord, help us resist the persistent temptation to make money an idol in our lives. We want to fully understand that You and You alone are the provider of all our needs. Whether we are in a season of financial abundance or difficulty, may we seek to keep our loving focus on You and worship You with what we've been given, just as the woman who anointed Your feet with oil. In Jesus's Name,

Amen.

Paul wraps up the chapter—and the letter—exhorting Timothy to avoid these temptations and actively to pursue godly things, fight for his faith, and focus on those things of eternal value: "But as for you, O man of God, flee these things. Pursue righteousness, godliness, faith, love, steadfastness, gentleness. Fight the good fight of the faith. Take hold of the eternal life to which you were called and about which you made the good confession in the presence of many witnesses" (6:11–13). Summarizing the letter's entire message, Paul reminds Timothy he is a man of God, and he must avoid the false teachers and their false teachings like the plague while vigorously pursuing holiness. Notably, Paul doesn't just instruct Timothy to casually turn away from these evil people and their teachings but to flee from them—denoting an urgency of sorts.

Paul's non-exhaustive list of Christian virtues mostly speaks for itself. Christians must strive to live morally pure lives, though they'll all fall short. They must pursue godliness, which is the natural result of a strong faith in Christ and the obedient and habitual exercise of the spiritual disciplines. Love is the core of Christianity, as Peter eloquently expresses: "Above all, keep loving one another earnestly, since love covers a multitude of sins" (1 Peter 4:8). In commanding Timothy to be steadfast, Paul is reminding him that perseverance is crucial to maintaining one's faith when encountering adversity and persecution. In Revelation Jesus affirms these ideas: "I know your works, your toil and your patient endurance, and how you cannot bear with those who are evil, but have tested those who call themselves apostles and are not, and found them to be false. I know you are enduring patiently and bearing up for my name's sake, and you have not grown weary" (Rev. 2:2–3).

But why does Paul commend "gentleness?" One reason is that when we are gentle and respectful in our dealings with opponents of the faith, we will increase the likelihood that they will come to repentance and be reconciled with God.[77] It is the same advice Peter gave to those defending the faith: "But in your hearts honor Christ the Lord as holy, always being prepared to make a defense to anyone who asks you for a reason for the hope that is in you; yet do it with gentleness and respect" (1 Peter 3:15).

In encouraging Timothy to fight the good fight of the faith, Paul acknowledges that doing God's work of spreading the gospel is often going to involve a fight, but that it's a good, worthwhile, and noble fight. Don't shy away from a battle when the eternal lives of your fellow human beings are at stake. One's eternal life begins upon his conversion from unbelief to belief in Christ. He begins to enjoy the kingdom of God presently, though in imperfect form. It will be enjoyed fully and permanently upon Christ's return and our bodily resurrection with Christ.

Paul is telling Timothy to embrace this reality and to maintain a spiritual perspective while engaging in these arduous battles. To shore up Timothy's resolve, Paul is reminding him of the day he professed his faith and became a Christian. He must remember and embrace the overwhelming enthusiasm he had for the Lord at that special moment and always carry that with him as he fights the good fight of the faith. Some may find Paul's repetition unnecessary, but we should remember he is not in Timothy's presence, and he is giving him this permanent written encouragement in lieu of being with him physically throughout these struggles. The letters to Timothy will always be with him and strengthen him when he is down, just as they will always be available for the rest of us who do our lesser part in fighting the good fight.

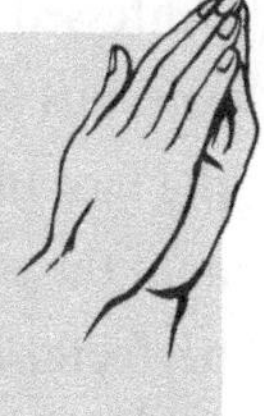

Prayer

Holy Spirit, we ask You to bring to our minds in this moment areas of our lives where the enemy is currently waging war against us. We know that because the devil hates everything

▶

that is good, he often attacks us in the very areas where God has plans to use us for His good purposes. We ask that You guard our hearts and minds against frustration and anger. May we keep in step with Paul's instruction to embrace gentleness even as we engage in spiritual warfare. We lean on You for our direction and strength.

AMEN.

Paul continues, "I charge you in the presence of God, who gives life to all things, and of Christ Jesus, who in his testimony before Pontius Pilate made the good confession, to keep the commandment unstained and free from reproach until the appearing of our Lord Jesus Christ, which he will display at the proper time—he who is the blessed and only sovereign, the King of kings and Lord of lords, who alone has immortality, who dwells in unapproachable light, whom no one has ever seen or can see. To him be honor and eternal dominion. Amen" (6:13–16).

To impress on Timothy the importance of the letter's contents, Paul tells him his commands (and Timothy's receipt of them) are in the presence of God and Jesus. If nothing else would get his attention, that would. Paul just reminded Peter of the time he confessed his faith in Christ. Now he is telling Timothy that Christ Himself made a similar profession, though His profession concerned His being the Messiah and Savior of all believers. Jesus confessed Himself even though by doing so He assured His own grievous suffering and death. As always Christ is our example in the face of adversity, suffering, and fear: "Let us run with endurance the race that is set before us looking to Jesus, the founder and perfecter of our faith, who for the joy that was set before him endured the cross, despising the shame, and is seated at the right hand of the throne of God. Consider him who endured from sinners such hostility against himself, so that you may not grow weary or fainthearted" (Heb. 12:1–3).

Timothy is to obey all the commands of this epistle until Jesus returns. This is an ongoing job and will never be finished until Christ's Second Coming. Our work as Christians has no earthly completion date. We are not excused from our calling and our duty to evangelize this side of eternity.

Paul rounds out this passage with a multi-faceted description of God and his majesty—blessed, the only sovereign, the King of kings and Lord of lords, and immortal. He then invokes the image of God as a light so bright that no one can see or approach it—a truth underscored throughout scripture beginning in Exodus, when Moses was only permitted a brief glimpse of God's glory (Exodus 33:18–23). Other examples include the Psalmist depicting God as having a face of light (Ps. 89:15); Isaiah prophesying that neither the sun nor the moon shall be our light because "the Lord will be your everlasting light" (Isaiah 60:18); and John declaring that the New Jerusalem will need no sunlight or moonlight because the glory of God itself will illuminate everything (Rev. 21:23).

One of our favorite revelations in scripture on this topic is John's confirmation that "no one has ever seen God; the only God, who is at the Father's side, he has made him known" (John 1:18). No one has seen God except Jesus, who is also God. But because we have seen Jesus in human form, we have effectively seen God. As we noted earlier, Jesus "is the radiance of the glory of God and the exact imprint of his nature" (Heb. 1:3). Just let that sink in. We can't approach God because His glory is simply too great. We will die if we see it directly. Yet, in another one of Christianity's most gratifying paradoxes, human beings *can* see God because they have seen Jesus in the flesh. The immortal, omnipresent, omniscient, omnibenevolent, and omnipotent God of the universe is completely unapproachable to us, except that His Son is completely accessible to us. Praise God and Jesus Christ.

Paul now returns to a discussion of the rich, whom he notably does not condemn but offers advice for proper living: "As for the rich in this present age, charge them not to be haughty, nor to set their hopes on the uncertainty of riches, but on God, who richly provides us with everything to enjoy. They are to do good, to be rich in good works, to be generous and ready to share, thus storing up treasure for themselves as a good foundation for the future, so that they may take hold of that which is truly life" (6:17–19).

It seems impossible to read this passage and conclude that God condemns the rich. Throughout Paul has warned of the serious traps waiting to ensnare the wealthy and given unequivocal commands that they should guard themselves against the enemy's temptations, to which they will be especially vulnerable. Here he reiterates that instruction, telling them to put their hopes on God, not on their wealth. But note that he is not telling them to get rid of their wealth but to do good with it—to be generous and sharing. If they do so, they will take hold of that which is truly life.

We should not interpret this to mean that the rich can earn their salvation through proper stewardship of their wealth. Instead, God is charging them with a kind of super stewardship. Just as they face inordinate temptations, they also are in a special position to do good. They will only do so if they are right with God, and their salvation depends on their saving faith. But to be Christlike in the management of their wealth, they must follow these commands, and their obedience will entitle them to rewards and evince their embrace of a richer life both on earth and in the eternal life through faith in Christ. "To be charitable for the sake of gaining heaven by it, is absurdity, for the selfish motive vitiates the act," writes D. Edmond Hiebert. "Rather, such good works are the evidence of faith and justification and as such assure us that we now possess genuine spiritual life. They also give us the assurance of a glorious future consummation, 'that they may lay hold on the life which is life indeed.'"[78]

In closing, Paul tells Timothy, "O Timothy, guard the deposit entrusted to you. Avoid the irreverent babble and contradictions of what is falsely called 'knowledge,' for by professing it some have swerved from the faith. Grace be with you" (6:20–21). Again, Paul is emphasizing the importance of Timothy's mission—calling it a deposit entrusted to him. A deposit is not something man has invented but which he has received by divine revelation. The false teachers have no deposit; they have ideas that they invented to puff themselves up—ideas that are not divine in origin but blasphemous. Paul has entrusted this deposit to Timothy, who is now a fiduciary of God's word—a daunting position that he must guard reverently.

An essential part of this duty is to resist the false teachers and their destructive, nonsensical babble that masquerades as knowledge. Just through exposure to it, some have turned toward it and away from the faith. Contemplating these mythological stories and genealogies makes people feel they have special knowledge, but it is not knowledge at all. It is poisonous misinformation that can lead to heresy. These seductive ideas are not just useless and time consuming but potentially dangerous to one's true faith and knowledge of God. Cyril of Jerusalem, a theologian of the early church, spoke to the importance of our correct understanding of scripture and knowledge of Christ: "And do you, my hearers, worship him alone as king, and flee every misguided heresy.... Flee the false Christ, and look for the true. You have been taught the way to be among those on his right hand at the judgment. Retain 'that which is committed to you' concerning Christ, and be adorned with good works."[79]

Throughout this letter, Paul has expressed his genuine concern about false teachings, so it is no surprise that he recapitulates this theme in closing—before signing off by offering grace to Timothy.

PRAYER

Lord, there are many items Paul reiterates throughout his letters, which to our minds can feel redundant. Help us to see Your divine plan and reasoning behind emphasizing this subject matter. As we read Your word, remind us to actively ask You questions in real time, recognizing Your word is living and that You speak to us—truly speak to us—through it. If we feel disengaged, use our confusion to pull us into an actual conversation with You. We know You can use anything to make an impact on our lives, so help us to believe it and to live as though we believe it. In Your Holy Name,

AMEN.

CHAPTER SIX

TITUS
QUALITIES OF A CHRISTLIKE LIFE

Although Paul himself is a master of doctrine…he is preeminently practical in his teaching. He often deals with the details of ordinary life. This is exceedingly noticeable in his Epistle to Titus.

—Charles Spurgeon[1]

Paul brought Titus to Christ and helped mold him into a mature Christian, evangelist, and pastor. The Book of Galatians informs us that Titus is a Gentile convert from Greece who had ministered to the Corinthian church (2 Cor. 7:6–7; 8:6, 16). Titus became one of Paul's closest friends, and Paul shows confidence in him by entrusting to him the stewardship of the newly formed churches in Crete. But as usual, he doesn't want to leave Titus ill-equipped for the task, especially considering obstacles he knows Titus will face in Crete, so he writes this letter to instruct Titus in teaching and strengthen him for this difficult mission. One of the main problems Titus faces is the Judaizers, who teach that Jewish practices must remain in the church. So Paul needs to give Titus guidance on matters of church organization and instructions on church leadership and Christian living, as well as advice to overcome the arguments of the Judaizers. Given Paul's impeccable credentials, this letter constitutes written authority for Titus to oversee these churches.

Titus is believed to have been written around the same time Paul wrote 1 Timothy—sometime after his first imprisonment in Rome, which is why we have placed it before 2 Timothy in this book for chronological purposes. The Cretan churches were formed some time earlier but are disorganized and floundering.[2] Titus' task will be particularly challenging because of the decadent morality of the Cretans and their influence on members of the churches. Paul wants to correct any church members who mistakenly believe that their salvation in Christ doesn't require them to live Christlike lives. He insists that Titus impress on them the importance of sound Christian doctrine and high moral behavior, as Christ's witnesses. Accordingly, Paul focuses on the essential connection between scriptural knowledge and wisdom, and on good conduct.

A provision in the Presbyterian constitution makes this point well: "Truth is in order to goodness; and the great touchstone of truth, its tendency to promote holiness, according to our Savior's rule 'By their fruits ye shall know them.'... We are persuaded that there is an inseparable connection between faith and practice, truth and duty. Otherwise, it would be of no consequence either to discover truth or to embrace it."[3] The underlying biblical authority for that provision is also the theme of Titus, as expressed in this verse: "The saying is trustworthy, and I want you to insist on these things, so that those who have believed in God may be careful to devote themselves to good works. These things are excellent and profitable for people" (Titus 3:8).

Gary Demarest articulates the interdependence of doctrine and good works that Paul lays out in this letter. "We have a tendency to emphasize one at the expense of the other," writes Demarest. "When either truth or doctrine becomes an end in itself, we produce a legalistic orthodoxy, often lacking in genuine love and care in action. However, when goodness is emphasized at the expense of truth ('it doesn't matter what you believe as long as you are sincere and loving'), we produce platitudes without power, often lacking in long-term commitment."[4]

As with many scriptural lessons, we must find a balance—that's the essence of biblical wisdom and prudence. We all know people who stress either doctrine or good works at the expense of the other. We may sometimes do it ourselves. We've heard people criticize fellow Christians for touting their Bible knowledge and not showing love in their lives, and some of those critics assert their criticism just to rationalize their own unwillingness to dive into scripture. But it's not that we actively choose one or the other. Paul is saying that by studying the Bible prayerfully and with deference to the empowerment of the Holy Spirit, good works will more likely follow. And while it is admirable to strive to do good works, we must not try to do so on our own power alone. We need scripture's wisdom and the Holy Spirit's power. Yet reading scripture alone does not end our duties. We must strive, through the aid of the Spirit walking beside us, to apply biblical principles to our lives, walk the Christian walk, tap into scriptural wisdom, and radiate the love of Christ.

CHAPTER 1

Paul begins the letter laying out its principal theme—the importance of teaching and learning biblical truth, which will lead to Christlike living. "Paul's ministry, then focused both on people's salvation and their sanctification," writes Duane Liftin.[5] He identifies himself, as usual, as an apostle of Jesus Christ and a servant of God. He has been assigned these roles "for the sake of the faith of God's elect and their knowledge of the truth, which accords with godliness, in hope of eternal life, which God, who never lies, promised before the ages began and at the proper time manifested in his word through the preaching with which I have been entrusted by the command of God our Savior" (1:3).

Notice that Paul's eyes are always on the prize—the gift of eternal life. His whole purpose as an apostle is to serve God's plan, formed before He created the world, to offer eternal life to those who place their faith in His Son. Again, this faith is directly connected to their "knowledge of the truth" and leads to godliness—as expressed in 2 Timothy 3:15, scripture makes us "wise for salvation through faith in Christ Jesus." This is a guarantee from our God "who never lies." As we explained in earlier chapters, "hope" means something different from its ordinary usage today. It is more than "a feeling of expectation and desire for a certain thing to happen," as our modern dictionaries define it. It is a rock-solid promise that we can rely on. "Biblical hope does not reflect a doubtful, tremulous wishing for that which may or may not occur," writes Thomas Lea. ". . . . Biblical hope is based on the immutable nature and promise of God and therefore results in encouragement, confidence, strength, and security for the believer."[6]

It's also notable that while Paul affirms that God's promise of eternal life was made before time began, it was not presented to man until "the proper time." People sometimes wonder why God split history, with Jesus Christ's incarnation thousands of years after man was created. That may not be for us to entirely understand, but here Paul is acknowledging that God did indeed wait until His appointed time, and only then did Christ appear, followed by the gospel message. It is no accident that the gospel was presented at a time most conducive to its rapid spread, given the relatively peaceful conditions and the facility of transportation and common language under the Roman Empire. "All history was the preparation for that revelation," writes

Hiebert. "The historical appropriateness of the time is evident from the existence of the Roman peace that gave a favorable setting for the preaching of the gospel and the development of Greek as the linguistic medium of its worldwide proclamation."[7]

Paul addresses Titus by name and calls him "my true child in a common faith." Commentators note that unlike certain other important people, Paul always expresses gratitude for those who helped him. He clearly trusts Titus and relies on him—a Gentile—to help his ministry to other Gentiles. We know Paul has affection for Titus, as he was "comforted by" his coming on one occasion (2 Cor. 7:6), and in another instance, he was troubled in spirit when Titus was not where Paul expected him to be (2 Cor. 2:13). So Paul clearly has a close relationship with Titus comparable to Timothy.

Paul next communicates his charge to Titus:

> This is why I left you in Crete, so that you might put what remained into order, and appoint elders in every town as I directed you—if anyone is above reproach, the husband of one wife, and his children are believers and not open to the charge of debauchery or insubordination. For an overseer, as God's steward, must be above reproach. He must not be arrogant or quick-tempered or a drunkard or violent or greedy for gain, but hospitable, a lover of good, self-controlled, upright, holy, and disciplined. He must hold firm to the trustworthy word as taught, so that he may be able to give instruction in sound doctrine and also to rebuke those who contradict it. (1:5–9)

Paul indicates he has already given these directions to Titus. We can imagine Paul thinking of these newly formed churches and knowing how difficult it is for any institution, in its infancy, to be effectively organized and to function smoothly. One critical part of that is, of course, leadership, so Paul is specific that Titus should appoint elders for every town if he hasn't already done so. From his list of qualifications, it is clear Paul is concerned both with the elders' character and their reputation in the community. It is important they be morally upright and that their peers recognize them as such. The obvious reason is that the church must be led by those who practice the Christian principles they preach. We know from our own times how fallen pastors, for example, can ruin the reputation of a church and its ability to grow and flourish.

The good reputation of the elders' children and their faith and good character are also essential. Titus should not appoint someone whose children are unbelievers, insubordinate, or ill-behaved, as this would reflect poorly on the elder's leadership and his ability to instill morality in his children. "For he who cannot be the instructor of his own children, how could he be the teacher of others?" asks Chrysostom. "For if he was unable to restrain them, it is a great proof of his weakness."[8] As Paul instructed Timothy, the elder must also be faithful to his wife (1 Tim. 3:2).

Paul next lists vices elders must shun—arrogance, intemperance, drunkenness, violence, and greed. All leaders are tempted by pride, and due to their weighty responsibilities, church leaders in particular must resist the temptation. We know from our own experience that people tend to put pastors on a pedestal and sometimes treat them as super-humans who are above temptation. But pastors are human, and the enemy has them in his sights. Pride was the devil's downfall and one of his best weapons against others. So we must recognize that pastors and church leaders are indeed vulnerable and keep them in our prayers.

Leading to other sins, pride is widely considered the worst offense. It is self-idolatry—if one is that impressed with himself, it's difficult for him to lean on God. Pride is also the antithesis of Christlike behavior, as Christ was the opposite of proud. Though God in the flesh, He was a humble servant. He did not lord his leadership and his sinlessness over others. He rejected the devil's seductive offer to become master of the world. One reason the Jews didn't recognize Him as the Messiah is that he did not come as a powerful military leader and conqueror but as one who would conquer the world through love.

Overall, Paul is saying that church leaders must display the fruit of the Spirit—and being quick-tempered, drunk, violent, or greedy is the opposite. Proverbs speaks to these vices: "A man of quick temper acts foolishly" (Prov. 14:17); "For the drunkard and the glutton will come to poverty, and slumber will clothe them with rags (Prov. 23:21); "Do not envy a man of violence and do not choose any of his ways" (Prov. 3:31); and "Such are the ways of everyone who is greedy for unjust gain; it takes away the life of its possessors" (Prov. 1:19).

Instead, church leaders must be hospitable, self-controlled, upright, holy, disciplined, and lovers of what is good. It's not enough simply to avoid evil and bad behavior. Like Jesus, they must show others hospitality (Romans 12:13). The writer of Hebrews cautions us, "Do not neglect to show hospitality to strangers, for thereby some have entertained angels unawares" (Heb. 13:2). Elders must display self-control and discipline, which are similar qualities, as are the requirements that they be upright and holy. Leaders must not be seen as reckless but in full control of their faculties and of sound and sober mind. They must, even more than other believers, be morally upright, as they are an example for all, believers and nonbelievers alike. Without such characteristics, the leaders will lack the credibility and moral authority to perform their sacred duties.

PRAYER

Jesus, regardless of how inspiring or godly a church leader might be, we ask that we never put our faith in men above our faith in You. Our personal relationship with You should not be tethered to or swayed by the personalities of mere mortals. Perhaps the best example of pastoral leadership was displayed by John the Baptist, who shepherded people back to Your divinity: "So John's disciples came to him and said, 'Rabbi, the man you met on the other side of the Jordan River, the one you identified as the Messiah, is also baptizing people. And everybody is going to him instead of coming to us.' John replied, 'No one can receive anything unless God gives it from heaven. You yourselves know how plainly I told you, "I am not the Messiah. I am only here to prepare the way for him." It is the bridegroom who marries the bride, and the bridegroom's friend is simply glad to stand with him and hear his vows. Therefore, I am filled with joy at his success. He must become greater and greater, and I must become less and less'" (26–30 NLT). May our hearts and the hearts of pastors around the world be convicted with this type of humility and selflessness. In Your Holy Name,

AMEN.

Paul explains that these positive traits in a church leader are essential to being a teacher of sound doctrine and a defender of the faith. We can't emphasize enough how important sound doctrine is to Paul and conversely, how poisonous false teaching is. Church leaders must not only have the wisdom and discernment to understand scripture but to recognize false teachers and have the ability and willingness to take them on. False doctrine inside the church can be more deadly to the body of Christ than outside attacks.

As such, Paul says, "For there are many who are insubordinate, empty talkers and deceivers, especially those of the circumcision party. They must be silenced, since they are upsetting whole families by teaching for shameful gain what they ought not to teach. One of the Cretans, a prophet of their own, said, 'Cretans are always liars, evil beasts, lazy gluttons.' This testimony is true. Therefore rebuke them sharply, that they may be sound in the faith, not devoting themselves to Jewish myths and the commands of people who turn away from the truth" (1:10–14).

Paul seems to equate false teaching with insubordination—that makes sense because those who follow their own counsel instead of the word of God are being rebellious. It's as if they think they know better than God what people ought to believe—a patent absurdity! As we read in Proverbs, "The way of a fool is right in his own eyes, but a wise man listens to advice" (Prov. 12:15). Furthermore, "Be not wise in your own eyes; fear the Lord, and turn away from evil" (Prov. 3:7). Paul says these types deceitfully engage in "empty talk," which recalls his admonition about those who spread myths and engage in foolish talk. But here he singles out "the circumcision party," indicating his particular concern about Jewish Christians who impose the requirements of Jewish law on believers.

These false teachers must be silenced because they are upsetting entire families by teaching false doctrine for personal gain. Paul doesn't mean the false teachers must be physically restrained but that they be rebuked, criticized, warned, and corrected. "Paul does not counsel dialogue or peaceful arbitration for the sake of preserving unity in the church," notes A. Kostenberger. "Rather, Titus's opponents must be silenced."[9] This may sound aggressive, but error cannot be promoted in the church because it will lead people away from God.

By teaching things "they ought not to teach," Paul may have been referring to the Jewish Christians' tendency to add a works requirement for salvation, which is anathema to Paul.[10] No teaching is more important than that pertaining to our salvation in Christ through faith alone, and Paul would not tolerate any distortion of that message. "This 'zero tolerance' is called for because these teachers are 'ruining whole households,' plunging their devotees into spiritual turmoil by overturning their previous convictions through persuasive argument," explains Kostenberger.[11]

Paul shares that Cretans had such horrible reputations that even one of their own prophets admitted they were always liars, evil beasts, and lazy gluttons. Providing secular corroboration of Paul's assessment, the ancient historian Polybius noted it was "almost impossible to find... personal conduct more treacherous or public policy more unjust than in Crete."[12] It isn't that Paul is randomly singling out Cretans but that he's facing opposition from these people and is calling on outside authority (one of their own) to substantiate his claim against the local troublemakers who are opposing the gospel.

Paul's criticism, however, is not without charity. He doesn't write off the Cretans. Rather, he says they must be sharply rebuked so they will see their error, return to the sound principles of the faith, and abandon the false teachings of those enamored with the Jewish myths. The "sharp rebuke" is not for the sake of harshness but to get their attention on a matter of vital spiritual importance. "Though exhibiting gentleness and care, the leader must not shrink from using strong words," writes Knute Larson.[13] "He needs to speak to the issue and clarify the wrong and evil into which the individual or group has fallen. The motive comes not from an enjoyment of confrontation, or from the heady position of pointing out faults, but from an earnest desire that people will be sound in the faith."

PRAYER

Father, we cling to Your word and seek justice for those who have been led astray by false teachers. You promise in Luke 8, "For all that is secret will eventually be brought into the open, and everything that is concealed will be brought to light and made known to all" (17 NLT), and You assure us in Proverbs 19:5, "A false witness will not go unpunished, nor will a liar escape" (NLT). May the wicked schemes of the enemy be snuffed out by the power of Your Holy Spirit. We pray for angelic protection to be sent to those of us who are more vulnerable to false teaching, and we ask You to place people in their lives who can help align their beliefs with the truth of Your word, not adding or taking away anything from it.

AMEN.

In closing the chapter Paul writes, "To the pure, all things are pure, but to the defiled and unbelieving, nothing is pure; but both their minds and their consciences are defiled. They profess to know God, but they deny him by their works. They are detestable, disobedient, unfit for any good work" (1:15–16). Many interpreters believe Paul is referring here to Jewish food laws. The Judaizers were causing much dissension in the church in promoting their dietary laws, and Paul counters this error in his other letters, insisting these restricted foods are not impure.

By arguing that we should strive for inward purity as opposed to external religiosity, Paul is echoing Jesus' teaching: "Now you Pharisees cleanse the outside of the cup and of the dish, but inside you are full of greed and wickedness. You fools! Did not he who made the outside make the inside also? But give as alms those things that are within, and behold, everything is clean for you" (Luke 11:39–41). Larson comments, "True purity resides not in the practice of ritual or in devotion to rules and regulations. Purity that

God recognizes and commends comes from within, and a person can attain this only through faith in Jesus Christ."[14]

The false teachers' sins were compounded by their profession of knowing God, though their works showed otherwise. The prophet Isaiah spoke of similar people: "And the Lord said: Because this people draw near with their mouth and honor me with their lips, while their hearts are far from me" (Isaiah 29:13). Of these people, C. S. Lewis said, "Of all bad men religious bad men are the worst."[15]

As bleak a picture as Paul paints of the Cretans, we must keep in mind that God did plant a church in Crete, and it was flourishing enough that Paul assigned his beloved Titus to oversee and nurture it. No one is irredeemable, and Christ doesn't want to lose any sheep. The great British pastor Charles Spurgeon reminds us that the gospel is fit for anyone, no matter the circumstances. Referring to Crete, he said, "This was bad soil, but it had to be plowed and to be sown. And with an almighty God at the back of the gospel plower and sower, a fruitful harvest came even in Crete. We do not need to be afraid of the adaptation of the gospel to the lowest of the low. If there is any quarter of the town where the people are more sunken in vice than anywhere else, there the gospel is to be carried with more prayer and more faith than anywhere else. Depend upon it, God can bless His word anywhere, among Cretans or among any other sort of degraded people."[16]

PRAYER

During his earthly ministry, Jesus was constantly ruffling feathers and confusing the religious leaders of His day. We learn in Luke 5 that while Jesus was eating with tax collectors, "the Pharisees and their teachers of religious law complained bitterly to Jesus' disciples, 'Why do you eat and drink with such scum?' Jesus answered them, 'Healthy people don't need a doctor—sick people do. I

▶

have come to call not those who think they are righteous, but those who know they are sinners and need to repent'" (30–31 NLT). Jesus, You amaze us! The level of compassion and mercy you offer sinners is difficult to fully comprehend. We ask that Your goodness flow through us—we want to experience life to the fullest by treating others with the grace and forgiveness You have shown us. We love You and offer our hearts to You in this moment,

AMEN.

CHAPTER 2

In this section, Paul gives instructions on Christian living for groups based on age, gender, and status (bondservants). He begins by telling Titus that, in contrast to the false teachers, he should "teach what accords with sound doctrine" (2:1). False teaching leads to behavior that is inconsistent with sound doctrine, whereas the teaching of biblical truth will lead to proper Christian living. If people are properly instructed in doctrine, they will not be easily seduced by false teachers.[17] The Bible is the ultimate barometer of truth—teachers must conform their teachings to biblical truth and their students should absorb these truths and live their lives accordingly. Above all, sound doctrine should be Christ centered.[18] So if Titus passes on correct biblical teaching, his congregants should conduct themselves properly.

Paul proceeds, then, to expound on what such proper behavior should be:

> Older men are to be sober-minded, dignified, self-controlled, sound in faith, in love, and in steadfastness. Older women likewise are to be reverent in behavior, not slanderers or slaves to much wine. They are to teach what is good, and so train the young women to love

> their husbands and children, to be self-controlled, pure, working at home, kind, and submissive to their own husbands, that the word of God may not be reviled. Likewise, urge the younger men to be self-controlled. Show yourself in all respects to be a model of good works, and in your teaching show integrity, dignity, and sound speech that cannot be condemned, so that an opponent may be put to shame, having nothing evil to say about us. Bondservants are to be submissive to their own masters in everything; they are to be well-pleasing, not argumentative, not pilfering, but showing all good faith, so that in everything they may adorn the doctrine of God our Savior. (2:2–10)

Among believers, older men should set an example. They've had the benefit of years of living to acquire wisdom and maturity, which should be evident in their behavior—sober-minded, dignified, etc. If elderly Christian men can't model exemplary behavior, young believers can hardly be expected to behave well. They must be temperate, self-controlled, and sound in their faith, love, and endurance. Paul specified similar qualities for elders in 1 Timothy 3.

Concerning "love," if Christians follow a set of rules perfectly but don't exhibit loving, caring, and giving hearts, then they'll reveal themselves to be outwardly obedient but inwardly impure. As Paul wrote to the Corinthians, "If I speak in the tongues of men and of angels, but have no love, I am a noisy gong or a clanging cymbal. And if I have prophetic powers, and understand all mysteries and all knowledge, and if I have all faith, so as to remove mountains, but have not love, I am nothing. If I give away all I have, and if I deliver up my body to be burned, but have not love, I gain nothing" (1 Cor. 13:1–3). Concerning "endurance," the elderly men must be so committed to the faith that they will bear whatever hardships that confront them and persevere.

PRAYER

Lord, we thank You for creating family and for designing men to function as righteous oaks whom future generations can look to for wisdom and support. We lift up the men in our families and ask that they will become like the men described in Psalm 112: "How joyful are those who fear the Lord and delight in obeying his commands. Their children will be successful everywhere; an entire generation of godly people will be blessed" (1–2 NLT). For those men in our lives who are lost, we ask that You bring them into Your loving arms. You never give up on us; therefore, we will stand in the gap for these men while we wait for them to have a revelation of who You are. We declare Psalm 92 over these men, believing in faith it will come to pass: "But the godly will flourish like palm trees and grow strong like the cedars of Lebanon. For they are transplanted to the Lord's own house. They flourish in the courts of our God. Even in old age they will still produce fruit; they will remain vital and green. They will declare, 'The Lord is just! He is my rock! There is no evil in him!'" (12–15 NLT).

AMEN.

Older women, like older men, are to be reverent, moderate, and temperate, and these dispositions will show the women are internally pure.[19] They are also tasked with teaching what is good, meaning that which is consistent with scripture. They must pass on their wisdom to young women, which must include instructions to love their husbands and children and to cultivate self-control, righteousness, industriousness, kindness, and submissiveness—all so the word of God may not be discredited. As we've noted, misbehaving

Christians reflect poorly on the faith and on the Bible, which informs the faith. We won't rehash the arguments concerning Paul's charge that women be submissive except to reiterate that the context is the husband's equal duty to love his wife sacrificially, as Christ loves the church.

PRAYER

As we lift up the men in our families, we now take time to lift up the women, both young and old. We pray that these women will put their self-worth and identity in You. Lord, guide them to become like the woman described in Proverbs 31, who the *Life Application Study Bible* describes as "of strong character, great wisdom, many skills, and great compassion." We also look to Mary's example of humility and submission. Just after the angel Gabriel gave her the news that she would carry God's child, she replied, "Behold, I am the servant of the Lord; let it be to me according to your word" (Luke 1:38). We ask You to grant Your daughters gentle and willing hearts to serve You with dignity and strength. In Your Holy Name,

AMEN.

Turning to younger men, Paul simply tells Titus that he must urge them to be self-controlled, although some commentators believe Paul's instructions to Titus on his own behavior are applicable to all younger men.[20] Young men are usually not as mature as young women, which may be why Paul emphasizes self-control. If young men show this quality, the other virtues are more likely to follow, and the vices will be more easily avoided.

Thus, Paul urges Titus to be a model for younger men. He must show integrity, dignity, and sound speech in his teaching. Ambrosiaster summarizes these two verses well: "Since young men have a habit of going astray and are therefore more prone to fall away, Paul orders them to be subjected to remedial discipline, so that what is unbridled [by nature] may be governed by divine laws. In order that this should not prove too difficult or arduous a task, he advises the master to set an example and show how the things which he teaches can be put into practice, so that those who are godless and enemies of the faith may be ashamed when they see that what he teaches in words he shows to be true in his deeds."[21] Paul adds that if Titus and younger men demonstrate this good behavior, it will put their opponents to shame, meaning it will discredit their pagan detractors and their criticism. In that way, their Christlike deportment will lend credence to the gospel and to the church.

PRAYER

Father, we petition You to empower us to teach and correct the younger men in our lives. We ask that You help us teach them hard lessons swiftly and to give them hearts that are willing to learn and be corrected. We look to Proverbs 10 and see many examples of the differences between wise and foolish men, but verses 8 and 9 especially move us: "The wise of heart will receive commandments but a babbling fool will come to ruin. Whoever walks in integrity walks securely, but he who makes his ways crooked will be found out." Grant Your sons wisdom, integrity, and patience. In Your Name we entrust them to You,

AMEN.

Next, Paul again commands bondservants to be submissive to their masters in everything, to be pleasant and not quarrelsome, not to steal their master's property, and be completely trustworthy so they will be ambassadors for the integrity and soundness of the gospel of Jesus Christ "our Savior." To reiterate what we've noted before, Paul's writings in no way sanction slavery as a God-ordained institution.[22] Spurgeon says it well: "I do not think for a moment Paul believed that the practice of slavery ought to exist. He believed to the fullest extent that the great principles of Christianity would overthrow slavery anywhere, and the sooner they did so the better pleased would he be. But, for the time being, as it was the custom to have slaves, they must do credit to the teaching of God their Savior in the position in which they were."[23]

Even the behavior of Christian slaves will have an impact on how Christianity and the gospel are perceived. Their walking the walk will have a powerful impact on nonbelievers, for it will show that their faith and loyalty to Jesus Christ transcend their tragic circumstances. But why does Paul add the command against stealing? Slaves dealt closely with their masters' property, and some historians claim theft was common. One could sympathize with slaves who might avail themselves of their masters' property because they were unfairly deprived of property ownership themselves. But in the end, Christian slaves are required to obey the law even when no one is looking—even if they can get away with crimes. Paul might be saying, "Even though you are in this unfair position and your impulse to steal is understandable, you have a higher duty as Christians. Your duty is to God, and you must honor that duty." This admirable obedience would not be lost on unbelievers and would advance the gospel. "Especially noteworthy is the fact that the exemplary behavior of those at the lowest level of society (i.e., slaves) has the effect of 'making attractive' [adorning] the gospel," writes Hayne Griffin. "Surely the gospel's transforming power in the lives of those who had every reason to be bitter would stand out clearer and brighter than in those who lived in freedom and dignity unknown to slaves."[24]

PRAYER

Jesus, we intercede for men and women across the world who are living under oppressive governmental systems that forbid people from freely worshiping You. We take comfort in Proverbs 5:21: "For the Lord sees clearly what a man does, examining every path he takes" (NLT). We know nothing is hidden from You, and in the end, You will bring justice to every situation. We ask You to comfort those who are suffering and to use their suffering as a means to seek You and know You more deeply. May they follow You and find hope in the rewards You have waiting for them in heaven. We thank You for the many blessings in our lives. May those of us who have freedom never take it for granted, and may we use it to help those who are not so fortunate. In Jesus' name,

AMEN.

Paul closes the chapter on a strong, positive note: "For the grace of God has appeared, bringing salvation for all people, training us to renounce ungodliness and worldly passions, and to live self-controlled, upright, and godly lives in the present age, waiting for our blessed hope, the appearing of the glory of our great God and Savior Jesus Christ, who gave himself for us to redeem us from all lawlessness and to purify for himself a people for his own possession who are zealous for good works. Declare these things; exhort and rebuke with all authority. Let no one disregard you" (2:11–15).

In a nutshell, Paul is laying out the theological basis for his prescriptions for Christian living described in the previous ten verses.[25] God, in His grace, has appeared—He became a man and sacrificially died so we could be saved. But there is more to Christianity than our salvation upon our earthly death. As Paul has been teaching throughout this letter and the other pastorals, we must grow in holiness from the moment of our conversion until we die. As such, we have to renounce the ways of the world and turn toward God, cultivating the Christian virtues and walking the Christian walk until Christ returns or until we reunite with Him when we physically die.

God cannot look upon sin (Hab. 1:13), so Christ died to make us holy, and we must accept that with the utmost seriousness. Until we are finally glorified with Christ, we will remain in our earthly bodies and will sin, but we must strive toward holiness. Our sanctification, or purification, is an ongoing process that will culminate when we meet with Him in eternity where we will be glorified and completely sinless. To that end, we must be zealous for good works, which will be pleasing to God.

Paul commands Titus to declare these things and to exhort people to obey and rebuke those who do not. No one may be permitted to ignore these teachings. Paul is telling Titus he must take himself seriously so that others will respect his authority and obey his teachings. Titus must set aside any insecurities he might have and rise to this higher calling, which God commissioned through His appointed apostle, Paul.

We must also note that this letter is intended to be read in the churches, so this warning to respect Titus' (and Paul's) teachings is intended for all who hear the epistle. John Calvin makes this point powerfully in the context of condemning the arrogance of those who believe the gospel message is not sophisticated enough for their self-perceived intellectuality. "Here [Paul] addresses the people rather than Titus," writes Calvin. "Because many had ears so delicate, that they despised the simplicity of the gospel; because they had such an itch for novelty, that hardly any space was left for edification; he beats down the haughtiness of such men, and strictly charges them to desist from despising, in any way, sound and useful doctrine. This confirms...that this Epistle was written to the inhabitants of Crete rather than to any single individual."[26]

CHAPTER 3

Paul instructs Titus to teach believers to obey government leaders and officials, which is consistent with his message to Timothy (1 Tim. 2:1) and to the Romans (13:1–7). The main reason is set forth in Romans—that civil authorities have been instituted by God, and respect for rulers promotes law, order, and peace, contributing to a positive reputation for the church.[27] This passage is subject to various interpretations. We certainly don't believe it precludes our resistance to government lawlessness or its trampling on our religious liberties. Moreover, in our constitutional republic, the people rule themselves, albeit through elected representatives. As such, the admonition that we obey our rulers doesn't negate our right to dissent from government rulings. Indeed, public input inheres in our system, and we have a duty to advocate and participate.

This biblical prescription is much more difficult when applied to people living under tyrannical governments, especially those that deny religious liberty and persecute Christians or members of other faiths. We should remember that the Bible also urges us to pray for our government leaders (1 Tim. 2:1–2). We don't believe this means we should pray for the implementation of harmful, misguided, or evil policies. Praying for leaders doesn't mean praying that they achieve destructive ends. When viewed in this light, these commands concerning obedience and prayer for government officials don't seem nearly as problematic. Regardless, we must bear in mind that the Bible is God's word, and we must obey it and never presume to substitute our judgment for God's.

Paul next tells Titus to instruct church members "to be obedient, to be ready for every good work, to speak evil of no one, to avoid quarreling, to be gentle, and to show perfect courtesy toward all people" (3:1–2). These commands are self-explanatory, but the context is probably that Paul wants believers to live peaceably and respectfully not only among themselves but with nonbelievers, as he taught the Romans (Rom. 12:18–21). We should not treat the pagan world as the enemy but as fellow human beings we are charged to love and to whom we have a duty to evangelize. Jesus was quite clear that we should love all people: "You have heard that it was said, 'You shall love your neighbor and hate your enemy.' But I say to you, love your enemies and pray for those who persecute you, so that you may be sons of your Father who is in heaven" (Matt. 5:43–44; c.f. Luke 6:27).

Prayer

Jesus, how can we truly love our enemies? It's statements like these that make us realize how much higher Your thoughts and ways are than our own (Isaiah 55). Reveal to us people in our lives who we may consider "enemies" but are in actuality our neighbors who are simply misguided and living apart from You. Show us specific ways we can pray for these people, and remind us to pray for them on a regular basis in the coming weeks. We know that You call us to forgive greatly because You Yourself have forgiven and paid for all our sins. When we begin to falter, bring Your answer to Peter's question in Matthew 18 to our minds: "Then Peter came to him and asked, 'Lord, how often should I forgive someone who sins against me? Seven times?' 'No, not seven times,' Jesus replied, 'but seventy times seven!'" (21–22 NLT).

Amen.

Paul provides another reason we should be charitable to nonbelievers. He humbly confesses that he (and Titus and other believers) used to be unbelievers and foolish, disobedient, and "led astray, slaves to various passions and pleasures, and passing our days in malice and envy, hated by others and hating one another" (3:3). Before becoming Christians they were guilty of all these things. Insofar as he persecuted and killed Christians, Paul was among the worst of sinners, as he elsewhere conceded (1 Tim. 1:15). And Paul adds that although he and other believers are no longer in that lost state, their deliverance is through no effort of their own. Believers are saved and redeemed by God's grace—period. "But when the goodness and loving kindness of God our Savior appeared," exclaims Paul, "he saved us, not because of works done by us in righteousness, but according to his own mercy, by the washing of regeneration and renewal of the Holy Spirit, whom he poured out on us richly through Jesus Christ our Savior, so that being justified by his grace we might become heirs according to the hope of eternal life" (3:4–7).

This is a concise and beautiful summary of the gospel. We were sinners, lost and dead in our sins, until God, because of His love, mercy, grace, and kindness, sent His Son to die for us, so that through faith in Him we are reborn through the power of the Holy Spirit and declared righteous and justified, heirs of the gift of eternal life. Let us never take for granted the magnitude of this unmerited gift. Let us never fail to appreciate and express our gratitude for our redemption and reconciliation with God.

In view of these verses and many others, some of which we have reviewed in this book, it is difficult to understand how any Bible reader can conclude that salvation is by anything other than faith in Jesus Christ alone. Paul hammers the point home over and over to ensure there is no mistaking it. He never wants us to forget that we owe our eternal lives to our loving, Triune God and that we did nothing to earn it. We do, however, have a duty to be forever grateful and to obediently place ourselves before God, exercise the spiritual disciplines, and grow more Christlike. Just because we don't earn our salvation, and our sanctification is through the power of the Holy Spirit, doesn't mean we don't have to strive to do good works, as Paul clarifies in the next verses: "The saying is trustworthy, and I want you to insist on these things, so that those who have believed in God may be careful to devote themselves to good works. These things are excellent and profitable for people" (3:8).

Though we are not saved by our good works, we must strive to lead good, moral lives in gratitude and obedience. Additionally, this is simply the right thing to do and is good for us—these are "excellent and profitable" things. Bruce Barton articulates this better than we can. "In this chapter, Paul stressed good works.... Paul understood good works as faithful service, acts of charity, and involvement in civil affairs," writes Barton. "While good works can't save us or even increase God's love for us, they are true indications of our faith and love for Christ. Paul did not make this aspect of discipleship 'optional.' Service to others is a requirement."[28]

PRAYER

Jesus, though we know Your sacrifice is the only thing that has saved us, may we also be reminded that You saved us so that we might live life abundantly, and a big part of that involves our actively working with You to bring goodness into the world. You told Your disciples the parable of the talents—which was a metaphor for people who take the gifts You have given them and put them to use contrasted with those who take Your gifts for granted and squander them. At the end of this parable, You told how the master responded to the servant who chose not to invest his gifts: "The master was furious. 'That's a terrible way to live! It's criminal to live cautiously like that! If

▶

you knew I was after the best, why did you do less than the least? The least you could have done would have been to invest the sum with the bankers, where at least I would have gotten a little interest. Take the thousand and give it to the one who risked the most. And get rid of this "play-it-safe" who won't go out on a limb'" (Matt 25:26–30, The MSG) This parable gives us insight into how seriously You feel about wasted opportunities. May we not miss our chance to be used by You to bear fruit and do good during the brief time we have here on earth. In Your Holy Name,

AMEN.

Paul sternly commands Titus to instruct believers to "avoid foolish controversies, genealogies, dissensions, and quarrels about the law, for they are unprofitable and worthless (3:9). While it is vitally important that we get our doctrine right—as Paul repeatedly emphasizes in these letters—we mustn't quibble over unimportant things because they generate strife and disharmony in the church and in society. More often about our own pride and egos than vindicating biblical truth, arguing over such matters has the opposite effect of correct doctrine because it draws us away from God. As for arguments with unbelievers, remember we will never argue anyone into the kingdom of God. We must defend the faith but do so winsomely and respectfully, not for the sake of winning an argument. We must give unbelievers the reasons for our belief without ridiculing their lack of faith (1 Peter 3:15). We are never going to persuade someone through reason alone; they must have a change of heart, and that requires the work of the Holy Spirit.

Paul is so adamant about preventing destructive quarrels in the church that he tells Titus, "As for a person who stirs up division, after warning him once and then twice, have nothing more to do with him, knowing that such a person is warped and sinful; he is self-condemned" (3:10–11). While this may sound harsh, remember the recurring theme of these letters concerning the paramount importance of correct doctrine and the necessity of purging false teachers and their teachings. These disciplinary measures are not punitive as much as they are needed to preserve unity in the church and the promotion of sound doctrine. "When the church cannot agree on the essentials of Christianity and is characterized by conflict and divisions, it is displeasing to God and ineffective to a lost world," writes Hayne Griffin.[29]

PRAYER

Father, You remind us of our fragility: "Come now, you who say, 'Today or tomorrow we will go into such and such a town and spend a year there and trade and make a profit'—yet you do not know what tomorrow will bring. What is your life? For you are a mist that appears for a little time and then vanishes. Instead you ought to say, 'If the Lord wills, we will live and do this or that'" (James 4:13–15). Since our time here is short and precious, guide us, today, to fix our eyes on what is true, pure, lovely, and admirable (Phil 4:8). May we not allow our minds to spiral into traps of petty quarrels; each day has enough trouble of its own and today, we choose to submit our hearts fully to Your hands.

AMEN.

Paul closes the letter with personal comments and greetings. He tells Titus to help Zenas the lawyer and Apollos proceed with their missionary journey and ensure that they lack nothing. The *ESV Study Bible* notes that these verses speak to the church's role in supporting missions, financially and otherwise. In closing, Paul repeats his call for believers to devote themselves to good works and to be productive. We must continue our path to holiness, contribute to the church and society, and serve our fellow human beings.

CHAPTER SEVEN

2 TIMOTHY

FINAL GUIDANCE FROM THE GREATEST EVANGELIST

The first epistle to Timothy is a "charge," this second one develops it into a challenge. It is a challenge to fortitude and faithfulness in face of present testings and of further testings which were yet to come.

—J. Sidlow Baxter[1]

This is the second of Paul's two epistles written to Timothy. Paul self-identifies as the author, which was largely unquestioned until a few centuries ago, when a group of revisionist scholars began casting doubt on Paul's authorship of this letter and other Pauline epistles. As Paul writes it, he's awaiting his death in a Roman prison. The letter's primary theme is encouraging Timothy to persevere in his fight for the faith no matter what hardships he encounters. Expecting his execution, Paul knows he must pass the torch to Timothy, as he also does in the first letter. Paul is not asking Timothy to do anything he wouldn't do himself, for he has already done it—and more.

Given Paul's imminent death, his close relationship with Timothy, and the stakes involved in Timothy's fully understanding and following his instructions, the letter is deeply personal. Paul reiterates themes from 1 Timothy and some of his other letters, particularly concerning the importance of understanding and teaching correct doctrine. Paul knows that Timothy understands how crucial it is to preserve the integrity of the gospel, yet he continues to reaffirm the theme.

The repetition illustrates that we all need constant encouragement and refreshers even on biblical principles with which we are intimately familiar. We must build one another other up in the face of challenges and emphasize the centrality of certain matters that may seem obvious. For example, we know how important Bible reading and prayer are, and we know it's vital that we always regard scripture as God's infallible revelation to us. But it is still wise for brothers in Christ to mutually reinforce these truths, which keep us grounded in the faith and our common mission in perspective. If Paul's entrusted lieutenant Timothy needs to be reminded of these essential truths and benefits from Paul's exhortations and encouragement, then so do we. We should be grateful to have one another for encouragement and that we have God's written record to forever remind us of what is most important.

As we read this letter, we should try to imagine what is going through Paul's mind as he writes it. Readers today know the historical record on the spread of the gospel, but Paul doesn't know how things will turn out. He trusts that God will arrange for the proliferation of the good news, but he also knows there will be obstacles because he is already experiencing them. At this point Paul must feel discouraged and anxious at times, wondering whether Timothy and others will press on with the same intensity and determination Paul has shown.

Paul feels conflicted, as he admits in his letter to the Philippians (Philip. 1:21–24). He knows his life on earth will end soon, which must be sad and difficult because he doesn't want to discontinue his work. But he is also looking forward to eternal life with Jesus Christ, "which is far better indeed." No matter how much he trusts God to superintend the work he began through Timothy, his letters reflect that he still believes he must do everything possible to impart his lessons to Timothy and to prepare him for inevitable conflicts.

What a poignant picture of the duality of Christian servants, who have one foot in the world and the other in God's kingdom. They recognize that while they trust God is in control, they have a duty to act on His behalf as long as they have life in them. And as we imagine Paul's mindset while penning this letter, we should also consider Timothy's thoughts and feelings when reading it—the combination of sorrow, joy, and the grave sense of duty and responsibility. While contemplating this epistle, we should try to capture its personal aspects, not just the doctrinal truths it teaches. God's lessons to us in scripture are not abstract, as in some written rule book or philosophical treatise. They are lessons wrapped in the lives of real people—human beings whose nature hasn't changed since mankind's beginning and who face the same types of problems and challenges we do. God bless Paul for his apostleship, his evangelism, and for leaving his written record for us, and God bless Timothy for rising to this divine challenge.

CHAPTER 1

Paul opens with a familiar reference to his divine appointment as an apostle, noting that it was by God's will according to the "promise of life that is in Christ Jesus." God's will is to save human beings who place their faith in Jesus Christ—and by save, we mean saving for eternal life. So it was God's will to appoint Paul to begin carrying the message to the entire world that He promises eternal life to those who trust the Son for it. He addresses the letter to Timothy, "my beloved child," showing again that Timothy is uniquely special to Paul—his spiritual son who will continue Paul's work.

Paul then thanks the God He serves with a clear conscience and notes that his ancestors served Him as well. The idea that Paul's Jewish ancestors served the same God might intrigue some readers, but as we've noted earlier, the Jews did worship and serve the God of the Bible—a God who was every bit as triune in Old Testament times as He is now. (Our eternal God has always been the same; He cannot change.) The Jews didn't recognize His triune nature and didn't accept Jesus Christ as the Son of God, but that doesn't change the fact that the God they served was indeed the same God Paul continued to serve. It's significant, however, that Paul tips his hat to his ancestors in this way, even after all he's been through for preaching a message about their God that they violently reject. Paul has longed his whole life for his fellow Jews to come to the full truth about God. That so many haven't yet is a source of great anguish for him (Romans 10:19–11:36).

Interpreters disagree about his reference to "a clear conscience," but most argue Paul is merely expressing his belief that he has acquitted himself well in his charge. He said the same thing when he defended himself before the chief priests and council: "I have lived my life before God in all good conscience up to this day" (Acts 23:1). He will also return to the theme later in this letter: "I have fought the good fight, I have finished the race, I have kept the faith" (2 Tim. 4:7). He knows he hasn't lived a sinless life since his conversion, but he has devoted himself entirely to Christ and has not the slightest doubt or pang of conscience about that.

Paul now gets personal with Timothy, telling him he prays for Timothy constantly, remembers his tears, and longs to see him so that he will be "filled with joy." He adds, "I am reminded of your sincere faith, a faith that dwelt first in your grandmother Lois and your mother Eunice and now, I am sure, dwells in you as well" (1:5). This is self-explanatory—Paul and Timothy are as lovingly close as father and son, and when they last parted Timothy was filled with sadness, probably because of Paul's imprisonment and their separation. So when they meet again they will both be joyful. Paul refers again to the faith of ancestors, but this time to Timothy's immediately preceding ancestors, and he notes that their firm faith was passed on to him. This seems natural because when Paul writes this—his last of thirteen epistles—he is nearing death and growing nostalgic, fondly remembering those who have gone before him and before Timothy. Moreover, Paul's appreciative reference to Timothy's faithful relatives shows the importance of teaching and modeling the faith to our own children. The saying "God has children but no grandchildren" is true—faith is a matter between each individual and God—but parental influence can be a major factor in a person's faith journey.

Prayer

Heavenly Father, thank You for the truth in Your promises. Deuteronomy 7:9 describes You as "the faithful God who keeps covenant and steadfast love with those who love him and keep his commandments, to a thousand generations." We know that each individual must come to know You on a personal level, but we also find many instances throughout Your word pointing to the significance of generational faith. Whatever our familial backgrounds, we ask that we will be part of an ongoing generation who will keep your commandments and love You steadfastly. Give us eyes to see beyond our own lives. Ignite our imaginations to have faith that our future descendants will be used in incredible ways for Your kingdom—that our lives are part of a large, multi-generational picture rather than just the seventy- to one hundred–year span through which the world measures them. Thank You for expanding our horizons and giving us fresh purpose. We pray these things in faith,

Amen.

Paul continues, "For this reason I remind you to fan into flame the gift of God, which is in you through the laying on of my hands, for God gave us a spirit not of fear but of power and love and self-control" (1:6–7). Paul clearly does not question Timothy's strong faith, but he'll need to elevate it further to assume Paul's work. Paul isn't suggesting Timothy has to resuscitate his faith as if it went dormant, but that he wants it to burn even brighter. "The command does not imply that Timothy had let his spiritual flame go out," writes Thomas Lea. "It is an appeal for a continual, vigorous use of spiritual gifts. Timothy was already using his gifts vigorously (2 Tim. 3:14)."[2] So Paul is treating Timothy respectfully. He isn't condescendingly ordering him to snap into action but gently reminding him of the gifts he is already using obediently. In case Timothy is in any sense timid, the courageous Paul is assuring him that fear is foreign to God's Holy Spirit (Romans 8:15), who infuses believers with power, love, and self-control (1:7).

Expanding on this theme that Timothy is to proceed fearlessly, Paul writes, "Therefore do not be ashamed of the testimony about our Lord, nor of me his prisoner, but share in suffering for the gospel by the power of God, who saved us and called us to a holy calling, not because of our works but because of his own purpose and grace, which he gave us in Christ Jesus before the ages began, and which now has been manifested through the appearing of our Savior Christ Jesus, who abolished death and brought life and immortality to light through the gospel, for which I was appointed a preacher and apostle and teacher, which is why I suffer as I do" (1:8–12).

Prayer

In their song "Fresh Fire," Maverick City Music sings of the fire that comes from a heart consumed with God. In one of the final stanzas, Brandon Lake sings that a "man on fire" does not care

▶

about appearances or his reputation or anyone's desires for his life but God's, so "God if I burn, I'll burn for You." What a beautiful depiction of a life lived in total pursuit of the Holy Spirit's calling. These words remind us of Paul's instructions to Timothy and his life lived on earth—no one can doubt Paul's burning heart for Jesus! Holy Spirit, we want this same type of passion for You. What would our lives look like if we cared more about what You think than what the world thinks of us? How much more joy would we experience if we set our hearts on knowing Your depths rather than continuously seeking to be blessed? Show us how we can please You, Lord. Reveal Your desires to us, that we might be truly set on making You smile. We love You and we bless Your Holy Name!

AMEN.

Paul is not worried about Timothy's being ashamed of the gospel any more than he was ashamed of it himself when he expressly said he wasn't (Romans 1:16). Chrysostom writes of the heretics and false teachers who, by contrast, *were* ashamed of the gospel, some of whom rejected the notion that Christ was actually human and endured physical suffering along with His other sufferings:

> Observe...how Marcion, and Manes, and Valentinus, and others who introduced heresies and pernicious doctrines into the church of God, measuring divine things by human reasonings, became ashamed of the divine economy. Yet it was not a subject for shame but rather for glorying; I speak of the cross of Christ.... For in themselves death and imprisonment and chains are matters of shame and reproach. But when the cause is added before us and mystery viewed aright, they will appear full of dignity and a matter for boasting. For it was that death on the cross that

> saved the world when it was perishing. That death connected earth with heaven; that death destroyed the power of the devil and made men…sons of God; that death raised our nature to the kingly throne. Those chains enabled the conversion of many.[3]

We include the long Chrysostom quote because it sublimely expresses that glorious Christian paradox that our sinless God triumphantly endured suffering for us so that we could live. He got down in the dirt for us in every respect; He was not ashamed to take on human form; He embraced it and drank in His suffering willingly, lovingly, and sacrificially. Far from being ashamed of the indignities as the heretics and false teachers were, Paul is honored and proud to proclaim the work Christ did for us while urging Timothy to keep it all in the proper perspective. As Ambrosiaster aptly observed, Christ's incarnation, death, and resurrection are not a cause of weakness but of power.[4] That's exactly right. How astonishingly off-base were the false teachers who completely missed the point. Christ's incarnation—His becoming a human being—is what allows us to be eternal, spiritual (and physical) beings.

Thus explaining that Christ's suffering was not shameful but a model for our own suffering for Him, Paul commands Timothy to share in that suffering for the gospel on God's behalf because God called us to holy service and saved us—not due to our works but because of His grace and His purpose, which He planned before time began. God's foreordained plan, Paul explains, has now come to fruition through Jesus' victory over death, and Paul has been appointed to preach and teach these truths, which is the direct cause of his suffering. But he relishes that suffering.

Paul repeats that he's not ashamed, even though he is imprisoned—something that would be shameful if it were a result of truly criminal and immoral acts. "Carrying out his stewardship had brought Paul much suffering, including his present imprisonment," writes Duane Liftin. "In the eyes of the world he was a common criminal (cf. 2 Tim. 2:9). Yet he was able to say, I am not ashamed." That's because Paul trusts that God will ultimately vindicate him. ("For I know whom I have believed, and I am convinced that he is able to guard until that day what has been entrusted to me" [1:12].)[5]

Paul instructs Timothy to "Follow the pattern of the sound words that you have heard from me, in the faith and love that are in Christ Jesus. By the Holy Spirit who dwells within us, guard the good deposit entrusted to you" (1:13–14). Here again, Paul underscores the importance of sound doctrine—the power of the word of God. The Holy Spirit, who indwells believers, will guard the word that has been entrusted to Paul, Timothy, and all believers. But specifically, Paul is reminding Timothy that he imparted the gospel to him, and Timothy should recognize that the Holy Spirit lives in him and will safeguard the word. This is powerful reassurance, for Paul is telling Timothy that he's not alone in this struggle to preserve correct doctrine. No less than God is right there within him to ensure he succeeds.

Augustine observes that we entrust to God's keeping His promise of salvation to us. But he adds that we pray to God to preserve the things we entrust to him—including faith. We love the idea that we can go to God in prayer and ask Him for anything, though we should always pray for outcomes that are within His sovereign will. But even as to faith, with which so many struggle, God won't leave us solely on our own. If we ask Him, He will strengthen our very faith. "Now what do we commend to God's keeping save those things which we pray he will preserve?" asks Augustine. "Is not our very faith among these? For what did the Lord commend for the apostle Peter, by his prayer for him, when he said to him, 'I have prayed for you, Peter, that your faith shall not fail'? This means that God would preserve his faith and that it would not fail by giving way to temptation."[6]

It is so comforting that Jesus Himself didn't berate Peter for any failings in his faith but prayed to His Father to protect Peter's faith. So let's not be too hard on ourselves when we experience doubts or our faith falters. Let's remember that Jesus, who experienced human life for us, understands what we're going through. He understands that our faith can waver, and he isn't judging us for it. He's lifting us up to enable us to get through it and to return us to full confidence in the Father, the Holy Spirit, and Himself.

PRAYER

Christian Holocaust survivor Corrie Ten Boom said, "With Jesus, even in our darkest moments the best remains and the very best is yet to be." Jesus, You are such a good friend! Thank You for standing in the gap, interceding for us even while our faith in Your goodness is found wanting. It's so comforting to know we never have to hide any of our faults or fears from You; if we don't tell You enough, we adore You for who You are. Thank You for being our constant in all things. You are our light, our life-source, and our hope! We love You.

AMEN.

Paul closes this chapter lamenting those, like Phygelus and Hermogenes, who turned away from him. Paul here reveals his human side. As strong as his faith is, he still feels the sting of those who abandoned him and even worse, who abandoned the gospel. The *ESV Study Bible* editors provide this valuable insight: "These details highlight the low situation in which Paul found himself and probably help explain why Timothy, the faithful one, was such a source of joy for Paul."[7] In contrast, Paul asks God for mercy on the household of Onesiphorus because he encouraged Paul and was unafraid of Paul's imprisonment. He even went out of his way to find Paul when he arrived in Rome, and he also rendered yeoman's service for the gospel at Ephesus.

CHAPTER 2

Paul begins this chapter directly commissioning Timothy to equip other men for ministry in the same way Paul equipped him. In turn they will be able to teach others, and the pattern will continue throughout the world and in perpetuity. "You then, my child, be strengthened by the grace that is in Christ Jesus, and what you have heard from me in the presence of many witnesses entrust to faithful men, who will be able to teach others also. Share in suffering as a good soldier of Christ Jesus. No soldier gets entangled in civilian pursuits, since his aim is to please the one who enlisted him. An athlete is not crowned unless he competes according to the rules. It is the hard-working farmer who ought to have the first share of the crops" (2:1–6).

Having cited positive and negative examples of colleagues, Paul is encouraging Timothy to imitate the positive one, the faithful Onesiphorus. By explaining the exponential effect of powerful preaching, he is demonstrating that Timothy's choice will have potentially unlimited consequences. If he remains strong through Christ's gracious empowerment and perseveres in teaching others and modeling such endurance and determination, others will do likewise, and the gospel will flourish throughout the generations. If instead he allows challenges to defeat him, his work will stop in its tracks. His poor witness will not advance the gospel and will even hinder it because others will devalue the faith if its main proponents wither in the face of obstacles.

So Paul doesn't merely provide "book knowledge" to Timothy but shows him how to walk the Christian walk even when it causes great personal pain. We must realize we won't always see the effects on others of our teaching and actions—both negative and positive—but we surely will have some effect, thus we must strive to be winsome witnesses for Christ. After all, our good works are not for our own gratification, so we can't be discouraged if we don't see immediate results in our evangelism. Sometimes many seeds must be planted before one ultimately takes root. There is nothing wrong, of course, in our natural human desire to see good come from our labors, but that can't be our primary focus. Like Paul, we must be obedient and persevere.

We should not try to please ourselves or others but "the One who enlisted" us (2:4). "The ambition of the Christian soldier must be that of pleasing the Commander," writes Hayne Griffin. "The phrase '[a good soldier of Christ Jesus]' is not merely a reference to someone's serving as a minister or full-time Christian worker. Paul desired that all believers live as solders."[8]

Imagine the frustration Paul must feel being physically restrained when he could be pounding the pavement for Christ. But at least he isn't silenced—he continues to preach, teach, and write prolifically during his house arrests, and his writings change the course of history. God is always in control. While it's much easier for us to write these words than to follow them, we must remain obedient to God's will. This includes spreading the good news because it is just as good as when it was first announced thousands of years ago. We believe Griffin is correct—Paul's charge applies to us as much as it does to Timothy. And like Timothy, we must follow the example of Paul, who pressed forward though many times when he couldn't see his impact firsthand.

We must also acknowledge that as American citizens our religious liberties are constitutionally guaranteed and, with certain exceptions, we don't endure suffering or persecution like the early Christians did or like those in many parts of the world today, including Communist China, still do. This is all the more reason we should obey our calling to be ambassadors for Christ.

PRAYER

The writer of Hebrews wrote, "Therefore, since we are surrounded by such a huge crowd of witnesses to the life of faith, let us strip off every weight that slows us down" (12:1 NLT). Bruce Barton observes, "These faithful people from the past now stand as so great a cloud of witnesses. Hebrews uses the athletic imagery of a Greek amphitheater that has rows and rows of spectators, a 'great cloud' or a large group. They do not 'witness' as if they were merely spectators... instead, they witness through the historical record of their faithfulness that constantly encourages those who follow them. We do not struggle alone, and we are not the first to struggle with problems, persecution, discouragement, even failure. Others have 'run the race' and crossed the finish line, and their witness stirs us to run and win also."

Jesus, thank You for being the first to run this great race for us. You are our ultimate goal post, cheerleader, and teammate in this battle of good versus evil. May we always remember we are never alone in our struggles because You go before us and stand behind us, beside us, and inside us. Give us the passion and energy needed to make a difference in the places where we live as well as places far away where Christians are truly persecuted for their beliefs. We ask for You to speak to us in specific ways, showing us how we can contribute to the fight against persecution. In Your Holy Name,

AMEN.

Paul now switches from a soldier metaphor to those of athletes and farmers, informing Timothy (and us) that God rewards hard work and obedience on behalf of Christ (2:5–6). Paul was more explicit in his second canonical letter to the Corinthians: "For we must all appear before the judgement seat of Christ, so that each one may receive what is due for what he has done in the body, whether good or evil" (2 Cor. 5:10). To the Galatians, Paul wrote, "Do not be deceived: God is not mocked, for whatever one sows, that will he also reap. For the one who sows to his own flesh will from the flesh reap corruption, but the one who sows to the Spirit will from the Spirit reap eternal life" (Gal. 6:7–8). The Old Testament expresses an identical principle: "The faithless will be fully repaid for their ways, and the good rewarded for theirs" (Prov. 14:14).

All three images—solider, athlete, and farmer—illustrate the same theme: we should be obedient and diligent in our work for Christ, staying motivated both to please God and to receive His rewards. Let's be clear: Paul is not contradicting his teaching that we are saved by faith alone and not by our works. "Our good works have nothing to do with keeping our salvation, no more than they had anything to do with our receiving our salvation," writes John MacArthur. "But they have everything to do with working out our salvation (Philip. 2:12).[9] Likewise, Gary Demarest notes, "Each one of us is called to a life of ministry. That ministry is done in the context of caring and supporting relationships. And it is always difficult. But in a life of discipline, like soldiers, athletes, and farmers, great are the joys and rewards of such a life. So it was for Paul. So it was for Timothy. And so it can be for us!"[10] Also bear in mind the words of Jesus here: "For the Son of Man is going to come with his angels in the glory of his Father, and then he will repay each person according to what he has done" (Matt. 16:27).

Paul then tells Timothy, "Think over what I say, for the Lord will give you understanding in everything" (2:7). Paul seems to acknowledge that his messages are sometimes complex and require deep thought and pondering. (Even the apostle Peter granted that some of Paul's writings are hard to understand [2 Peter 3:15–16].) But if we study, pray, and meditate on these writings, as with other scripture, God will enlighten our understanding. If we do our part, God will more than meet us halfway. God gave us our minds and intends for us to use them. Jesus said, "You shall love the Lord your God with all your heart and with all your soul and with all your mind" (Matt. 22:34). We must witness and defend our faith wisely, while leaning on the Holy Spirit to aid our understanding and our teaching of the word. We marvel at God's word in so many ways, but one major one is that while its message is simple enough for children to understand, it is also complex enough that we can spend a lifetime studying it and never uncover all its riches.

Prayer

Regarding Paul's writing in 2 Timothy 2:7, the *Life Application Study Bible* instructs, "As you read the Bible, ask God to show you His timeless truths and the application to your life. Then consider what you have read by thinking it through and meditating on it. God will give you understanding." Father, when it comes to spending time with You in Your word, quality means so much more than quantity. Many of us push ourselves to read as much as we can rather than using our time in the word as an opportunity to truly commune with You. It's so important that we use the Bible as a gateway to Your presence, inviting You into our lives, seeking to receive insight from You. We so desperately need to slow down. Help us to be rid of the religious mentality that focuses on achievement-based, goal-oriented Bible study rather than genuine intimacy and conversation with You. May we take time now to read 2 Timothy in our Bibles and invite You to instruct us, even if it's just about a singular verse in the chapter.

Amen.

Now Paul tells Timothy, "Remember Jesus Christ, risen from the dead, the offspring of David, as preached in my gospel, for which I am suffering, bound with chains as a criminal. But the word of God is not bound! Therefore I endure everything for the sake of the elect, that they also may obtain the salvation that is in Christ Jesus with eternal glory" (2:8–10).

As we mentioned above, though Paul is in prison, his work continues, and its impact multiplies exponentially because "the word of God is not bound!" He is telling Timothy to keep his eyes focused on the essence of the gospel message. One component of it is that Jesus was the promised Messiah in the line of King David who died and was resurrected so that those who place their faith in Him would be resurrected with Him. Paul confesses his own suffering but testifies that his work is worth hardship because he is leading people to Christ and eternal life. If we put our faith in Him, we will be resurrected by Him and live with Him. As summarized by the *Preacher's Outline and Sermon Bible*, "Just imagine living forever in eternal glory! Such a life is beyond our imagination, yet it is exactly what the gospel is all about. Therefore, no matter what it costs—no matter how much suffering we have to bear—we must endure it all for the salvation of people."[11]

Paul rounds out this theme with what many scholars believe is a hymn of the early church: "The saying is trustworthy, for: If we have died with him, we will also live with him; if we endure, we will also reign with him; if we deny him, he also will deny us; if we are faithless, he remains faithful—for he cannot deny himself" (2:11–13).[12] We can bank on God's promise of eternal life if we trust in His Son. We will even reign along with Him (Rev. 3:21; 5:10; 20:4).

Christ doesn't force us to trust in Him or follow Him. If we choose to reject Him, He will honor our choice. Jesus said Himself, "So everyone who acknowledges me before men, I also will acknowledge before my Father who is in heaven, but whoever denies me before men, I also will deny before my Father who is in heaven" (Matt. 10:32–33); But if we do truly place our faith in Him for salvation, He will grant us life even if we sin, as all believers do. He will not deny His promise of salvation to believers because God never lies (Titus 1:2). God's character is unchanging (Mal. 3:6; He. 13:8). "Even when believers fail the Savior, He remains loyal," says E. D. Radmacher. "For Christ to abandon us would be contrary to His faithful nature. Christ's relationship with Peter is a fitting example of God's faithfulness."[13] Paul is not saying that a temporary lapse in faith or denial of Christ will result in a forfeiture of eternal life.[14] Those Christ denies are probably those who never genuinely trusted Him in the first place.[15] "True believers might be faithless and weak at times;" writes Barton, "they might falter when giving a testimony, but they would never disown their Lord."[16]

Paul tells Timothy to remind his congregation of the lessons he is imparting in this letter. This is a change in emphasis—whereas before he had mainly been telling Timothy what Timothy should think, remember, and do, now he's telling Timothy to make sure his congregation remembers these things as well.[17] The point is that these lessons are for all Christians. Note that Paul is often telling Timothy (and now the church members) various doctrinal truths. If they already know these things, why does he find it so important to remind them? We alluded to this earlier in the chapter—we know from our own experience that we have been previously exposed to many biblical principles, yet when we hear preaching and teaching on many of these subjects we realize we don't always have top-of-the-mind awareness, which we need to apply these principles to our lives.

That's one reason verse memorization is a cherished spiritual discipline. The Bible is so full of life-changing messages, but we just can't keep them all in our heads, so it is vital that we read, re-read, study, meditate, and contemplate scripture, and listen to and read what others say. This is why we should cultivate the practice of daily scripture reading. The Bible not only tells us how to live but informs us of God's will, His plan, and His righteousness, which we are to emulate. The longer we neglect this discipline, the more the principles fade from our conscious minds. We should interact with scripture every day to ensure that its message remains an integral part of our lives.

PRAYER

Holy Spirit, thank You for living in us, never neglecting to watch over us. As the Psalmist described in Psalm 121, "The Lord himself watches over you! The Lord stands beside you as your protective shade. The sun will not harm you by day, nor the moon at night. The Lord keeps you from all harm and watches over your life. The Lord keeps watch over you as you come and go, both now and forever" (5–8 NLT). We read this Psalm and meditate on the fact that You are always watching over us. Therefore, we should be moved to include You in every aspect of our daily lives: our coming and our going, our waking and sleeping. Help us to speak to You sometimes in whispers throughout our day, making prayer less of a formal activity and more of an ongoing conversation with You. We want You to be our best friend and to always feel connected to You. We love You, Lord!

AMEN.

Paul adds that Timothy must command the congregants before God to stop quarreling over words, as it is futile and destructive. As we've said, Paul insists some arguments are worth having, such as correcting the doctrinal errors of the false teachers, but petty squabbles over minor matters or words are damaging. Such disputes are usually driven by those who want to prove themselves brilliant rather than vindicating the word of God. Argument for its own sake about supposedly spiritual matters does not build up but is harmful to the participants and to the cause of Christ.

Instead, says Paul, Timothy should set a good example before God: "Do your best to present yourself to God as one approved, a worker who has no need to be ashamed, rightly handling the word of truth. But avoid irreverent babble, for it will lead people into more and more ungodliness, and their talk will spread like gangrene. Among them are Hymenaeus and Philetus, who have swerved from the truth, saying that the resurrection has already happened. They are upsetting the faith of some. But God's firm foundation stands, bearing this seal: 'The Lord knows those who are his,' and 'Let everyone who names the name of the Lord depart from iniquity'" (2:15–19).

The meaning of the first sentence is plain enough: Timothy should do God's work in a way that will gain His approval. False teachers do precisely the opposite, behaving in a way that displeases God. These heretics probably aren't even motivated to please God but themselves and other people. As long as Timothy consciously conducts himself to please God, he is more likely actually to please Him. Specifically, and above all, his exemplary work should be in correctly understanding, communicating, and applying the gospel message and the entirety of scripture ("the word of truth").

Correctly handling the word of truth means to present it without adding or subtracting from it to suit your own agenda and without distorting or perverting its meaning. "For many distort the text of Scripture and pervert it in every way, and many additions are made to it," writes Chrysostom. "With the sword of the Spirit cut off from your preaching, as from a thong, whatever is superfluous and foreign to it."[18] The *Preacher's Outline and Sermon Bible* explains, "We are not to mishandle the Word of God: twist it to fit what we think or want it to say; over-emphasize or underemphasize its teachings; add to or take away from it. Any person who mishandles God's Word is not approved of God."[19] Pray that the Holy Spirit will illuminate God's word for you, then read it, study it, and treat it sacredly, for it is sacred, as God's infallible word to us. Rightly handling the word of truth will insulate Timothy—and all other preachers and teachers—from the type of shame that should attach to false teachers.

Paul's command to Timothy—to avoid irreverent babble that will lead people into ungodliness, upset their faith, and spread like gangrene—is a grave warning. Hymenaeus and Philetus have violated this principle by insisting that the resurrection has already happened, which is undermining some people's faith. Scholars argue that Paul's command means Timothy should "turn his back" on these babblings—not just avoid them but hold them in contempt.[20] It's fine to engage in serious discussions about doctrine in a genuine quest to discover its true meaning, but to bicker over words in the spirit of ego-driven arguments rather than seeking the truth is not constructive and potentially divisive and destructive. We also don't want to sow doubt among our fellow believers or increase the doubts of nonbelievers by giving too much credence to fallacious ideas. To do so leads away from godliness rather than toward it. And these kinds of pseudo-intellectual exchanges will spawn further negative discussions, which Paul likens to spreading gangrene. Interpreters note that Paul chooses his words carefully because this analogy not only captures the image of rapid spreading of the practice but its spiritually deadly potential.[21] Paul's readers will understand that gangrene in their day is almost always fatal to the human body, just as false teaching can be fatal to one's spiritual condition and to the church.[22]

Paul again singles out Hymenaeus as a false teacher (he had mentioned him in verse 1:20), but this time he adds Philetus as another one. Paul is especially intolerant of their spreading the abominable heresy that the resurrection had already occurred. Greek philosophers reject Christ's humanity and his bodily resurrection because they believe the spiritual world is pure and the material world is evil, and that the physical body temporarily imprisons the immortal soul.[23] These false teachers claim believers are spiritually resurrected upon their conversion, and there will be no future bodily resurrection. Their heresy is upsetting the faith of some people, so central is it to Christian doctrine.

It is critical to one's Christian faith that one believes Christ is both human and divine, that he was bodily resurrected, and that He will bodily resurrect those who have faith in Him. This is a non-negotiable Christian truth, and Paul will not allow the slightest deviation from it. Paul's firm words to the Corinthians should be permanently etched in our minds: "Now if Christ is proclaimed as raised from the dead, how can some of you say that there is no resurrection of the dead? But if there is no resurrection of the dead, then not even Christ has been raised. And if Christ has not been raised, then our preaching is in vain and your faith is in vain.... And if Christ has not been raised, your faith is futile and you are still in your sins. Then those also who have fallen asleep in Christ have perished. If in Christ we have hope in this life only, we are of all people most to be pitied" (1 Cor. 15:12–14, 17–19). This is a perfect example of a subject that Paul does argue about—in fact, it is a hill to die on.

Despite these false teachings, Paul assures Timothy that God's church remains solid, and the Lord knows who are and aren't genuine believers. Paul is letting Timothy know that God is in control and can be relied on to seal the hearts of believers. Those who are in Christ, warns Paul, should have nothing to do with these false teachers and their lies—they should abandon them, put all their faith in the true God, and follow correct doctrine. If you claim you belong to God, then act like it, and don't even flirt with these heresies.

Paul continues, "Now in a great house there are not only vessels of gold and silver but also of wood and clay, some for honorable use, some for dishonorable. Therefore, if anyone cleanses himself from what is dishonorable, he will be a vessel for honorable use, set apart as holy, useful to the master of the house, ready for every good work" (2:20–21). Some interpreters believe Paul uses this metaphor to describe two types of believers. There are the spiritually mature believers who adhere to correct doctrine and don't engage in these petty quarrels; there are also those less mature who allow these heresies to infect their thinking. Other scholars believe Paul is referring to believers in the church and unbelievers. Either way, Paul is encouraging Timothy and all readers to avoid those who spread false teachings and bond with those who don't spread such errors. Community among believers is essential for the spiritual health of individual believers and for the church. Followers of Christ should keep themselves from impurities and live lives of holiness, thus being useful to God and for every good work.

Paul then counsels, "So flee from youthful passions and pursue righteousness, faith, love, and peace, along with those who call on the Lord from a pure heart. Have nothing to do with foolish, ignorant controversies; you know that they breed quarrels. And the Lord's servant must not be quarrelsome but kind to everyone, able to teach, patiently enduring evil, correcting his opponents with gentleness. God may perhaps grant them repentance leading to a knowledge of the truth, and they may come to their senses and escape from the snare of the devil, after being captured by him to do his will" (2:22–26).

Paul is warning Timothy to pursue the Christian virtues instead of worldly temptations that typically attract the young and immature. "Youthful desires are contrary [to faith] because they are worldly lusts which are tied up with all sorts of temptations," writes Ambrosiaster. "For that reason, they must be avoided by the servant of God. Paul orders Timothy to aim for things which seem odd and hard to someone who is young."[24] One thing that makes Paul and his teachings so unique is that he doesn't just list things to avoid but usually adds things to pursue. He ends the chapter on a typically encouraging note, telling Timothy to actively seek holiness.

Paul is reiterating that Timothy shouldn't engage in these silly, trivial discussions, which will lead to petty quarrels. Even so, he should show humility and respect to everyone, even his opponents. Paul doesn't want opponents to be humiliated or punished. He instructs Timothy to correct them gently—hoping they will repent, come to know the truth, and see the error of false teachings. He genuinely wants them to snap out of their unreasonableness and escape the devil's clutches, though they have been captive to him and doing his will.

Paul apparently wants opponents to be treated respectfully because it's the right thing to do and also because it will increase the likelihood they will repent and turn from Satan to Christ. In short, avoid the false teachings, but don't necessarily abandon the false teachers or those who have fallen under their spell. If approached with Christlike care, some will come to repentance and abandon their errors. And the best antidote to false teaching is correct teaching. "The best prescription for avoiding enticing errors is a proper presentation of the truth," says Hayne Griffin.[25] Bear in mind that the Bible, being truth, is a great weapon to advance truth. And remember Paul's teaching to the Ephesians that the word of God is "the sword of the Spirit" (Eph. 6:17).

PRAYER

Basil the Great once warned of the temptation to let our emotions drive us when correcting others, writing, "The superior should not administer a rebuke to wrongdoers when his own passions are aroused. By admonishing a brother with anger and indignation, he does not free him from his faults but involves himself in the error."[26] Lord, when we are clearly called to correct or rebuke another, help us to take a pause, inviting the Holy Spirit to give us the direction we need to handle such situations with proper care. If we show no restraint in regard to our heightened emotions, we will most assuredly give the enemy a foothold in these situations. Guard our hearts and help us to submit our plans to You. With reverence for Your knowledge and authority over all things we lift these things to You.

AMEN.

CHAPTER 3

Paul turns now to a prophecy of the prevalence of godlessness in the last days: "But understand this, that in the last days there will come times of difficulty. For people will be lovers of self, lovers of money, proud, arrogant, abusive, disobedient to their parents, ungrateful, unholy, heartless, unappeasable, slanderous, without self-control, brutal, not loving good, treacherous, reckless, swollen with conceit, lovers of pleasure rather than lovers of God, having the appearance of godliness, but denying its power" (3:1–5).

The reference to "the last days" is sometimes misunderstood. This wasn't necessarily a reference to the distant future, for scripture refers to "the last days" as those beginning when the Holy Spirit came at Pentecost (Acts 2:17). "Last days includes the whole time from the writing of this letter until the return of Christ," writes E. D. Radmacher.[27] Similarly, Douglas Moo notes that the phrase "later times" is synonymous with "the last days," and they each refer to the period beginning with Christ's coming, then intensifying with His resurrection and the coming of the Spirit, and continuing until His return.[28] There is certainly other scriptural warrant for this, as the writer of Hebrews said, "But in these last days he has spoken to us by his Son, whom he appointed the heir of all things, through whom also he created the world" (Heb. 1:2). Some scholars, however, insist "the last days" refers only to the period before Christ returns to establish His kingdom, though acknowledging that Christians living during the New Testament period believed they were already living in the last days.[29]

Regardless, conditions certainly have continued to intensify in our modern era. Considering the decadence of modern culture, it's a little chilling to read the comments on this verse by early Christian author Tertullian. "The conquering power of evil is on the increase," he writes. "This is characteristic of the last times. Innocent babies are now not even allowed to be born, so corrupted are the moral standards. Or if born, no one educates them, so desolate are studies. Or if trained, no one enforces the training, so impotent are the laws. In fact, the case for modesty which we are now beginning to treat, has in our time become an obsolete subject."[30]

The ominous vices in this passage all seem to flow from the first one—the love of self. "When the center of gravity in an individual shifts from God to self, a plethora of sins can spring up," writes Thomas Lea.[31] A quick review of the remaining vices bears this out. This is a fairly comprehensive list of sins, and with little imagination we can readily see how turning away from God toward an inordinate focus on self could lead to all of them.

The last vice may be less self-evident so we should more closely examine it—"having the appearance of godliness, but denying its power." We find this especially interesting in view of the quasi-religious zeal with which some promote secular causes in the modern culture. Paul is talking here about people who are nominally Christians but don't really embrace the faith. However, it is hauntingly descriptive of many in our popular culture today who reject the Christian faith but evangelize various secular enterprises with militant fervor. Bruce Barton's description of these nominal Christians during New Testament times is instructive. "Often these evil characteristics appear in the context of respectability," writes Barton. "Religion is not gone; in fact these character qualities are frequently exhibited by people known for their 'religiousness.' However, as Paul wrote, they practice a form of godliness—that is, using godliness as a cloak of respectability while denying God's power over their lives."[32]

We can see how things have indeed intensified in our modern era when you modify Barton's description to remove God from the equation altogether. The secular zealots today display all the faith of a monk but are totally detached from the God of the Bible as they advocate, protest, and moralize. They often disdain the Christian faith and Christians themselves due to our supposed intolerance. Yet bereft of self-awareness, they are more judgmental than the most legalistic of Christians. They also reject many of the moral standards prescribed in scripture while proclaiming their own superior morality. Like the counterfeit Christians of New Testament times, today's secular warriors are often unapologetic practitioners of sins from Paul's list. While not under the umbrella of the Christian church, they are nevertheless false teachers who prey on spiritually vulnerable people who do not have God in their lives but have a hole in their hearts that must be filled with something.

Paul plainly commands Timothy to avoid these compromised people: "For among them are those who creep into households and capture weak women, burdened with sins and led astray by various passions, always learning and never able to arrive at a knowledge of the truth. Just as Jannes and Jambres opposed Moses, so these men also opposed the truth, men corrupted in mind and disqualified regarding the faith. But they will not get very far, for their folly will be plain to all, as was that of those two men" (3:6–9).

Note that Paul is again indicting the false teachers who lead people into sin, and again, the analogies to our modern secular culture are striking. They "creep into households," meaning they deceive their victims into believing they hold the key to godliness and moral principles. They prey upon weak women burdened with sins and those always thirsting for knowledge but never finding the truth. Once the false teachers gain a foothold, they "capture" or seize control of their victims. "They had entered homes under false pretenses," explains Lea. "Once admitted, they proceeded to 'gain control.'... In this context the terms suggest that the false teachers had gained a complete psychological dominance over their victims."[33] Sadly, in our modern culture, so many fall prey to the false teachings of the secular zealots who have gained such psychological dominance over those they indoctrinate and intimidate that their victims no longer exhibit any ability to think for themselves.

Jannes and Jambres are not mentioned in the Old Testament, but extra-biblical Jewish writings describe them as Egyptian magicians who opposed Moses and thus became symbols of opposition to God.[34] By referring to these two hucksters, Paul is saying that the false teachers and those under their spell are "disqualified regarding the faith," meaning they have no authentic saving faith. Such people, however, will eventually expose themselves through the obviousness of their foolish teaching and practices.

PRAYER

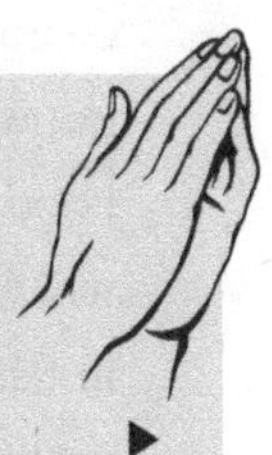

Holy Spirit, increase in us the ability to discern evil disguised as good in modern culture. Help us to be patient as we absorb ▶

information in the news, taking time to allow You to speak to us and instruct us on where we should stand on current cultural matters. We don't want to get swept up by popular narratives, however well-meaning they may appear to be at surface-level. Remind us to test these things against scripture and to seek counsel from wise leaders who wait to receive guidance from You on complex issues.

AMEN.

Paul keeps returning to positive themes, and now we come to another one of our favorite passages of scripture thanks to its affirmation that the Bible is divinely inspired, wholly reliable, and spiritually, morally, and intellectually edifying. After describing the false teachers and the tragic results of their teachings on the body of Christ and individual believers, Paul praises Timothy for his obedience and for honoring God's word and living out its principles:

> You, however, have followed my teaching, my conduct, my aim in life, my faith, my patience, my love, my steadfastness, my persecutions and sufferings that happened to me at Antioch, at Iconium, and at Lystra—which persecutions I endured; yet from them all the Lord rescued me. Indeed, all who desire to live a godly life in Christ Jesus will be persecuted, while evil people and impostors will go on from bad to worse, deceiving and being deceived. But as for you, continue in what you have learned and have firmly believed, knowing from whom you learned it and how from childhood you have been acquainted with the sacred writings, which are able to make you wise for salvation through faith in Christ Jesus. All Scripture is breathed out by God and profitable for teaching, for reproof, for correction, and for

training in righteousness, that the man of God may be complete, equipped for every good work." (3:10–17)

Here Paul holds himself up as the prime example of how a Christian should lead, teach, and live, which stands in stark contrast to the picture he paints of the false teachers. Note the first clause, which other translations render more clearly as, "You however, know all about my teaching" (3:10). Paul is not saying that Timothy has already followed his teaching but that he is aware of it and understands it, as he was Paul's spiritual student. Again, Paul has no interest in proudly lifting himself up. He seeks no credit for this, but he does want Timothy to understand that Paul has modeled this behavior, and Timothy should emulate it. Far from egotistical, Paul is reassuring Timothy that living out Christian principles is an achievable goal. Paul's words aren't entirely encouraging, of course, because they realistically warn Timothy of persecution that inevitably awaits him if he follows Paul's path. Even so, the Lord always rescues Paul and everyone profits in the end—Paul's listeners and Paul himself.

We find it especially gratifying that Paul doesn't candy-coat problems inherent in living and preaching the faith. If he were merely trying to win converts, he might promise nothing but rainbows, but he does the opposite, which enhances his credibility. He isn't trying to win superficial allies to the faith but spiritual warriors grounded in scripture, steeped in their faith in Christ, filled with the Holy Spirit, and prepared to endure hardship—whatever it takes to advance the glorious gospel. Augustine puts into proper perspective Paul's transparency, as distinguished from those who would promise only good things for believers. "What sort of people, though, are those who, being afraid to offend the ones they are talking to, not only don't prepare them for the trials that are looming ahead but even promise them a well-being in this world which God himself hasn't promised to the world?" he asks. "He foretells distress upon distress coming upon the world right up to the end, and do you wish the Christian to be exempt from these distresses? Precisely because he's a Christian, he is going to suffer more in this world."[35]

PRAYER

Lord, thank You for being a perfect Father to us who, when necessary, gives us the hard truth we need to steer us from the wayward path. We acknowledge that You are wonderfully complex, and throughout Your word You instruct us with different tones for every type of occasion. Good earthly fathers know when to be firm and when to show compassion, and that discernment actually comes from You! You are the best Father, teacher, and companion, and we adore You for all that You are to us.

AMEN.

Now Paul directly instructs Timothy to stay the course, remembering what he's learned about Christ and who taught him. He acknowledges that Timothy has been raised up on scripture, which is "able to make you wise for salvation through faith in Christ Jesus." Remember that Paul here is mostly talking about Old Testament writings, which he is saying lead to salvation through faith in Christ. Some interpreters hold that Paul might also be referring to early records of Jesus' words and perhaps some apostolic writings,[36] but Paul is primarily talking about the Old Testament.

This might seem counterintuitive. Since the days when he was persecuting Christians, however, Paul has learned that the Old Testament is all about Jesus Christ. In my (David's) book *The Emmaus Code*, I walked through the Old Testament to show how every book in countless ways points to Christ. Jesus, of course, affirmed that the Old Testament scripture is all about Him when he met two people on the road to Emmaus in one of His resurrection appearances: "And beginning with Moses and all the Prophets, [Christ] interpreted to them in all the Scriptures the things concerning himself" (Luke 24:27). Griffin explains, "The aim of the content of the sacred writings is to relate God's saving purpose in Christ. Timothy's study of the Scriptures had grounded him in that wisdom and enlightenment that lead to faith in Jesus Christ. The Scriptures lead to salvation but only as they point to Christ."[37] Recall that the Old Testament also "points to Christ" by illuminating for us our total inadequacy to meet God's standards apart from Christ. It primes us for faith in Christ as it underscores the impossibility of our perfectly obeying God's perfect law.

The next verse is exciting for Bible lovers: "All Scripture is breathed out by God and profitable for teaching, for reproof, for correction, and for training in righteousness, that the man of God may be complete, equipped for every good work" (3:16). We noted that in the previous verse, "the sacred writings" primarily refers to the Old Testament but that it also could be applied to the New Testament. Scholars agree that the phrase "all Scripture" in verse 16 refers to the Old Testament. Paul is saying that the entire Old Testament is inspired by God even though it was written through human authors.

The main question for us, however, shouldn't be what Paul's intent is but what God's is. Through divine inspiration Paul writes these words. But around the same time, Paul's canonical writings are becoming understood as scripture. Peter proclaimed as much when he wrote, "And count the patience of our Lord as salvation, just as our beloved brother Paul also wrote to you according to the wisdom given him, as he does in all his letters when he speaks in them of these matters. There are some things in them that are hard to understand, which the ignorant and unstable twist to their own destruction, as they do the other Scriptures" (2 Tim. 3:15–16). "The other Scriptures" is the critical phrase here, indicating Peter viewed Paul's letters as scripture. Thus Paul's statement that all scripture is God-breathed now incorporates his own canonical writings, whether he knows or intended that to be the case. God breathed out that truth through Paul. "Originally Paul's statement referred to the inspiration of the Old Testament, but the term Scripture came to be used also in reference to New Testament writings," states David Black.[38] Other New Testament passages also show that the New Testament is scripture. "For the Scripture says, 'You shall not muzzle an ox when it treads out the grain,' and 'The Laborer deserves his wages'" (1 Tim. 5:18). Paul is paraphrasing Jesus here from Luke 10:7.

Paul is making a bold statement in these verses. Scripture is unique in the world of literature. In fact, it is far more than literature. It is breathed out by God, meaning that "God's words were given through men superintended by the Holy Spirit so that their writings are without error," writes Liftin.[39] "[Scripture] is a divine revelation, which we may depend upon as infallibly true," writes renowned Bible scholar Matthew Henry. "The same Spirit that breathed reason into us breathes revelation among us: For the prophecy came not in old time by the will of man, but holy men spoke as they were moved or carried by the Holy Ghost, 2 Peter 1:21. The prophets and apostles did not speak from themselves, but what they received of the Lord that they delivered unto us."[40]

The Bible is God's word. God inspired it, and it can bring men to salvation in Jesus Christ. It leads people to eternal life; it teaches; it lays down God's moral laws and principles; it molds our moral character and leads us to righteousness; it shows sinners the error of their ways and leads them to correct their mistakes and to restoration, redemption, and reconciliation with God; and it leads to men's growth in Jesus Christ and equips them for good works—the Christian walk. The Bible is sufficient in itself to teach man how to live a holy life. Isn't it interesting that the Bible reveals that God breathed out scripture similar to the way he breathed the material world into existence: "By the word of the Lord the heavens were made, and by the breath of his mouth all their host" (Psalm 33:6). And isn't it also interesting that Jesus, the second person of the Holy Trinity, is called the Word (John 1:1–4), and that He (the Word) was the active agent in creation?

Much has been written on the mystery of God's giving us His word through human authors in the writing of the thirty-nine books of the Old Testament and twenty-seven books of the New Testament. Most scholars agree that though God inspired these human authors through His Holy Spirit, He allowed them the freedom of their own individuality and personality in penning these words.[41] The Holy Spirit guided them into truth and ensured that God's divine message be written. Edmond Hiebert elaborates further, saying God's "inspiration was not mechanical. The Holy Spirit did not destroy the personality and individual characteristics of the individual writers but rather so worked through the entire being of the writer that the very words used, although truly the words of the human author, were yet the very words of the Spirit intended to be employed to express the divine truths being recorded."[42]

To us, it is yet another marvel of our Holy God. There are so many complicated mysteries and paradoxes that enhance rather than detract from our faith. Consider the Holy Trinity, for example, and the wholly divine and wholly human nature of Jesus Christ. As to the latter, we see an analogy between Jesus' being fully human and fully divine, and the Bible's being written by God yet through fully human authors whom God allowed to be themselves in penning His word. We have found our thought here is not original, which is affirming to us. No less a Bible scholar and apologist than my (David's) friend, the late Norman Geisler, put it well. "There is an analogy between the Written Word of God and the Living Word," wrote Geisler. "While neo-evangelicals say that error is due to the introduction of human thought and human language, they must somehow account for the fact that Jesus Christ was both fully human and fully divine, yet without sin. In both cases the human and divine are wedded, yet the human aspects have no imperfections. This suggests that sin and error are not necessary consequences of humanity; they are only accidental. God can produce both a Person and a Book that are without error."[43]

No other verses of the Bible are more illuminating about the nature of scripture, its divine authority, and its usefulness to man than 2 Timothy 3:16–17. They are critically important because our view of the Bible will affect our view of and relationship with our Creator. That said, it is not a one-off revelation. Many figures in both the Old and New Testaments attest that the Bible is the word of God.

- ★ David: "The Spirit of the Lord speaks by me; his word is on my tongue." (2 Samuel 23:2)
- ★ The prophet Jeremiah: "Then the Lord put out his hand and touched my mouth. And the Lord said to me, 'Behold, I have put my words in your mouth.'" (Jer. 1:9)
- ★ The prophet Habakkuk: "Write the vision; make it plain on tablets, so he may run who reads it." (Hab. 2:2)
- ★ The prophet Zechariah: "Then the word of the Lord came to me, saying...." (Zech. 4:8)

- ★ Jesus: "When the Spirit of truth comes, he will guide you into all the truth, for he will not speak on his own authority, but whatever he hears he will speak, and he will declare to you the things that are to come." (John 16:13)
- ★ Jesus: "The Scripture cannot be broken." (John 10:34–35)
- ★ Jesus: "You search the Scriptures because you think that in them you have eternal life; and it is they that bear witness about me, yet you refuse to come to me that you may have life" (John 5:39–40)

The writers of the New Testament also confirm the divine authority of Old Testament writings, for example: "All this took place to fulfil what the Lord had spoken by the prophet: 'Behold, the virgin shall conceive and bear a son, and they shall call his name Immanuel'" (Matt. 1:22–23); and "Brothers, the Scripture had to be fulfilled, which the Holy Spirit spoke beforehand by the mouth of David concerning Judas, who became a guide to those who arrested Jesus" (Acts 1:16).

So we must ask ourselves: do we have a high view of scripture? Do we believe it—and treat it—as the word of God?

PRAYER

Father in heaven, we thank You for breathing Your word onto pages abundantly accessible to us, that we might know You and learn from You. The Bible itself is truly a million little miracles wrapped into one book. We love that Psalm 119, placed almost dead-center in the Bible, is both the longest Psalm and the longest chapter and is all about the beauty of Your word! We are in awe of the

▶

mystery of Your word, how Your very words brought the earth into existence (Gen 1), and how their power continues to touch the lives of every person who comes into contact with them. Help us to memorize and carry more scripture in our hearts and minds, so that we might be used to share it with those who so desperately need it. In Your Name,

AMEN.

CHAPTER 4

Having established the unique nature of the Bible, Paul now instructs Timothy to build on that foundation: "I charge you in the presence of God and of Christ Jesus, who is to judge the living and the dead, and by his appearing and his kingdom: preach the word; be ready in season and out of season; reprove, rebuke, and exhort, with complete patience and teaching. For the time is coming when people will not endure sound teaching, but having itching ears they will accumulate for themselves teachers to suit their own passions, and will turn away from listening to the truth and wander off into myths. As for you, always be sober-minded, endure suffering, do the work of an evangelist, fulfill your ministry" (4:1–5).

It's as if Paul is saying, "Now that you understand its origin, its essence, its importance, its power, and its ability to change lives, go out and preach it far, wide, and always. Use it wisely as a divine tool in all the ways I have told you it is useful—to reprove, rebuke, and exhort. Make sure you stay true to the word. Always preach and teach sound doctrine. Do it now because the time is coming when people won't be as receptive to the word, and they'll be even more vulnerable to false teachers and their myths. But you must remain serious about this charge and willing to endure opposition and hardship. This is a matter of dire importance, which is why I am issuing you this command in the presence of God and Jesus Christ, who, after all, is the ultimate Judge and will be judging all of mankind when He returns and sets up His kingdom."

Think about this. Paul, an apostle directly appointed by Jesus Christ, is commanding Timothy, his prized pupil in the faith, as the Father and the Son are looking on, to preach the very word of God because his hearers' lives hang in the balance. Paul further commands him to be sober-minded in carrying out this mission and to be prepared to face hardship on the way. He can't worry about pleasing man. He must always keep his sights on God and pleasing Him. Many whom he approaches will be resistant because they have "itching ears"—unlike Timothy, they will be tempted to follow false teachers, and they'll yearn to hear what pleases them and satisfies their perverse desires rather than the sometimes-hard truths of scripture. "They are the specious words of lovers of matter and the body, who say that pleasure is a good, 'itching at their ears and running after myths,'" writes early Christian scholar Origen.[44]

Timothy must remember that above all, he is an evangelist. His charge is to win souls for Christ. He must do it unceasingly, in and out of season. "Let it always be your season, not merely in peace and security and when sitting in the church," writes Chrysostom.[45] We should remember this charge applies not just to Timothy and the evangelists of early Christian history but all believers, as difficult and impractical as it may seem. As some of the most inspiring evangelists of our day remind us through their example, you can creatively turn all kinds of situations into opportunities to spread the gospel. "Every occasion constitutes an opportune time for preaching," writes fourth-century Christian theologian Theodore of Mopsuestia.[46]

Paul continues, "For I am already being poured out as a drink offering, and the time of my departure has come. I have fought the good fight, I have finished the race, I have kept the faith. Henceforth there is laid up for me the crown of righteousness, which the Lord, the righteous judge, will award to me on that day, and not only to me but also to all who have loved his appearing" (4:6–8).

Scholars note that Paul is adding another reason for urgency—his impending death. Timothy already has the weight of the world on his shoulders, having been delegated to assume Paul's ministry as Paul remains imprisoned. But the weight will soon be even heavier, as Paul is telling him his time left on earth is short. But Paul is comforted in knowing he has obeyed his calling, and though it took its earthly and physical toll on him, he will be rewarded in heaven along with all believers who long for Christ's coming. He completed his part of the race and acquitted himself well.

Paul isn't giving himself credit as much as acknowledging that he has placed himself before Christ as His servant, and Christ accomplished these good works through him as His vessel. He has kept the faith both by staying true to the gospel and by honoring God in performing the assigned tasks. "An expectation of reward is...insert thin space herea recognition of God's grace," writes Lea. "Those who anticipate reward will not be able to boast, 'Look at my accomplishments.' They should be able to offer praise to God by saying, 'Thank you, Lord, for what you have produced in me.' The very expectation of reward is an acknowledgment of God's grace."[47]

Paul pens an extended personal closing to this letter, twice asking Timothy to visit him—apparently because he suspects he won't live much longer. He singles out Demas for abandoning him due to "love with this present world" (4:9). He also notes that some others have left him and the only one remaining is Luke, the physician and author of Acts and the Gospel of Luke (Col. 4:14). He urges Timothy to bring Mark with him because "he is very useful to me for ministry" (4:11). Scholars take interest in the reference to Mark because Paul had earlier fallen out with him, considering him untrustworthy (Acts 15:36–40). Paul and Barnabas went their separate ways, disagreeing about Mark, and it now appears Barnabas' faith in Mark has been vindicated.[48]

Paul further asks Timothy to bring some personal items to him when he comes and then warns him to avoid Alexander the coppersmith, who opposed the gospel message (4:13–14). Without expressing personal animus, he leaves Alexander's punishment in God's hands, saying, "The Lord will repay him according to his deeds" (4:14). Paul then notes, without bitterness, that no one stood by him at his first defense (probably referring to his preliminary hearing before the Roman authorities during his second imprisonment) (4:16).[49] He is even sympathetic to the deserters' human weaknesses, insisting, "May it not be charged against them!" (4:16). Besides, says Paul, the Lord stood by him and gave him strength, not for Paul's sake but so he could continue to be used to proclaim the gospel message so that "all the Gentiles might hear it. So I was rescued from the lion's mouth" (4:17–18).

Yes, he was spared from physical death, but now he shifts gears, once again acknowledging his inevitable death. Even this, however, he regards as a matter of God's rescuing him: "The Lord will rescue me from every evil deed and bring me safely into his heavenly kingdom. To him be the glory forever and ever. Amen" (4:18). So whether in sparing his physical life or permitting him to finally be killed, Paul always honors, respects, and appreciates God's will like the extraordinary Christ-centered servant he is. It's as if Paul is saying, "Whatever God decides to do, I'm perfectly fine with it and subservient to His perfect will. I know that He will use me as His instrument as long as He deems necessary, then He will mercifully take me into His loving arms in eternal bliss."

Paul ends the letter with some final greetings and his second request that Timothy come to see him—before winter. In closing he offers this final encouragement, showing his typical concern for others over himself and his overarching interest in the continued spread of the gospel: "The Lord be with your spirit. Grace be with you" (4:22). Touchingly, these are probably the final words to have survived from the great apostle to the Gentiles and the fiercest Christian warrior in history.[50]

PRAYER

Lord, we thank You for Your incredible servant Paul, whose divinely-inspired writings have brought countless people to faith in Jesus Christ. As this book comes to a close, we're especially grateful for the man You created Paul to be, that once-lost person whom You pulled out of darkness and used as a vessel for some of the brightest light in Your kingdom to be spread across the earth throughout the centuries. May we always remember that Paul was in fact just a man who was used by You, Jesus. Because You believed in Paul, he was able to rise from a state of faithlessness to one of irrepressible faith, spreading the good news of the gospel throughout the world, creating and maintaining church unity, preserving Your truth within those churches, and giving You all the glory for these things. To quote Your parable of the talents, "The servant who had received the two bags of silver came forward and said, 'Master, you gave me two bags of silver to invest, and I have earned two more.' The master said, 'Well done, good and faithful servant! You have been faithful with a few things; I will put you in charge of many things. Come and share your master's happiness!'" (Matt. 25:22–23 NLT). May the same be said of each of us when our earthly lives come to a close. As we live another day, we seek to continually grow into servants who are Your light in the world, running our individual races with the hope and knowledge that You are with us in every trial, and one day we will be face to face with You "sharing in Your happiness."

AMEN.

CONCLUSION

We sincerely hope this book is as meaningful to readers as writing it has been for us. As always, the goal here is to help our fellow lay Bible readers and students better understand scripture and inspire them to make Bible reading a daily practice.

With this book we have covered the epistles of Paul not covered in *Jesus Is Risen*. In our next book, we intend to cover the eight non-Pauline, or general epistles, of the New Testament: Hebrews, James, 1 Peter, 2 Peter, 1 John, 2 John, 3 John, and Jude. We are really looking forward to beginning the research and writing for that book.

We realize we are not Bible scholars, but we both love reading scripture and doing everything we can to help explain it and inspire others to love and read it. We pray that we have been true and faithful to God in doing this joyful work.

It has been so gratifying to work on this book together as father and daughter as we learn from and inspire each other. We are both blessed beyond measure. We hope you all have enjoyed it.

ACKNOWLEDGMENTS

This is my eleventh and Christen's first book—every one of them with Regnery Publishing, with which I've had a wonderful and gratifying relationship. Special thanks to Tom Spence, who has been so great to work with. Since taking over at Regnery he has done an amazing job, and Regnery continues to thrive. My friend Harry Crocker has been with me from the beginning, and there is no one better in this industry. He has always been in my corner, and he is always a joy to work with. Sincere thanks also to the design and art departments for the great work they do in layout and jacket covers. My sincere gratitude to Laura Swain for her excellent work copy editing, proofreading, and shepherding this manuscript through production.

Profuse thanks to my friend Jack Langer for editing this book, which makes this the eighth book we've worked on together. Jack has been a joy to work with and has made every one of my books read more clearly and smoothly. I have learned so much from him over the years and have become much better at self-editing, but he is in no danger of making himself obsolete. As I've said before, I am blown away by his ability to strip unnecessary words from the manuscript, even when I think I've already purged them all through many rounds of self-editing. I told Christen about Jack's skills and now she has witnessed them firsthand, which will make her a better writer as well. These books simply would not be as good without his special touch. He also functions as an objective reader, makes suggestions, and asks questions that inevitably lead to greater clarity and readability. In addition to his professional skills, he is so easy to work with, so flexible and accommodating, and so punctual. I pray he remains my editor and our editor for as long as we're privileged to write books.

Thanks, as always, to my wife and Christen's mom, Lisa, for always being supportive, patient, and understanding in this demanding process. Her prayers and encouragement behind the scenes have carried each of us along our faith journeys in immeasurable ways. We love you so much.

Thanks, as always, to my very good friend Frank Turek, an extraordinary apologist and mentor to me, for reviewing this manuscript and offering his valuable insight. We really appreciate it so much.

My longtime friend Sean Hannity has always been supportive of all my books and other professional endeavors. His mentorship and overwhelming support in Christen's career have also been invaluable. Sean remains a humble, kind, and generous man despite his celebrity and phenomenal success. We are proud to call him our close friend and are eternally appreciative of his encouragement. We couldn't have a more loyal ally.

I greatly appreciate the friendship and steadfast support of Mark Levin, upon whom I can always depend. I am extremely grateful for his support of this project—as always.

I reserve special thanks for my brother Rush who will always mean more to me than I can adequately express. Beyond his brotherly love, he opened so many doors for me professionally. I dare say my law practice wouldn't have gone in the wonderful direction it has without his influence, and I may not have ever had the confidence to write books.

Christen offers the following acknowledgments:

To my husband, Sam, your peace, strength, and love for the Lord have blessed my life in ways I cannot put into words. Thank you for always encouraging me to persist past every difficulty in this lifelong race. You are the best friend, partner, coach, and husband. I am lucky to call you mine. I love you!

Warmest thanks to my dear friend (and Dad's dear friend as well) Ainsley Earhardt. Your loving mentorship has been a guidepost and constant inspiration for me. You have helped pave the way for many in the media to speak freely about their faith and always make it look fun and easy. I'm grateful to know you and to follow along your path in a small way.

To my friend and spiritual mentor Kate Hillegeist, your wisdom and search for God's heart have transformed my own relationship with Jesus, and I am forever grateful. Thank you for your encouragement, consistency, grace, and mountain-moving faith. You are such an inspiration, and I thank God He put you in my life.

Most of all, Christen and I are grateful to God—the Father, the Son, and the Holy Spirit—for His countless blessings. We realize the solemn duty we have in properly handling His word and presenting it as accurately as we can. It is a joy to dig into scripture and grow closer to God in the process. Writing books is always hard work but nothing compared to the joy we feel in writing about scripture.

NOTES

INTRODUCTION

1. Dale Leschert, *The Flow of the New Testament* (Fearn, UK: Christian Focus Publications, 2002), 23.
2. G. C. Martin and W. F. Adeney, eds., *Ephesians, Colossians, Philemon, & Philippians* (Edinburgh; London: T. C. & E. C. Jack, 1902), 9.
3. L. R. Farley, *The Prison Epistles: Philippians, Ephesians, Colossians, Philemon* (Chesterton, Indiana: Ancient Faith Publishing, 2003), 12.
4. B. B. Barton, D. Veerman, and N. S. Wilson, *1 Timothy, 2 Timothy, Titus* (Wheaton, Illinois: Tyndale House Publishers, 1993), 7.
5. *Crossway Bibles. The ESV Study Bible* (Wheaton, Illinois: Crossway Bibles, 2008), 2321, 2335.
6. Barton, Veerman, and Wilson, *1 Timothy, 2 Timothy, Titus*, x.

7. J. P. Lilley, *The Pastoral Epistles*, eds. M. Dods and Whyte Alexander (Edinburgh: T&T Clark, 1901), 23.
8. J. N. D. Kelly, *The Pastoral Epistles* (London: Continuum, 1963), 2.
9. Barton, Veerman, and Wilson, *1 Timothy, 2 Timothy, Titus*, viii.
10. J. P. Lilley, *The Pastoral Epistles* (M. Dods, Whyte Alexander, Eds.) (Edinburgh: T&T Clark, 1901), 22.
11. William Hendriksen and S. J. Kistemaker, *Exposition of the Pastoral Epistles*, vol. 4, 1953–2001 (Grand Rapids: Baker Book House, 1957), 35.

CHAPTER 1

COLOSSIANS: A DEFENSE AGAINST EARLY HERESIES

1. Bruce Barton and P. W. Comfort, *Philippians, Colossians, Philemon* (Tyndale House Publishers, 1995), 132–34.
2. Crossway Bibles, *The ESV Study Bible* (Wheaton, Illinois: Crossway Bibles, 2008), 2291.
3. G. F. Hawthorne, R. P. Martin, and D. G. Reid, eds., *Dictionary of Paul and His Letters* (Downers Grove, Illinois: InterVarsity Press, 1993), 147.
4. Richard R. Melick, *Philippians, Colossians, Philemon* (Nashville, Tennessee: Broadman & Holman Publishers, 1991), 32:161.
5. D. J. Moo, "The Letters and Revelation," in *NIV Biblical Theology Study Bible*, ed. D. A. Carson (Grand Rapids, Michigan: Zondervan, 2018), 2138.
6. S. B. Ferguson and J. I. Packer in *New Dictionary of Theology* (Downers Grove, Illinois: InterVarsity Press, 2000), 6.

7. D. Brown, "Docetism" in *The Lexham Bible Dictionary*, eds. J. D. Barry et al. (Bellingham, Washington: Lexham Press, 2016).
8. H. D. McDonald, "Apollinarianism" in *New Dictionary of Theology: Historical and Systematic*, eds. M. Davie et al., 2nd ed. (London; Downers Grove, Illinois: InterVarsity Press, 2016), 48–49.
9. Donald Tinder, "The Doctrine of the Trinity: Its Historical Development and Departures," *Emmaus Journal* 13, no. 1 (2004): 121–149; James B. Walker, "Arianism," in *The Dictionary of Historical Theology* (Carlisle, Cumbria, UK: Paternoster Press, 2000), 30; L. A. Nichols, G. A. Mather, and A. J. Schmidt, *Encyclopedic Dictionary of Cults, Sects, and World Religions* (Grand Rapids, Michigan: Zondervan, 2006), 362.
10. *Encyclopedia Britannica*, Logos ed. (Chicago, Illinois: Encyclopedia Britannica, 2016).
11. Ferguson and Packer, *New Dictionary of Theology*, 442.
12. F. L. Cross and E. A. Livingstone, eds., *The Oxford Dictionary of the Christian Church*, 3rd rev. ed. (Oxford; New York: Oxford University Press, 2005), 1112; J. Warner Wallace goes into more detail on these various heresies in his article "Historic Heresies Related to the Nature of Jesus," *Cold Case Christianity*, November 17, 2017, https://coldcasechristianity.com/writings/historic-heresies-related-to-the-nature-of-jesus/.
13. Bruce Barton et al., *Life Application New Testament Commentary* (Wheaton, Illinois: Tyndale, 2001), 879.
14. Barton and Comfort, *Philippians, Colossians, Philemon* (Wheaton, Illinois: Tyndale House Publishers, 1995), 132.

15. E. Hindson and E. Caner, *The Popular Encyclopedia of Apologetics: Surveying the Evidence for the Truth of Christianity* (Eugene, Oregon: Harvest House Publishers, 2008).
16. Melick, *Philippians, Colossians, Philemon*, 162.
17. John F. MacArthur Jr., *Colossians* (Chicago, Illinois: Moody Press, 1992), 14.
18. Barton et al., *Life Application New Testament Commentary* (Wheaton, Illinois: Tyndale, 2001), 870.
19. John Woodhouse, *Colossians and Philemon: So Walk in Him* (Ross-shire, Great Britain: Christian Focus, 2011), 23–24.
20. Ibid., 24.
21. E. K. Simpson and F. F. Bruce, *The Epistles to the Ephesians and the Colossians* (Grand Rapids, Michigan: Wm. B. Eerdmans Publishing Co., 1957), 182.
22. J. D. Barry et al., *Faithlife Study Bible* (Bellingham, Washington: Lexham Press, 2016, 2012).
23. Woodhouse, *Colossians and Philemon*, 46–47.
24. S. R. Leach, "The Epistle of Paul the Apostle to the Colossians" in R. N. Wilkin, ed., *The Grace New Testament Commentary* (Denton, Texas: Grace Evangelical Society, 2010), 912.
25. Ibid., 911.
26. Simpson and Bruce, *Epistles to the Ephesians and the Colossians*, 185–86.
27. F. F. Bruce, *The Epistles to the Colossians, to Philemon, and to the Ephesians* (Grand Rapids, Michigan: Wm. B. Eerdmans Publishing Co., 1984), 50.
28. M. R. De Haan, *Studies in Revelation* (Grand Rapids, Michigan: Kregel Publications, 1998), 103.
29. C. S. Lewis, *Mere Christianity* (New York: HarperOne, 2001), 52.

30. Crossway Bibles, *The ESV Study Bible* (Wheaton, Illinois: Crossway Bibles, 2008), 2020.
31. Peter Gorday, ed., *Colossians, 1–2 Thessalonians, 1–2 Timothy, Titus, Philemon* (Downers Grove, Illinois: InterVarsity Press, 2000), 10.
32. Barry et al., *Faithlife Study Bible.*
33. Crossway Bibles, *ESV Study Bible*, 2294.
34. Barry et al., *Faithlife Study Bible.*
35. Peter Gorday, ed., *Colossians, 1–2 Thessalonians, 1–2 Timothy, Titus, Philemon* (Downers Grove, Illinois: InterVarsity Press, 2000), 10.
36. Crossway Bibles, *ESV Study Bible*, 2294.
37. E. D. Radmacher, R. B., Allen, and H. W. House, *The Nelson Study Bible: New King James Version* (Nashville, Tennessee: T. Nelson Publishers, 1997).
38. David L. Allen, *The New American Bible Commentary, Hebrews* (Nashville, Tennessee: B & H Publishing Group, 2010), 119.
39. William L. Lane, *World Biblical Commentary, Hebrews 1–8* (Dallas, Texas: Word, Incorporated, 1991), 47A:14.
40. David L. Allen, *The New American Bible Commentary, Hebrews* (Nashville, Tennessee: B & H Publishing Group, 2010), 122.
41. Bruce B. Barton et al., *Hebrews* (Wheaton, Illinois: Tyndale House Publishers, 1997), 5.
42. Arnold G. Fruchtenbaum, *The Messianic Bible Study Collection* (Tustin, California: Ariel Ministries, 1983), 100:13.
43. John R. W. Stott, *The Cross of Christ* (Downers Grove, Illinois: InterVarsity Press, 1986), 329.
44. Barton et al., *Hebrews*, 179.

45. Scot McKnight, *The Letter to the Colossians*, eds. N. B. Stonehouse et al. (Grand Rapids, Michigan: Wm. B. Eerdmans Publishing Company, 2018), 209–10.
46. John Woodhouse, *Colossians and Philemon: So Walk in Him* (Ross-shire, Great Britain: Christian Focus, 2011), 94.
47. Ibid., 95.
48. Ibid.
49. Douglas J. Moo, *The Letters to the Colossians and to Philemon* (Grand Rapids, Michigan: William B. Eerdmans Pub. Co., 2008), 175–77.
50. Barry et a., *Faithlife Study Bible*; Richard R. Melick, *Philippians, Colossians, Philemon* (Nashville, Tennessee: Broadman & Holman Publishers, 1991), 32:257.
51. Charles H. Spurgeon, *Christ in the Old Testament: Sermons of the Foreshadowing of our Lord in Old Testament History, Ceremony, and Prophecy* (Chattanooga, Tennessee: AMG Publishers, 1998), 370.
52. Bruce Barton et al., *Hebrews*, Life Application Bible Commentary, (Wheaton, Illinois: Tyndale House Publishers, 1997), 21.
53. John F. MacArthur, *Hebrews*, MacArthur New Testament Commentary (Chicago: Moody Press, 1983), 57.
54. John F. MacArthur, *Galatians* (Chicago: Moody Press, 1983), 129.
55. Martin Luther, *Galatians* (Wheaton, Illinois: Crossway Books, 1998), 241.
56. Warren W. Wiersbe, *Wiersbe's Expository Outlines on the New Testament* (Wheaton, Illinois: Victor Books, 1992), 527.
57. C. Vaughan, "Colossians" in *The Expositor's Bible Commentary: Ephesians through Philemon*, ed. F. E. Gaebelein (Grand Rapids, Michigan: Zondervan Publishing House, 1981), 11:205.

58. Peter Gorday, ed., *Colossians, 1–2 Thessalonians, 1–2 Timothy, Titus, Philemon* (Downers Grove, Illinois: InterVarsity Press, 2000), 41.
59. John F. MacArthur Jr., *Colossians* (Chicago: Moody Press., 1992), 122.
60. MacArthur, *Colossians*, 123.
61. Barry et al., *Faithlife Study Bible.*
62. David Limbaugh, *The True Jesus: Uncovering the Divinity of Christ in the Gospels* (Washington, D.C.: Regnery Publishing, 2017), location 2751.
63. Grant R. Osborne, *Colossians & Philemon: Verse by Verse* (Bellingham, Washington: Lexham Press, 2016), 91.
64. John F. MacArthur Jr., ed, *The MacArthur Study Bible* (Nashville, Tennessee: Word Pub. 1997), 1836.
65. Ibid., 1835.
66. Osborne, *Colossians & Philemon: Verse by Verse*, 91.
67. Warren W. Wiersbe, *The Bible Exposition Commentary* (Wheaton, Illinois: Victor Books, 1996), 2:133.
68. J. P. Arthur, *Christ All-Sufficient: Colossians and Philemon Simply Explained* (Darlington, England: Evangelical Press, 2007), 135.
69. Ibid., 136.
70. Norman L. Geisler, "Colossians" in *The Bible Knowledge Commentary: An Exposition of the Scriptures*, eds. J. F. Walvoord & R. B. Zuck (Wheaton, Illinois: Victor Books, 1985), 2:681.
71. Sam Storms, *Biblical Studies: Colossians* (Edmond, Oklahoma: Sam Storms, 2016).
72. Geisler, "Colossians," 2:681.
73. Ibid., 2:682.

74. John Phillips, *Exploring Colossians & Philemon: An Expository Commentary* (Kregel Publications; WORDsearch Corp., 2009).
75. Moo, "The Letters and Revelation," 2146.
76. J. Moffatt, *Love in the New Testament* [London, 1929], 191, from F. F. Bruce, *The Epistles to the Colossians, to Philemon, and to the Ephesians* (Grand Rapids, Michigan: Wm. B. Eerdmans Publishing Co, 1984).
77. Woodhouse, *Colossians and Philemon*, 208.
78. Melick, *Philippians, Colossians, Philemon*, 32:307.
79. Ibid., 32:310.
80. Ibid., 32:312.
81. Crossway Bibles, *The ESV Study Bible*, 2299.
82. Ibid., 2273.
83. E. K. Simpson and F. F. Bruce, *The Epistles to the Ephesians and the Colossians* (Grand Rapids, Michigan: Wm. B. Eerdmans Publishing Co., 1957), 171.
84. Bruce Barton et al., *Life Application New Testament Commentary*, 886.
85. Crossway Bibles, *The ESV Study Bible*, 2201.

CHAPTER 2

PHILEMON: "NO MORE AS A SLAVE"

1. Richard Melick, *Philippians, Colossians, Philemon* (Nashville, Tennessee: Broadman & Holman Publishers, 1991), 32:334–35.
2. E. C. Deibler, "Philemon" in *The Bible Knowledge Commentary: An Exposition of the Scriptures*, eds. J. F. Walvoord and R. B. Zuck, (Wheaton, Illinois: Victor Books, 1985), 2:769.

3. Peter Gorday, ed., *Colossians, 1–2 Thessalonians, 1–2 Timothy, Titus, Philemon* (Downers Grove, Illinois: InterVarsity Press, 2000), 257.
4. F. F. Bruce, *The Epistles to the Colossians, to Philemon, and to the Ephesians* (Grand Rapids, Michigan: Wm. B. Eerdmans Publishing Co, 1984), 205.
5. R. C. H. Lenski, *The Interpretation of St. Paul's Epistles to the Colossians, to the Thessalonians, to Timothy, to Titus and to Philemon* (Columbus, Ohio: Lutheran Book Concern, 1937), 954.
6. John F. MacArthur, *Philemon* (Chicago, Illinois: Moody Press, 1992), 213.
7. Scot McKnight, *The Letter to Philemon*, eds. N. B. Stonehouse et al. (Grand Rapids, Michigan: William B. Eerdmans Publishing Company, 2017), 70–71.
8. Bruce B. Barton & P. W. Comfort, *Philippians, Colossians, Philemon* (Wheaton, Illinois: Tyndale House Publishers, 1995), 255.
9. Melick, *Philippians, Colossians, Philemon*, 32:355.
10. MacArthur, *Philemon*, 214.
11. Gorday, *Colossians, 1–2 Thessalonians, 1–2 Timothy, Titus, Philemon*, 315.
12. Barton and Comfort, *Philippians, Colossians, Philemon*, 261–62.
13. Peter T. O'Brien, *Colossians, Philemon* (Dallas, Texas: Word, Incorporated, 1982), 44:297.
14. Joseph B. Lightfoot, *Saint Paul's Epistles to the Colossians and to Philemon*, 8th ed. (London; New York: Macmillan and Co., 1886), 341.
15. O'Brien, *Colossians, Philemon*, 44:299.
16. Lightfoot, *Saint Paul's Epistles to the Colossians*, 341.1.

17. Barton and Comfort, *Philippians, Colossians, Philemon*, 263.
18. Robert W. Wall, *Colossians and Philemon* (Downers Grove, Illinois: InterVarsity Press, 1993).
19. William Hendriksen and S. J. Kistemaker, *Exposition of Colossians and Philemon*, vol. 6 (Grand Rapids: Baker Book House, 1953–2001), 222.
20. James D. G. Dunn, *The Epistles to the Colossians and to Philemon: A Commentary on the Greek Text* (Grand Rapids, Michigan: Wm. B. Eerdmans Publishing, 1996), 340.
21. Seth M. Ehorn, *Philemon*, eds. H. W. House and W. H. Harris (Bellingham, Washington: Lexham Press, 2011).
22. Ibid.
23. N. T. Wright, *Colossians and Philemon: An Introduction and Commentary* (Downers Grove, Illinois: InterVarsity Press, 1986), 12:195.
24. O'Brien, *Colossians, Philemon*, 44:301.
25. McKnight, *Letter to Philemon*, 107.
26. Dunn, *Epistles to the Colossians and to Philemon*, 340.
27. Lenski, *Interpretation of St. Paul's Epistles*, 971–72.
28. D. Ellis, "Commentary on the Book of Philemon" in *1 Thessalonians through Philemon*, ed. R. E. Picirilli, 1st ed. (Nashville, Tennessee: Randall House Publications, 1990), 438.
29. Daniel L. Migliore, *Philippians and Philemon*, eds. A. P. Pauw and W. C. Placher, 1st ed. (Louisville, Kentucky: Westminster John Knox Press, 2014), 242.
30. Craig S. Keener and J. H. Walton, eds., *NIV Cultural Backgrounds Study Bible: Bringing to Life the Ancient World of Scripture* (Grand Rapids, Michigan: Zondervan, 2016), 2137.
31. Migliore, *Philippians and Philemon*, 244.
32. L. Gatiss, B. G. Green, and T. George, eds., *1–2 Thessalonians, 1–2 Timothy, Titus, Philemon: New Testament* (Downers Grove, Illinois: InterVarsity Press, 2019), 12:317.

33. Gordon D. Fee and Douglas K. Stuart, *How to Read the Bible Book by Book: A Guided Tour* (Grand Rapids, Michigan: Zondervan, 2002), 389.

CHAPTER 3

EPHESIANS: A BLUEPRINT FOR SPIRITUAL EMPOWERMENT

1. Walter L. Liefeld, *Ephesians* (Downers Grove, Illinois: InterVarsity Press, 1997), vol. 10.
2. "Pastor-A Tour through the Treasure House," *Ministry Magazine*, February 1954, https://www.ministrymagazine.org/archive/1954/02/pulpit.
3. John F. MacArthur Jr., *Ephesians* (Chicago, Illinois: Moody Press, 1986), vii.
4. Dale Leschert, *The Flow of the New Testament* (Fearn, Great Britain: Christian Focus Publications, 2002), 347.
5. Gary H. Everett, *The Epistle of Ephesians* (Gary Everett, 2011), 4.
6. Matthew Henry, *Matthew Henry's Commentary on the Whole Bible: Complete and Unabridged in One Volume* (Peabody, Massachusetts: Hendrickson, 1994), 2307.
7. Robert E. Picirilli, "Commentary on the Book of Ephesians and Philippians" in *Galatians through Colossians*, ed. R. E. Picirilli, 1st ed. (Nashville, Tennessee: Randall House Publications, 1988), 119.
8. Leschert, *Flow of the New Testament*, 347.
9. Bruce B. Barton and P. W. Comfort, *Ephesians* (Wheaton, Illinois: Tyndale House Publishers, 1996), 7.
10. P. J. Achtemeier, "Harper & Row and Society of Biblical Literature" in *Harper's Bible Dictionary*, 1st ed. (San Francisco: Harper & Row, 1985), 766.

11. M. J. Edwards, ed., *Galatians, Ephesians, Philippians* (Downers Grove, Illinois: InterVarsity Press, 1999), 108.
12. F. F. Bruce, *The Epistles to the Colossians, to Philemon, and to the Ephesians* (Grand Rapids, Michigan: Wm. B. Eerdmans Publishing Co., 1984), 254.
13. Barton and Comfort, *Ephesians*, 22.
14. Crossway Bibles, *The ESV Study Bible* (Wheaton, Illinois: Crossway Bibles, 2008), 2263.
15. R. C. H. Lenski, *The Interpretation of St. Paul's Epistles to the Galatians, to the Ephesians and to the Philippians* (Columbus, Ohio: Lutheran Book Concern, 2037), 395.
16. Edwards, *Galatians, Ephesians, Philippians*, 121.
17. Paul Gardner, *Ephesians: Grace and Joy in Christ* (Rossshire, Great Britain: Christian Focus Publications, 2007), 37.
18. John F. MacArthur Jr., *Ephesians* (Chicago, Illinois: Moody Press, 1986), 49.
19. D. W. Appleby and G. Ohlschlager, "Introduction: The Call to Transformational Living" in *Transformative Encounters: The Intervention of God in Christian Counseling and Pastoral Care* (Westmont, Illinois: IVP Academic, 2013), 39–40.
20. Ibid., 40.
21. T. F. George, "General Introduction" in *Galatians, Ephesians: New Testament*, eds. G. L. Bray & S. M. Manetsch (Downers Grove, Illinois: IVP Academic, 2001), 10:273.
22. MacArthur, *Ephesians*, 49.
23. Bruce, *Epistles to the Colossians, to Philemon, and to the Ephesians*, 277.
24. Edwards, *Galatians, Ephesians, Philippians*, 126.
25. Douglas J. Moo, "The Letters and Revelation" in *NIV Biblical Theology Study Bible*, ed. D. A. Carson (Grand Rapids, Michigan: Zondervan, 2018), 2119.

26. Ambrosiaster, *Commentaries on Galatians–Philemon*, eds. T. C. Oden and G. L. Bray, trans. G. L. Bray (Downers Grove, Illinois: InterVarsity Press, 2009), 39.
27. C. S. Lewis, *Mere Christianity* (Harper Collins, Kindle Edition, 1952), 41.
28. Edwards, *Galatians, Ephesians, Philippians*, 137.
29. Gardner, *Ephesians*, 65.
30. Bruce B. Barton, D. Veerman, and N. S. Wilson, *Romans* (Wheaton, Illinois: Tyndale House Publishers, 1992), 157.
31. Moo, "The Letters and Revelation," 2120.
32. Peter T. O'Brien, *The Letter to the Ephesians* (Grand Rapids, Michigan: Wm. B. Eerdmans Publishing Co., 1999), 221.
33. Warren W. Wiersbe, *The Bible Exposition Commentary* (Wheaton, Illinois: Victor Books, 1996), 2:25.
34. H. W. Hoehner, "Ephesians," in J. F. Walvoord and R. B. Zuck, eds., *The Bible Knowledge Commentary: An Exposition of the Scriptures* (Wheaton, IL: Victor Books, 1985), vol. 2, 628.
35. D. Haines, "God's Incomprehensibility" in *Lexham Survey of Theology*, eds. M. Ward et al. (Bellingham, Washington: Lexham Press, 2018).
36. Lenski, *Interpretation of St. Paul's Epistles*, 480; MacArthur, *Ephesians*, 96.
37. John Phillips, *Exploring Proverbs 1–19: An Expository Commentary* (Kregel Publications; WORDsearch Corp, 2009), vol. 1.
38. Lenski, *Interpretation of St. Paul's Epistles*, 480; MacArthur, *Ephesians*, 464.
39. MacArthur, *Ephesians*, 100.
40. Bruce, *Epistles to the Colossians, to Philemon, and to the Ephesians*, 329.

41. Steve M. Baugh, *Ephesians: Evangelical Exegetical Commentary*, eds. W. H. House, H. W. Harris III, and A. W. Pitts (Bellingham, Washington: Lexham Press, 2015), 279–80.
42. John Calvin and W. Pringle, *Commentaries on the Epistles of Paul to the Galatians and Ephesians* (Bellingham, Washington: Logos Bible Software, 2010), 267.
43. J. O. F. Murray, ed., *The Epistle of Paul the Apostle to the Ephesians* (Cambridge: Cambridge University Press, 1914), 63.
44. Gardner, *Ephesians*, 97.
45. Hoehner, "Ephesians," 2:633.
46. MacArthur, *Ephesians*, 130.
47. Kenneth L. Boles, *Galatians and Ephesians* (Joplin, Missouri: College Press, 1993).
48. Barton et al., *Life Application New Testament Commentary* (Wheaton, Illinois: Tyndale House Publishers, 2001), 819.
49. Boles, *Galatians and Ephesians*.
50. Ibid.
51. Graham Kendrick, "Meekness and Majesty," Copyright © 1986 Thankyou Music.
52. Warren W. Wiersbe and David Wiersbe, *The Elements of Preaching: The Art of Biblical Preaching Clearly and Simply Presented* (Wheaton, Illinois: Tyndale House Publishers, 1986), 61.
53. Crossway Bibles, *ESV Study Bible*, 2269.
54. Ambrosiaster, *Commentaries on Galatians–Philemon*, 51.
55. R. B. Callahan Sr., *Following Christ: An Expository Commentary Based upon Paul's Letter to the Ephesians (4:17–32)* (Eugene, Oregon: Resource Publications, 2012), 5:46.
56. E. K. Simpson and F. F. Bruce, *The Epistles to the Ephesians and the Colossian* (Grand Rapids, Michigan: Wm. B. Eerdmans Publishing Co., 1957), 104.

57. J. R. Franke, "Still the Way, the Truth, and the Life," *Christianity Today*, 2009, 53 (12), 27–31.
58. Barton and Comfort, *Ephesians*, 94.
59. Crossway Bibles, *ESV Study Bible*, 2270.
60. *NIV Life Application Study Bible*, 2nd ed. (Tyndale House Publishers, Inc.. Kindle Edition), 6229.
61. Crossway Bibles, *ESV Study Bible*, 2376.
62. H. C. G. Moule, *Commentary on Ephesians* (Cambridge Bible; Cambridge, 1884).
63. Bruce, *Epistles to the Colossians, to Philemon, and to the Ephesians*, 372.
64. Crossway Bibles, *ESV Study Bible*, 2270.
65. Walter L. Liefeld, *Ephesians*, vol. 10 (Downers Grove, Illinois: InterVarsity Press, 1997).
66. MacArthur, *Ephesians*, 202.
67. Richard D. Phillips, *Ephesians* (Ross-shire, Scotland: Mentor, 2016), 378–79.
68. Barton and Comfort, *Ephesians*, 104.
69. Hoehner, "Ephesians," 2:639.
70. Edwards, *Galatians, Ephesians, Philippians*, 191.
71. Ibid.
72. John F. Walvoord, *The Holy Spirit* (Galaxie Software, 2008), 155.
73. Got Questions Ministries, *Got Questions? Bible Questions Answered* (Bellingham, Washington: Logos Bible Software, 2002–2013).
74. Barton and Comfort, *Ephesians*, 110.
75. Ibid., 119.
76. H. D. M. Spence-Jones, ed. *Ephesians* (London; New York: Funk & Wagnalls Company, 1909), 257.
77. MacArthur, *Ephesians*, 316.

78. Leadership Ministries Worldwide, *Galatians–Colossians* (Chattanooga, Tennessee: Leadership Ministries Worldwide, 1996), 215–16.
79. Edwards, ed., *Galatians, Ephesians, Philippians*, 203.
80. Ibid., 209.
81. Hoehner, "Ephesians," 2:643.
82. Charles Hodge, *Ephesians* (Wheaton, Illinois: Crossway Books, 1994).
83. MacArthur, *MacArthur Study Bible*, 1815.
84. Max Anders, *Galatians–Colossians*, vol. 8 (Nashville, Tennessee: Broadman & Holman Publishers, 1999), 191.
85. Gardner, *Ephesians*, 173.
86. Barton et al., *Life Application New Testament Commentary* (Wheaton, Illinois: Tyndale House Publishers, 2001), 834.

CHAPTER 4

PHILIPPIANS: REJOICE IN CHRIST

1. Gordon D. Fee, *Paul's Letter to the Philippians* (Grand Rapids, Michigan: Wm.B . Eerdmans Publishing Co., 1995), 52–53.
2. Crossway Bibles, *The ESV Study Bible* (Wheaton, Illinois: Crossway Bibles, 2008), 2275.
3. Fee, *Paul's Letter to the Philippians*, 52–53.
4. Richard R. Melick, *Philippians, Colossians, Philemon* (Nashville, Tennessee: Broadman & Holman Publishers, 1991), 32:28.
5. Ambrosiaster, *Commentaries on Galatians–Philemon*, eds. T. C. Oden and G. L. Bray, trans. G. L. Bray (Downers Grove, Illinois: InterVarsity Press, 2009), 64.

6. Jacobus J. Muller, *The Epistles of Paul to the Philippians and to Philemon* (Grand Rapids, Michigan: Wm. B. Eerdmans Publishing Co., 1955), 35.
7. Max Anders, *Galatians–Colossians* (Nashville, Tennessee: Broadman & Holman Publishers, 1999), 8:208.
8. Ibid., 8:209.
9. M. J. Edwards, ed., *Galatians, Ephesians, Philippians* (Downers Grove, Illinois: InterVarsity Press, 1999), 225.
10. Ibid.
11. Bruce B. Barton and P. W. Comfort, *Philippians, Colossians, Philemon* (Wheaton, Illinois: Tyndale House Publishers, 1995), 38.
12. Ambrosiaster, *Commentaries on Galatians–Philemon*, 67.
13. John Calvin and J. Pringle, *Commentaries on the Epistles of Paul the Apostle to the Philippians, Colossians, and Thessalonians* (Bellingham, Washington: Logos Bible Software, 2010), 47.
14. Crossway Bibles, *ESV Study Bible*, 2282.
15. F. F. Bruce, *The Book of the Acts* (Grand Rapids, Michigan: Wm. B. Eerdmans Publishing Co, 1988), 118.
16. "2 Corinthians" in *The Bible Knowledge Commentary: An Exposition of the Scriptures*, eds. J. F. Walvoord and R. B. Zuck (Wheaton, Illinois: Victor Books, 1985), 2:554.
17. Bruce B. Barton and N. S. Wilson, *Romans* (Wheaton, Illinois: Tyndale House Publishers, 1992), 100.
18. Matthew Henry, *Matthew Henry's Commentary on the Whole Bible: Complete and Unabridged in One Volume* (Peabody, Massachusetts: Hendrickson, 1994), 2323.
19. Wayne A. Grudem, *Christian Beliefs: Twenty Basics Every Christian Should Know*, ed. E. Grudem(Grand Rapids, Michigan: Zondervan, 2005), 70.

20. J. D. Barry et al., *Faithlife Study Bible* (Bellingham, Washington: Logos Bible Software, 2012).
21. Charles C. Ryrie, *Basic Theology, A Popular Systematic Guide to Understand Biblical Truth* (Chicago, Illinois: Moody Press, 1999, 1986), 237.
22. Guy P. Duffield and Nathaniel M. Van Cleave, *Foundations of Pentecostal Theology* (Los Angeles, California: L.I.F.E. Bible College, 1983), 186.
23. David Limbaugh, *Jesus on Trial: A Lawyer Affirms the Truth of the Gospel* (Washington, D.C.: Regnery Publishing, 2014), Kindle Location 2521.
24. Leon Morris, *The Gospel According to John* (Grand Rapids, Michigan: Wm. B. Eerdmans Publishing Co., 1995), 584–85.
25. M. J. Gorman, "'Although/Because He Was in the Form of God': The Theological Significance of Paul's Master Story (Phil 2:6–11)," *Journal of Theological Interpretation* 1 (2007): 1–2.
26. Crossway Bibles, *ESV Study Bible*, 2283.
27. John MacArthur Jr., ed., *The MacArthur Study Bible* (Nashville, Tennessee: Word Pub, 1997), 1823.
28. Melick, *Philippians, Colossians, Philemon*, 32:106.
29. R. P. Lightner, "Philippians" in *The Bible Knowledge Commentary: An Exposition of the Scriptures*, eds. J. F. Walvoord and R. B. Zuck (Wheaton, Illinois: Victor Books, 1985), 2:654.
30. Crossway Bibles, *ESV Study Bible*, 2283.
31. Melick, *Philippians, Colossians, Philemon*, 32:111.
32. Edwards, *Galatians, Ephesians, Philippians*, 258.
33. F. F. Bruce, *Philippians* (Peabody, Massachusetts: Baker Books, 2011), 84–85.

34. David Chapman, *Philippians: Rejoicing and Thanksgiving* (Ross-shire, Scotland: Christian Focus, 2012), 160.
35. MacArthur, *Philippians*, 191.
36. Ibid., 193.
37. Lightner, "Philippians," 2:65–57).
38. Barton and Comfort, *Philippians, Colossians, Philemon*, 74.
39. Bruce, "Philippians," 98.
40. Ibid.
41. John Chrysostom, "Homilies of St. John Chrysostom, Archbishop of Constantinople, on the Epistle of St. Paul the Apostle to the Philippians" in *Saint Chrysostom: Homilies on Galatians, Ephesians, Philippians, Colossians, Thessalonians, Timothy, Titus, and Philemon*, ed. P. Schaff, trans. W. C. Cotton and J. A. Broadus, vol.13 (New York: Christian Literature Company, 1889), 229.
42. R. C. H. Lenski, *The Interpretation of St. Paul's Epistles to the Galatians, to the Ephesians and to the Philippians* (Columbus, Ohio: Lutheran Book Concern, 1937), 828.
43. Ibid., 829.
44. Moises Silva, *Philippians*, 2nd ed. (Grand Rapids, Michigan: Baker Academic, 2005), 149.
45. Calvin and Pringle, *Commentaries on the Epistles*, 89.
46. Barton and Comfort, *Philippians, Colossians, Philemon*, 87.
47. Thomas Hale, *The Applied New Testament Commentary* (Colorado Springs, Colorado; Ontario, Canada; East Sussex, England: David C. Cook, 1996), 763.
48. Ibid.
49. Edwards, *Galatians, Ephesians, Philippians*, 272–73.
50. H. D. M. Spence, ed., *1 John* (London; New York: Funk & Wagnalls Company, 1909), 5.
51. Ibid.5.

52. Johnson Oatman Jr., "I'm Pressing on the Upward Way," https://hymnary.org/text/im_pressing_on_the_upward_way.
53. Ralph P. Martin, *Philippians: An Introduction and Commentary* (Downers Grove, Illinois: InterVarsity Press, 1987), 11:163.
54. Edwards, *Galatians, Ephesians, Philippians*, 277.
55. J. Vernon McGee, *Thru the Bible Commentary: The Epistles (Philippians/Colossians)*, vol. 48 (Nashville: Thomas Nelson, 1991), 81.
56. Melick, *Philippians, Colossians, Philemon*, 32:143–44.
57. Edwards, *Galatians, Ephesians, Philippians*, 278.
58. Fee, *Paul's Letter to the Philippians*, 384.
59. Lightner, "Philippians," 2:663.
60. MacArthur, *Philippians*, 283.
61. I-Jin Loh and E. A. Nida, *A Handbook on Paul's Letter to the Philippians* (New York: United Bible Societies, 1995), 130.
62. Muller, *Epistles of Paul to the Philippians and to Philemon*, 142–43.
63. Leadership Ministries Worldwide, *Galatians–Colossians* (Chattanooga, Tennessee: Leadership Ministries Worldwide, 1996), 317.
64. Norman L. Geisler, *Systematic Theology, Volume One: Introduction, Bible* (Minneapolis, Minnesota: Bethany House Publishers, 2002), 109.
65. Ibid., 115.
66. Ibid.
67. Fee, *Paul's Letter to the Philippians*, 417.
68. Ibid., 417–18.
69. Bruce, *Philippians*, 146.
70. Lightner, "Philippians," 2:664.

71. J. H. Michael, *The Epistle of Paul to the Philippians*, ed. J. Moffatt, (New York; London: Harper and Brothers Publishers, 1927), 204.
72. Chapman, *Philippians*, 254.
73. Barton and Comfort, *Philippians, Colossians, Philemon*, 118.
74. Melick, *Philippians, Colossians, Philemon*, 32:151.
75. MacArthur, *MacArthur Study Bible*, 1828.
76. Edwards, *Galatians, Ephesians, Philippians*, 284.
77. Michael, *Epistle of Paul to the Philippians*, 217.
78. Markus Bockmuehl, *The Epistle to the Philippians* (London: Continuum, 1997), 266.
79. Edwards, *Galatians, Ephesians, Philippians*, 289.

CHAPTER 5

1 TIMOTHY: SOUND DOCTRINE AND CHRISTIAN LIVING

1. Irving L. Jensen, *Jensen's Survey of the New Testament: Search and Discover* (Chicago, Illinois: Moody Press, 1981), 373.
2. D. Edmond Hiebert, *First Timothy* (Chicago, Illinois: Moody Press 1957), 9.
3. Duane Litfin, "1 Timothy" in *The Bible Knowledge Commentary: An Exposition of the Scriptures*, eds. J. F. Walvoord and R. B. Zuck, (Wheaton, Illinois: Victor Books, 1985), 2:726.
4. Douglas J. W. Milne, *1 Timothy, 2 Timothy, Titus* (Scotland; Great Britain: Christian Focus Publications, 1996), 26.
5. Thomas D. Lea and David Alan Black, *The New Testament: Its Background and Message*, 2nd ed. (Nashville, Tennessee: Broadman & Holman Publishers, 2003), 473.

6. Thomas D. Lea and Hayne P. Griffin, *1, 2 Timothy, Titus*, vol. 34 (Nashville, Tennessee: Broadman & Holman Publishers, 1992), 66.
7. Samuel Rutherford and Andrew Bonar, *Letters of Samuel Rutherford: with a Sketch of his Life and Biographical Notices of his Correspondents* (Edinburgh, Scotland: Oliphant, Anderson & Ferrier, 1891), 280.
8. R. Gilmour, *Samuel Rutherford: A Study, Biographical and Somewhat Critical, in the History of the Scottish Covenant* (Edinburgh, Scotland: Oliphant, Anderson & Ferrier, 1904), 230.
9. Bruce B. Barton, D. Veerman, and N. S. Wilson, *1 Timothy, 2 Timothy, Titus* (Wheaton, Illinois: Tyndale House Publishers, 1993), 23.
10. Peter Gorday, ed., *Colossians, 1–2 Thessalonians, 1–2 Timothy, Titus, Philemon* (Downers Grove, Illinois: InterVarsity Press, 2000), 135–36.
11. Douglas J. W. Milne, *1 Timothy, 2 Timothy, Titus* (Scotland; Great Britain: Christian Focus Publications, 1996), 29–30.
12. John F. MacArthur, Jr., *1 Timothy* (Chicago: Moody Press, 1995), 21.
13. Warren W. Wiersbe, *The Bible Exposition Commentary* (Wheaton, IL: Victor Books, 1996), V1, 538-539.
14. Milne, *1 Timothy, 2 Timothy, Titus*, 30.
15. Warren W. Wiersbe, *Wiersbe's Expository Outlines on the New Testament* (Wheaton, Illinois: Victor Books, 1992), 620.
16. Crossway Bibles, *The ESV Study Bible* (Wheaton, Illinois: Crossway Bibles, 2008), 2326.
17. Gorday, *Colossians, 1–2 Thessalonians, 1–2 Timothy, Titus, Philemon*, 143.
18. Ibid.

19. Ibid., 146.
20. George M. Wieland, *The Significance of Salvation: A Study of Salvation Language in the Pastoral Epistles* (Milton Keynes, UK: Paternoster, 2006), 44.
21. Douglas Moo, *The Epistle to the Romans* (Grand Rapids, Michigan: Wm. B. Eerdmans Publishing Co., 1996), 556.
22. Robert H. Mounce, *Romans*, vol. 27 (Nashville, Tennessee: Broadman & Holman Publishers, 1995), 232.
23. Arnold G. Fruchtenbaum, *The Messianic Bible Study Collection* (Tustin, California: Ariel Ministries, 1983), 143:18.
24. J. A. Witmer, "Romans" in *The Bible Knowledge Commentary: An Exposition of the Scriptures*, eds. J. F. Walvoord and R. B. Zuck (Wheaton, Illinois: Victor Books, 1985), 2:488.
25. Barton, Veerman, and Wilson, *1 Timothy, 2 Timothy, Titus*, 36.
26. Robert W. Yarbrough, *The Letters to Timothy and Titus*, ed. D. A. Carson (Grand Rapids, Michigan: William B. Eerdmans Publishing Company, 2018), 147.
27. Crossway Bibles, *ESV Study Bible*, 2327.
28. Tyndale House Publishers, *Life Application Study Bible* (Grand Rapids, Michigan: Zondervan Publishing House, 1991).
29. Yarbrough, *Letters to Timothy and Titus*, 162.
30. Barton, Veerman, and Wilson, *1 Timothy, 2 Timothy, Titus*, 47.
31. G. M. Burge, *The New Testament in Antiquity* (Grand Rapids, Michigan: Zondervan, 2009), 369.
32. Milne, *1 Timothy, 2 Timothy, Titus* (Scotland; Great Britain: Christian Focus Publications, 1996), 54.
33. Barton, Veerman, and Wilson, *1 Timothy, 2 Timothy, Titus*, 48.

34. Philip H. Towner, *The Letters to Timothy and Titus* (Grand Rapids, Michigan: Wm. B. Eerdmans Publishing Co., 2006), 213.
35. Ibid.
36. Lea and Griffin, *1, 2 Timothy, Titus*, vol. 34 (Nashville, Tennessee: Broadman & Holman Publishers, 1992), 105.
37. Ibid., 102.
38. John F. MacArthur Jr., *1 Timothy* (Chicago, Illinois: Moody Press, 1995), 89–90.
39. Walter C. Kaiser Jr., et. al., *Hard Sayings of the Bible* (Downers Grove, Illinois: InterVarsity, 1996), 670–71.
40. Barton, Veerman, and Wilson, *1 Timothy, 2 Timothy, Titus*, 57.
41. Gorday, *Colossians, 1–2 Thessalonians, 1–2 Timothy, Titus, Philemon*, 172.
42. Lea and Griffin, *1, 2 Timothy, Titus*, vol. 34 (Nashville, Tennessee: Broadman & Holman Publishers, 1992), 114.
43. Milne, *1 Timothy, 2 Timothy, Titus* (Scotland; Great Britain: Christian Focus Publications, 1996), 68.
44. Thomas Lea and David Allan Black, *The New Testament: Its Background and Message*, 2nd ed. (Nashville, Tennessee: Broadman & Holman Publishers, 2003), 479.
45. Walter C. Kaiser Jr., *The Promise-Plan of God: A Biblical Theology of the Old and New Testaments* (Grand Rapids, Michigan: Zondervan, 2008), 347.
46. Calvin and Pringle, *Commentaries on the Epistles to Timothy, Titus, and Philemon* (Bellingham, Washington: Logos Bible Software, 2010), 92.
47. *NIV Life Application Bible* (Carol Stream, Illinois: Tyndale House Publishers, 1988–2005), 2828; Crossway Bibles, *ESV Study Bible*, 2331.

48. Warren W. Wiersbe, *The Bible Exposition Commentary* (Wheaton, Illinois: Victor Books, 1996), 2:225.
49. Lea and Griffin, *1, 2 Timothy, Titus*, vol. 34 (Nashville: Broadman & Holman Publishers, 1992), 132.
50. Gorday, *Colossians, 1–2 Thessalonians, 1–2 Timothy, Titus, Philemon*, 187.
51. Litfin, "1 Timothy," 2:740.
52. Ambrosiaster, *Commentaries on Galatians–Philemon*, 132.
53. Gorday, *Colossians, 1–2 Thessalonians, 1–2 Timothy, Titus, Philemon*, 190.
54. *NIV Life Application Bible*, 2828; Crossway Bibles, *ESV Study Bible*, 7951.
55. Fee, *1 and 2 Timothy, Titus*, 107–8.
56. Lea and Griffin, *1, 2 Timothy, Titus*, vol. 34, 141.
57. Crossway Bibles, *ESV Study Bible*, 2332.
58. Gorday, *Colossians, 1–2 Thessalonians, 1–2 Timothy, Titus, Philemon*, 196.
59. Ibid.
60. Litfin, "1 Timothy," 2:742.
61. Calvin and Pringle, *Commentaries on the Epistles to Timothy, Titus, and Philemon*, 125.
62. MacArthur, *1 Timothy*, 201–2.
63. Towner, *Letters to Timothy and Titus*, 359.
64. Litfin, *1 Timothy*, 2:744.
65. Gorday, *Colossians, 1–2 Thessalonians, 1–2 Timothy, Titus, Philemon*, 206.
66. Crossway Bibles, *ESV Study Bible*, 2333.
67. Lea and Griffin, *1, 2 Timothy, Titus*, vol. 34, 162.
68. William Hendriksen and Simon J. Kistemaker, *Exposition of the Pastoral Epistles*, vol. 4 (Grand Rapids, Michigan: Baker Book House, 1953–2001), 192.

69. Bruce B. Barton, D. Veerman, and N. S. Wilson, *1 Timothy, 2 Timothy, Titus* (Wheaton, Illinois: Tyndale House Publishers, 1993), 120.
70. Philip H. Towner, *The Letters to Timothy and Titus* (Grand Rapids, Michigan: Wm. B. Eerdmans Publishing Co., 2006), 399.
71. Gordon J. Keddie, *The Practical Christian: The Message of James* (Darlington, England: Evangelical Press, 1989), 182.
72. Barton, Veerman, and Wilson, *1 Timothy, 2 Timothy, Titus*, 127.
73. Gorday, *Colossians, 1–2 Thessalonians, 1–2 Timothy, Titus, Philemon*, 217.
74. Barton, Veerman, and Wilson, *1 Timothy, 2 Timothy, Titus*, 127.
75. Lea and Griffin, *1, 2 Timothy, Titus*, vol. 34, 169.
76. Bruce Barton, *Matthew* (Wheaton, Illinois: Tyndale House Publishers, 1996), 505.
77. Towner, *Letters to Timothy and Titus*, 410.
78. Hiebert, *First Timothy*, 122.
79. Gorday, *Colossians, 1–2 Thessalonians, 1–2 Timothy, Titus, Philemon*, 226.

CHAPTER 6

TITUS: QUALITIES OF A CHRISTLIKE LIFE

1. Charles Spurgeon, *Spurgeon Commentary: Titus*, ed. E. Ritzema (Bellingham, Washington: Lexham Press, 2014), 265.
2. D. E. Hiebert, "Titus" in *The Expositor's Bible Commentary: Ephesians through Philemon*, ed. F. E. Gaebelein, vol. 11 (Grand Rapids, Michigan Zondervan Publishing House, 1981), 423.

3. *Book of Church Order of the Presbyterian Church in the USA*, "Form of Government" (Andesite Press, 2017), 1.0304.
4. Gary W. Demarest and L. J. Ogilvie, *1, 2 Thessalonians / 1, 2 Timothy / Titus*, vol. 32 (Nashville, Tennessee: Thomas Nelson Inc., 1984), 305.
5. Duane Litfin, "Titus" in *The Bible Knowledge Commentary: An Exposition of the Scriptures*, eds. J. F. Walvoord and R. B. Zuck (Wheaton, Illinois: Victor Books, 1985), 2:761.
6. Thomas D. Lea and H. P. Griffin, *1, 2 Timothy, Titus*, vol. 34 (Nashville, Tennessee: Broadman & Holman Publishers 1992), 268.
7. Hiebert, "Titus," 427–28.
8. Peter Gorday, ed., *Colossians, 1–2 Thessalonians, 1–2 Timothy, Titus, Philemon* (Downers Grove, Illinois: InterVarsity Press, 2000), 287.
9. A. Kostenberger, "Titus" in *The Expositor's Bible Commentary: Ephesians–Philemon (Revised Edition)*, eds. T. Longman III and D. E. Garland, vol. 12 (Grand Rapids, Michigan: Zondervan, 2006), 609.
10. Lea and Griffin, *1, 2 Timothy, Titus*, 289.
11. Kostenberger, "Titus," 609.
12. Crossway Bibles, *The ESV Study Bible* (Wheaton, Illinois: Crossway Bibles, 2008), 2349.
13. Knute Larson, *I & II Thessalonians, I & II Timothy, Titus, Philemon*, vol. 9 (Nashville, Tennessee: Broadman & Holman Publishers, 2000), 346.
14. Ibid., 347.
15. C. S. Lewis, *Reflections on the Psalms* (London: Collins, 1961), 32.
16. Spurgeon, *Spurgeon Commentary*, 291.

17. Bruce B. Barton, D. Veerman, and N. S. Wilson, *1 Timothy, 2 Timothy, Titus* (Wheaton, Illinois: Tyndale House Publishers, 1993) 266.
18. Ibid.
19. Philip H. Towner, *The Letters to Timothy and Titus* (Grand Rapids, Michigan: Wm. B. Eerdmans Publishing Co., 2006), 723.
20. Ibid., 730.
21. Ambrosiaster, *Commentaries on Galatians–Philemon*, eds. T. C. Oden and G. L. Bray, trans. G. L. Bray (Downers Grove, Illinois: InterVarsity Press, 2009), 158.
22. Lea and Griffin, *1, 2 Timothy, Titus*, 306.
23. Spurgeon, *Spurgeon Commentary*, 300.
24. Lea and Griffin, *1, 2 Timothy, Titus*, 308.
25. Crossway Bibles, *ESV Study Bible*, 2350.
26. John Calvin and W. Pringle, *Commentaries on the Epistles to Timothy, Titus, and Philemon* (Bellingham, Washington: Logos Bible Software, 2010), 323.
27. J. N. D. Kelly, *The Pastoral Epistles* (London: Continuum, 1963), 249.
28. Barton, Veerman, and Wilson, *1 Timothy, 2 Timothy, Titus*, 290.
29. Lea and Griffin, *1, 2 Timothy, Titus*, 329.

CHAPTER 7

2 TIMOTHY: FINAL GUIDANCE FROM THE GREATEST EVANGELIST

1. J. Sidlow Baxter, *Explore the Book* (Grand Rapids, Michigan: Zondervan, 1986), 1638.

2. Thomas D. Lea and Hayne P. Griffin, *1, 2 Timothy, Titus*, vol. 34 (Nashville, Tennessee: Broadman & Holman Publishers, 1992), 188.
3. Peter Gorday, ed., *Colossians, 1–2 Thessalonians, 1–2 Timothy, Titus, Philemon* (Downers Grove, Ilinois: InterVarsity Press, 2000), 234.
4. Ambrosiaster, *Commentaries on Galatians–Philemon*, eds. T. C. Oden and G. L. Bray, trans. G. L. Bray (Downers Grove, Illinois: InterVarsity Press, 2009), 143.
5. Duane Litfin, "1 Timothy" in *The Bible Knowledge Commentary: An Exposition of the Scriptures*, eds. J. F. Walvoord and R. B. Zuck (Wheaton, Illinois: Victor Books, 1985), 2:751.
6. Gorday, *Colossians, 1–2 Thessalonians, 1–2 Timothy, Titus, Philemon*, 236.
7. Crossway Bibles, *ESV Study Bible* (Wheaton, Illinois: Crossway Bibles, 2008), 2339.
8. Thomas D. Lea and Hayne P. Griffin, *1, 2 Timothy, Titus*, vol. 34 (Nashville, Tennessee: Broadman & Holman Publishers, 1992), 203.
9. John F. MacArthur Jr., *2 Timothy* (Chicago, Illinois: Moody Press, 1995), 48.
10. Gary W. Demarest and L. J. Ogilvie, *1, 2 Thessalonians / 1, 2 Timothy / Titus*, vol. 32 (Nashville, Tennessee: Thomas Nelson Inc., 1984), 262.
11. Leadership Ministries Worldwide, *1 Thessalonians–Philemon* (Chattanooga, Tennessee: Leadership Ministries Worldwide, 2006), 235.
12. Ibid., 236.
13. E. D. Radmacher, R. B. Allen, and H. W. House, *The Nelson Study Bible: New King James Version* (Nashville, Tennessee: T. Nelson Publishers, 1997).

14. Lea and Griffin, *1, 2 Timothy, Titus*, 211.
15. Walter C. Kaiser Jr., *The Promise-Plan of God: A Biblical Theology of the Old and New Testaments* (Grand Rapids, Michigan: Zondervan, 2008), 354.
16. Barton, Veerman, and Wilson, *1 Timothy, 2 Timothy, Titus*, 188–89.
17. Crossway Bibles, *ESV Study Bible*, 2340.
18. Gorday, *Colossians, 1–2 Thessalonians, 1–2 Timothy, Titus, Philemon*, 249.
19. Leadership Ministries Worldwide, *1 Thessalonians–Philemon*, 238.
20. R. C. H. Lenski, *The Interpretation of St. Paul's Epistles to the Colossians, to the Thessalonians, to Timothy, to Titus and to Philemon* (Columbus, Ohio: Lutheran Book Concern, 1937), 800.
21. Crossway Bibles, *ESV Study Bible*, 2340.
22. Barton, Veerman, and Wilson, *1 Timothy, 2 Timothy, Titus*, 192–93.
23. Litfin, "1 Timothy," 2:754.
24. Ambrosiaster, *Commentaries on Galatians–Philemon*, 149.
25. Lea and Griffin, *1, 2 Timothy, Titus*, vol. 34, 222.
26. Gorday, *Colossians, 1–2 Thessalonians, 1–2 Timothy, Titus, Philemon*, 257.
27. E. D. Radmacher, R. B. Allen, and H. W. House, *The Nelson Study Bible: New King James Version* (Nashville, Tennessee: T. Nelson Publishers, 1997).
28. Douglas J. Moo, "The Letters and Revelation" in *NIV Biblical Theology Study Bible*, ed. D. A. Carson (Grand Rapids, Michigan: Zondervan, 2018), 2182.
29. J. D. Barry et al, *Faithlife Study Bible* (Bellingham, Washington: Lexham Press, 2016, 2012).

30. Gorday, *Colossians, 1–2 Thessalonians, 1–2 Timothy, Titus, Philemon*, 258.
31. Lea and Griffin, *1, 2 Timothy, Titus*, 222.
32. Barton, Veerman, and Wilson, *1 Timothy, 2 Timothy, Titus*, 207.
33. Lea and Griffin, *1, 2 Timothy, Titus*, 227.
34. Crossway Bibles, *ESV Study Bible*, 2341.
35. Gorday, *Colossians, 1–2 Thessalonians, 1–2 Timothy, Titus, Philemon*, 266.
36. Barton, Veerman, and Wilson, *1 Timothy, 2 Timothy, Titus*, 216.
37. Lea and Griffin, *1, 2 Timothy, Titus*, 234.
38. Lea and Black, *New Testament*, 71.
39. Litfin, "2 Timothy," 2:757.
40. Leadership Ministries Worldwide, *1 Thessalonians–Philemon*, 259.
41. Milne, *1 Timothy, 2 Timothy, Titus*, 169.
42. Hiebert, *Second Timothy*, 101.
43. Norman L. Geisler and R. M. Brooks, *When Skeptics Ask* (Wheaton, Illinois: Victor Books, 1990), 152.
44. Gorday, *Colossians, 1–2 Thessalonians, 1–2 Timothy, Titus, Philemon*, 272.
45. Ibid., 271.
46. Ibid.
47. Lea and Griffin, *1, 2 Timothy, Titus*, 249.
48. Litfin, "2 Timothy," 2:759.
49. Crossway Bibles, *ESV Study Bible*, 2343.
50. Litfin, "2 Timothy," 2:760.

10 Gordon, *Colossians*, *1–2 Thessalonians*, *1 and 2 Timothy*, *Titus*, *Philemon*, [illegible].
11 Lea and Griffin, *1, 2 Timothy, Titus*, [illegible].
12 Barton, Veerman, and Wilson, *1 Timothy, 2 Timothy, Titus*, [illegible].
13 Lea and Griffin, *1, 2 Timothy, Titus*, [illegible].
14 Conway, *Bible Study Guide*, [illegible].
15 Gordon, *Colossians*, *1–2 Thessalonians*, *1 and 2 Timothy*, *Titus*, *Philemon*, [illegible].
16 Barton, Veerman, and Wilson, *1 Timothy, 2 Timothy, Titus*, [illegible].
17 Lea and Griffin, *1, 2 Timothy, Titus*, [illegible].
18 [illegible]
19 [illegible] *Timothy*, [illegible].
20 [illegible]
21 [illegible] *Timothy*, [illegible].
22 [illegible]
23 Norman [illegible] (Wheaton, Illinois: Victor Books, [illegible]), [illegible].
24 Gordon, *Colossians*, *1–2 Thessalonians*, *1 and 2 Timothy*, *Titus*, *Philemon*, [illegible].
25 Ibid., [illegible].
26 Ibid.
27 Lea and Griffin, *1, 2 Timothy, Titus*, [illegible].
28 [illegible] *Timothy*, [illegible].
29 Conway, *Bible Study Guide*, [illegible].
30 [illegible] *Timothy*, [illegible].

INDEX

S

T